ABOUT THIS PUBLICATION

FOR SERVICE ASSISTANCE

Customer Service
1.704.898.0770

North Carolina General Statues is published by The Muliti-Media Group of Greater Charlotte in Charlotte, North Carolina. Copyright 2015 by the Multi-Media Group of Greater Charlotte. This book or parts thereof may not be reproduced in any form, stored in a retrieval system, or transmitted in any form by any means—electronic, mechanical, photocopy, recording or otherwise—without prior written permission of the publisher, except as provided by United States of America copyright law.

The records required by U.S. Code 2257(a) through (c) and the pertinent regulations 28 C.F.R. Cli. 1, Part 75 with respect to this publication and all materials associated with such records are maintained by The Multi-Media Group of Greater Charlotte, Publisher and available for review by Attorney General.

www.visionbooks.org

Copyright © 2015 by MMGGC
All rights reserved!

TID: 5061763
ISBN (10) digit: 1502915618
ISBN (13) digit: 978-1502915610

123-4-56789-01239-Paperback
123-4-56789-01239-Hardback

First Edition

090520140547

Printed in the United States of America

2015 EDITION

North Carolina Criminal Law And Procedure-Pamphlet # 52

Printed In conjunction with the Administration of the Courts

North Carolina Criminal Law and Procedure
Pamphlet Reference Guide

Chapters	Pamphlet
Chapter 1 Civil Procedure	1
Chapter 1 Civil Procedure (Continue)	2
Chapter 1A Rules of Civil Procedure	2
Chapter 1B Contribution.	2
Chapter 1C Enforcement of Judgments.	2
Chapter 1D Punitive Damages.	2
Chapter 1E Eastern Band of Cherokee Indians.	2
Chapter 1F North Carolina Uniform Interstate Depositions and Discovery Act.	2
Chapter 2 - Clerk of Superior Court [Repealed and Transferred.]	3
Chapter 3 - Commissioners of Affidavits and Deeds [Repealed.]	3
Chapter 4 - Common Law	3
Chapter 5 - Contempt [Repealed.]	3
Chapter 5A - Contempt	3
Chapter 6 - Liability for Court Costs	3
Chapter 7 - Courts [Repealed and Transferred.]	3
Chapter 7A – Judicial Department	3
Chapter 7A – Continuation (Judicial Department)	4
Chapter 7A – Continuation (Judicial Department)	5
Chapter 7B - Juvenile Code	5
Chapter 8 - Evidence	6
Chapter 8A - Interpreters for Deaf Persons [Recodified.]	6
Chapter 8B - Interpreters for Deaf Persons	6
Chapter 8C - Evidence Code	6
Chapter 9 - Jurors	6
Chapter 10 - Notaries [Repealed.]	6
Chapter 10A - Notaries [Recodified.]	6
Chapter 10B - Notaries	6
Chapter 11 - Oaths	6
Chapter 12 - Statutory Construction	6
Chapter 13 - Citizenship Restored	6
Chapter 14 - Criminal Law	7
Chapter 14 –Criminal Law (Continuation)	8
Chapter 15 - Criminal Procedure	9
Chapter 15A - Criminal Procedure Act (Continuation)	10
Chapter 15A - Criminal Procedure Act (Continuation)	11
Chapter 15B - Victims Compensation	11
Chapter 15C - Address Confidentiality Program	11
Chapter 16 - Gaming Contracts and Futures	11
Chapter 17 - Habeas Corpus	11

Chapter 17A - Law-Enforcement Officers [Recodified.]	11
Chapter 17B - North Carolina Criminal Justice Education and Training System [Recodified.] Chapter 17C - North Carolina Criminal Justice Education and Training Standards Commission	11
	11
Chapter 17D - North Carolina Justice Academy	11
Chapter 17E - North Carolina Sheriffs' Education and Training Standards Commission	11
Chapter 18 - Regulation of Intoxicating Liquors [Repealed.]	12
Chapter 18A - Regulation of Intoxicating Liquors [Repealed.]	12
Chapter 18B - Regulation of Alcoholic Beverages	12
Chapter 18C - North Carolina State Lottery	12
Chapter 19 - Offenses against Public Morals	12
Chapter 19A - Protection of Animals	12
Chapter 20 - Motor Vehicles	13
Chapter 20 - Motor Vehicles (Continuation)	14
Chapter 20 - Motor Vehicles (Continuation)	15
Chapter 20 - Motor Vehicles (Continuation)	16
Chapter 21 - Bills of Lading	17
Chapter 22 - Contracts Requiring Writing	17
Chapter 22A - Signatures	17
Chapter 22B - Contracts Against Public Policy	17
Chapter 22C - Payments to Subcontractors	17
Chapter 23 - Debtor and Creditor.	17
Chapter 24 – Interest	17
Chapter 25 – Uniform Commercial Code	18
Chapter 25 – Uniform Commercial Code (Continuation)	19
Chapter 25A – Retail Installment Sales Act	20
Chapter 25B - Credit	20
Chapter 25C - Sales of Artwork	20
Chapter 26 - Suretyship	20
Chapter 27 - Warehouse Receipts [Repealed.]	20
Chapter 28 - Administration [Repealed.]	20
Chapter 28A - Administration of Decedents' Estates	20
Chapter 28B - Estates of Absentees in Military Service	20
Chapter 28C - Estates of Missing Persons	20
Chapter 29 - Intestate Succession	21
Chapter 30 - Surviving Spouses	21
Chapter 31 - Wills	21
Chapter 31A - Acts Barring Property Rights	21
Chapter 31B - Renunciation of Property and Renunciation of Fiduciary Powers Act	21
Chapter 31C - Uniform Disposition of Community Property Rights at Death Act	21
Chapter 32 - Fiduciaries	21
Chapter 32A - Powers of Attorney	21
Chapter 33 - Guardian and Ward [Repealed and Recodified.]	21

Chapter 33A - North Carolina Uniform Transfers to Minors Act	21
Chapter 33B - North Carolina Uniform Custodial Trust Act	21
Chapter 34 - Veterans' Guardianship Act	22
Chapter 35 - Sterilization Procedures	22
Chapter 35A - Incompetency and Guardianship	22
Chapter 36 - Trusts and Trustees [Repealed.]	22
Chapter 36A - Trusts and Trustees	22
Chapter 36B - Uniform Management of Institutional Funds Act [Repealed.]	22
Chapter 36C - North Carolina Uniform Trust Code	22
Chapter 36D - North Carolina Community Third Party Trusts, Pooled Trusts	23
Chapter 36E - Uniform Prudent Management of Institutional Funds Act	23
Chapter 37 - Allocation of Principal and Income [Repealed.]	23
Chapter 37A - Uniform Principal and Income Act	23
Chapter 38 - Boundaries	23
Chapter 38A - Landowner Liability	23
Chapter 39 - Conveyances	23
Chapter 39A - Transfer Fee Covenants Prohibited	23
Chapter 40 - Eminent Domain [Repealed.]	23
Chapter 40A - Eminent Domain	23
Chapter 41 - Estates	23
Chapter 41A - State Fair Housing Act	23
Chapter 42 - Landlord and Tenant	23
Chapter 42A - Vacation Rental Act	23
Chapter 43 - Land Registration	23
Chapter 44 - Liens	24
Chapter 44A - Statutory Liens and Charges	24
Chapter 45 - Mortgages and Deeds of Trust	24
Chapter 45A - Good Funds Settlement Act	24
Chapter 46 - Partition	24
Chapter 47 - Probate and Registration	25
Chapter 47A - Unit Ownership	25
Chapter 47B - Real Property Marketable Title Act	25
Chapter 47C - North Carolina Condominium Act	25
Chapter 47D - Notice of Settlement Act [Expired.]	25
Chapter 47E - Residential Property Disclosure Act	25
Chapter 47F - North Carolina Planned Community Act	25
Chapter 47G - Option to Purchase Contracts	25
Chapter 47H - Contracts for Deed	25
Chapter 48 - Adoptions +	26
Chapter 48A - Minors	26
Chapter 49 - Bastardy	26
Chapter 49A - Rights of Children	26
Chapter 50 - Divorce and Alimony	26
Chapter 50A - Uniform Child-Custody Jurisdiction and	

Enforcement Act	26
Chapter 50B - Domestic Violence	26
Chapter 50C - Civil No-Contact Orders	26
Chapter 51 - Marriage	26
Chapter 52 - Powers and Liabilities of Married Persons	27
Chapter 52A - Uniform Reciprocal Enforcement of Support Act [Repealed.]	27
Chapter 52B - Uniform Premarital Agreement Act	27
Chapter 52C - Uniform Interstate Family Support Act	27
Chapter 53 - Banks	27
Chapter 53A - Business Development Corporations and North Carolina Capital Resource Corporations	28
Chapter 53B - Financial Privacy Act	28
Chapter 54 - Cooperative Organizations	28
Chapter 54A - Capital Stock Savings and Loan Associations [Repealed.]	28
Chapter 54B - Savings and Loan Associations	29
Chapter 54C - Savings Banks	29
Chapter 55 - North Carolina Business Corporation Act	30
Chapter 55A - North Carolina Nonprofit Corporation Act	31
Chapter 55B - Professional Corporation Act	31
Chapter 55C - Foreign Trade Zones	31
Chapter 55D - Filings, Names, and Registered Agents for Corporations, Nonprofit Corporations, and Partnerships	31
Chapter 56 - Electric, Telegraph and Power Companies [Repealed.]	31
Chapter 57 - Hospital, Medical and Dental Service Corporations [Recodified.]	31
Chapter 57A - Health Maintenance Organization Act [Recodified.]	31
Chapter 57B - Health Maintenance Organization Act [Recodified.]	31
Chapter 57C - North Carolina Limited Liability Company Act.	31
Chapter 58 - Insurance.	32
Chapter 58 - Insurance (Continuation)	33
Chapter 58 - Insurance (Continuation)	34
Chapter 58 - Insurance (Continuation)	35
Chapter 58 - Insurance (Continuation)	36
Chapter 58 - Insurance (Continuation)	37
Chapter 58 - Insurance (Continuation)	38
Chapter 58A - North Carolina Health Insurance Trust Commission [Recodified.]	38
Chapter 59 - Partnership.	39
Chapter 59B - Uniform Unincorporated Nonprofit Association Act.	39
Chapter 60 - Railroads and Other Carriers [Repealed and Transferred.]	39
Chapter 61 - Religious Societies	39
Chapter 62 - Public Utilities	39

Chapter 62 - Public Utilities (Continuation)	40
Chapter 62A - Public Safety Telephone Service And Wireless Telephone Service	40
Chapter 63 - Aeronautics	40
Chapter 63A - North Carolina Global TransPark Authority	40
Chapter 64 - Aliens	40
Chapter 65 – Cemeteries	40
Chapter 66 - Commerce and Business	41
Chapter 67 - Dogs	41
Chapter 68 - Fences and Stock Law	41
Chapter 69 - Fire Protection	41
Chapter 70 - Indian Antiquities, Archaeological Resources and Unmarked Human Skeletal Remains Protection	42
Chapter 71 - Indians [Repealed.]	42
Chapter 71A - Indians	42
Chapter 72 - Inns, Hotels and Restaurants	42
Chapter 73 - Mills	42
Chapter 74 - Mines and Quarries	42
Chapter 74A - Company Police [Repealed.]	42
Chapter 74B - Private Protective Services Act [Repealed.]	42
Chapter 74C - Private Protective Services	42
Chapter 74D - Alarm Systems	42
Chapter 74E - Company Police Act	42
Chapter 74F - Locksmith Licensing Act	42
Chapter 74G - Campus Police Act	42
Chapter 75 - Monopolies, Trusts and Consumer Protection	42
Chapter 75A - Boating and Water Safety	43
Chapter 75B - Discrimination in Business	43
Chapter 75C - Motion Picture Fair Competition Act	43
Chapter 75D - Racketeer Influenced and Corrupt Organizations	43
Chapter 75E - Unlawful Activities in Connection With Certain Corporate Transactions	43
Chapter 76 - Navigation	43
Chapter 76A - Navigation and Pilotage Commissions	43
Chapter 77 - Rivers, Creeks, and Coastal Waters	43
Chapter 78 - Securities Law [Repealed.]	43
Chapter 78A - North Carolina Securities Act	43
Chapter 78B - Tender Offer Disclosure Act [Repealed.]	43
Chapter 78C - Investment Advisers	43
Chapter 78D - Commodities Act	43
Chapter 79 - Strays [Repealed.]	43
Chapter 80 - Trademarks, Brands, etc.	44
Chapter 81 - Weights and Measures [Recodified.]	44
Chapter 81A - Weights and Measures Act of 1975.	44
Chapter 82 - Wrecks [Repealed.]	44
Chapter 83 - Architects [Recodified.]	44

Chapter 83A - Architects	44
Chapter 84 - Attorneys-at-Law	44
Chapter 84A - Foreign Legal Consultants	44
Chapter 85 - Auctions and Auctioneers [Repealed.]	44
Chapter 85A - Bail Bondsmen and Runners [Recodified.]	44
Chapter 85B - Auctions and Auctioneers	44
Chapter 85C - Bail Bondsmen and Runners [Recodified.]	44
Chapter 86 - Barbers [Recodified.]	44
Chapter 86A - Barbers	44
Chapter 87 - Contractors	44
Chapter 88 - Cosmetic Art [Repealed.]	44
Chapter 88A - Electrolysis Practice Act	44
Chapter 88B - Cosmetic Art	45
Chapter 89 - Engineering and Land Surveying [Recodified.]	45
Chapter 89A - Landscape Architects	45
Chapter 89B - Foresters	45
Chapter 89C - Engineering and Land Surveying	45
Chapter 89D - Landscape Contractors	45
Chapter 89E - Geologists Licensing Act	45
Chapter 89F - North Carolina Soil Scientist Licensing Act	45
Chapter 89G - Irrigation Contractors	45
Chapter 90 - Medicine and Allied Occupations	45
Chapter 90 - Medicine and Allied Occupations (Continuation)	46
Chapter 90 - Medicine and Allied Occupations (Continuation)	47
Chapter 90 - Medicine and Allied Occupations (Continuation)	48
Chapter 90A - Sanitarians and Water and Wastewater Treatment Facility Operators	48
Chapter 90B - Social Worker Certification and Licensure Act	48
Chapter 90C - North Carolina Recreational Therapy Licensure Act	48
Chapter 90D - Interpreters and Transliterators	48
Chapter 91 - Pawnbrokers [Repealed.]	48
Chapter 91A - Pawnbrokers Modernization Act of 1989	48
Chapter 92 - Photographers [Deleted.]	48
Chapter 93 - Certified Public Accountants	48
Chapter 93A - Real Estate License Law	49
Chapter 93B - Occupational Licensing Boards	49
Chapter 93C - Watchmakers [Repealed.]	49
Chapter 93D - North Carolina State Hearing Aid Dealers and Fitters Board.	49
Chapter 93E - North Carolina Appraisers Act	49
Chapter 94 - Apprenticeship	49
Chapter 95 - Department of Labor and Labor Regulations	49
Chapter 95 - Department of Labor and Labor Regulations (Continuation)	50
Chapter 96 - Employment Security	50
Chapter 97 - Workers' Compensation Act	50
Chapter 97 - Workers' Compensation Act (Continuation)	51

Chapter 98 - Burnt and Lost Records	51
Chapter 99 - Libel and Slander	51
Chapter 99A - Civil Remedies for Criminal Actions	51
Chapter 99B - Products Liability	51
Chapter 99C - Actions Relating to Winter Sports Safety and Accidents	51
Chapter 99D - Civil Rights	51
Chapter 99E - Special Liability Provisions	51
Chapter 100 - Monuments, Memorials and Parks	51
Chapter 101 - Names of Persons	51
Chapter 102 - Official Survey Base	51
Chapter 103 - Sundays, Holidays and Special Days	51
Chapter 104 - United States Lands	51
Chapter 104A - Degrees of Kinship	51
Chapter 104B - Hurricanes or Other Acts of Nature	51
Chapter 104C - Atomic Energy, Radioactivity and Ionizing Radiation [Repealed and Recodified.]	51
Chapter 104D - Southern States Energy Compact	51
Chapter 104E - North Carolina Radiation Protection Act	51
Chapter 104F - Southeast Interstate Low-Level Radioactive Waste Management Compact [Repealed]	51
Chapter 104G - North Carolina Low-Level Radioactive Waste Management Authority Act of 1987 [Repealed]	51
Chapter 105 - Taxation	51
Chapter 105 - Taxation (Continuation)	52
Chapter 105 - Taxation (Continuation)	53
Chapter 105 - Taxation (Continuation)	54
Chapter 105A - Setoff Debt Collection Act	55
Chapter 105B - Defaulted Student Loan Recovery Act	55
Chapter 106 - Agriculture	55
Chapter 106 - Agriculture (Continue)	56
Chapter 106 - Agriculture (Continue)	57
Chapter 107 - Agricultural Development Districts [Repealed.]	57
Chapter 108 - Social Services [Repealed and Recodified.]	57
Chapter 108A - Social Services	57
Chapter 108B - Community Action Programs	58
Chapter 108C Medicaid and Health Choice Provider Requirements.	58
Chapter 108D Medicaid Managed Care for Behavioral Health Services.	58
Chapter 109 - Bonds [Recodified.]	58
Chapter 110 - Child Welfare	58
Chapter 111 - Aid to the Blind	58
Chapter 112 - Confederate Homes and Pensions [Repealed.]	58
Chapter 113 - Conservation and Development	58
Chapter 113 - Conservation and Development (Continuation)	59

Chapter 113A - Pollution Control and Environment	59
Chapter 113A - Pollution Control and Environment (Continuation)	60
Chapter 113B - North Carolina Energy Policy Act of 1975	60
Chapter 114 - Department of Justice	60
Chapter 115 - Elementary and Secondary Education [Repealed.]	60
Chapter 115A - Community Colleges, Technical Institutes, and Industrial Education Centers [Repealed.]	60
Chapter 115B - Tuition and Fee Waivers	60
Chapter 115C - Elementary and Secondary Education	60
Chapter 115C - Elementary and Secondary Education (Continuation)	61
Chapter 115C - Elementary and Secondary Education (Continuation)	62
Chapter 115C - Elementary and Secondary Education (Continuation)	63
Chapter 115D - Community Colleges	63
Chapter 115E - Private Educational Facilities Finance Act [Recodified]	63
Chapter 116 - Higher Education	63
Chapter 116 - Higher Education (Continuation)	63
Chapter 116A - Escheats and Abandoned Property [Repealed.]	64
Chapter 116B - Escheats and Abandoned Property	64
Chapter 116C - Continuum of Education Programs	64
Chapter 116D - Higher Education Bonds	64
Chapter 117 - Electrification	64
Chapter 118 - Firemen's and Rescue Squad Workers' Relief and Pension Funds [Recodified.]	64
Chapter 118A - Firemen's Death Benefit Act [Repealed.]	64
Chapter 118B - Members of a Rescue Squad Death Benefit Act [Repealed.]	64
Chapter 119 - Gasoline and Oil Inspection and Regulation	64
Chapter 120 - General Assembly	65
Chapter 120 - General Assembly (Continuation)	66
Chapter 120 - General Assembly (Continuation)	67
Chapter 120C - Lobbying	67
Chapter 121 - Archives and History	67
Chapter 122 - Hospitals for the Mentally Disordered [Repealed.]	67
Chapter 122A - North Carolina Housing Finance Agency	67
Chapter 122B - North Carolina Agricultural Facilities Finance Act [Repealed.]	67
Chapter 122C - Mental Health, Developmental Disabilities, and Substance Abuse Act of 1985	67
Chapter 122C - Mental Health, Developmental Disabilities, and Substance Abuse Act of 1985 (Continuation)	68
Chapter 122D - North Carolina Agricultural Finance Act	68

Chapter 122E - North Carolina Housing Trust and Oil Overcharge Act	68
Chapter 123 - Impeachment	69
Chapter 123A - Industrial Development [Repealed.]	69
Chapter 124 - Internal Improvements	69
Chapter 125 - Libraries	69
Chapter 126 - State Personnel System	69
Chapter 127 - Militia [Repealed.]	69
Chapter 127A - Militia	69
Chapter 127B - Military Affairs	69
Chapter 127C - Advisory Commission on Military Affairs	69
Chapter 128 - Offices and Public Officers	69
Chapter 128 - Offices and Public Officers (Continuation)	70
Chapter 129 - Public Buildings and Grounds	70
Chapter 130 - Public Health [Repealed.]	70
Chapter 130A - Public Health	70
Chapter 130A - Public Health (Continuation)	71
Chapter 130A - Public Health (Continuation)	72
Chapter 130B - Hazardous Waste Management Commission [Repealed.]	72
Chapter 131 - Public Hospitals [Repealed.]	72
Chapter 131A - Health Care Facilities Finance Act	72
Chapter 131B - Licensing of Ambulatory Surgical Facilities [Repealed.]	72
Chapter 131C - Charitable Solicitation Licensure Act [Repealed.]	72
Chapter 131D - Inspection and Licensing of Facilities	72
Chapter 131E - Health Care Facilities and Services	72
Chapter 131E - Health Care Facilities and Services (Continuation)	73
Chapter 131F - Solicitation of Contributions	73
Chapter 132 - Public Records	73
Chapter 133 - Public Works	74
Chapter 134 - Youth Development [Recodified.]	74
Chapter 134A - Youth Services [Repealed.]	74
Chapter 135 - Retirement System for Teachers and State Employees; Social Security; Health Insurance Program for Children	74
Chapter 135 - Retirement System for Teachers and State Employees; Social Security; Health Insurance Program for Children	75
Chapter 136 - Transportation	75
Chapter 136 - Transportation (Continuation)	76
Chapter 137 - Rural Rehabilitation [Repealed.]	76
Chapter 138 - Salaries, Fees and Allowances	76
Chapter 138A - State Government Ethics Act	76
Chapter 139 - Soil and Water Conservation Districts	76

Chapter 140 - State Art Museum; Symphony and Art Societies	76
Chapter 140A - State Awards System	76
Chapter 141 - State Boundaries	76
Chapter 142 - State Debt	76
Chapter 143 - State Departments, Institutions, and Commissions	77
Chapter 143 - State Departments, Institutions, and Commissions (Continuation)	78
Chapter 143 - State Departments, Institutions, and Commissions (Continuation)	79
Chapter 143 - State Departments, Institutions, and Commissions (Continuation)	80
Chapter 143A - State Government Reorganization	80
Chapter 143B - Executive Organization Act of 1973	80
Chapter 143B - Executive Organization Act of 1973 (Continuation)	81
Chapter 143B - Executive Organization Act of 1973 (Continuation)	82
Chapter 143C - State Budget Act	83
Chapter 143D - The State Governmental Accountability and Internal Control Act	83
Chapter 144 - State Flag, Official Governmental Flags, Motto, and Colors	83
Chapter 145 - State Symbols and Other Official Adoptions.	83
Chapter 146 - State Lands	83
Chapter 147 - State Officers	83
Chapter 148 - State Prison System	84
Chapter 149 - State Song and Toast	84
Chapter 150 - Uniform Revocation of Licenses [Repealed.]	84
Chapter 150A - Administrative Procedure Act [Recodified.]	84
Chapter 150B - Administrative Procedure Act	84
Chapter 151 - Constables [Repealed.]	84
Chapter 152 - Coroners	84
Chapter 152A - County Medical Examiner [Repealed.]	84
Chapter 152A - County Medical Examiner [Repealed.] (Continuation)	85
Chapter 153 - Counties and County Commissioners [Repealed.]	85
Chapter 153A - Counties	85
Chapter 153B - Mountain Resources Planning Act	85
Chapter 153C - Uwharrie Regional Resources Act	85
Chapter 154 - County Surveyor [Repealed.]	85
Chapter 155 - County Treasurer [Repealed.]	85
Chapter 156 - Drainage	85
Chapter 156 – Drainage (Continuation)	86

Chapter 157 - Housing Authorities and Projects	86
Chapter 157A - Historic Properties Commissions [Transferred.]	86
Chapter 158 - Local Development	86
Chapter 159 - Local Government Finance	86
Chapter 159 - Local Government Finance (Continuation)	87
Chapter 159A - Pollution Abatement and Industrial Facilities Financing Act [Unconstitutional.]	87
Chapter 159B - Joint Municipal Electric Power and Energy Act	87
Chapter 159C - Industrial and Pollution Control Facilities Financing Act	87
Chapter 159D - The North Carolina Capital Facilities Financing Act	87
Chapter 159E - Registered Public Obligations Act	87
Chapter 159F - North Carolina Energy Development Authority [Repealed.]	87
Chapter 159G - Water Infrastructure	87
Chapter 159H - [Reserved.]	87
Chapter 159I - Solid Waste Management Loan Program and Local Government Special Obligation Bonds	87
Chapter 160 - Municipal Corporations [Repealed And Transferred.]	87
Chapter 160A - Cities and Towns	88
Chapter 160A - Cities and Towns (Continuation)	89
Chapter 160B - Consolidated City-County Act	89
Chapter 160C - Baseball Park Districts [Repealed.]	90
Chapter 161 - Register of Deeds	90
Chapter 162 - Sheriff	90
Chapter 162A - Water and Sewer Systems	90
Chapter 162B Continuity of Local Government in Emergency.	90
Chapter 163 Elections and Election Laws.	90
Chapter 163 Elections and Election Laws. (Continuation)	91
Chapter 164 Concerning the General Statutes of North Carolina.	92
Chapter 165 Veterans.	92
Chapter 166 Civil Preparedness Agencies [Repealed.]	92
Chapter 166A North Carolina Emergency Management Act.	92
Chapter 167 State Civil Air Patrol [Repealed.]	92
Chapter 168 Persons with Disabilities.	92
Chapter 168A Persons With Disabilities Protection Act.	92

§ 105-129.71. (See note for repeal) Credit for income-producing rehabilitated mill property.

(a) Credit. - A taxpayer who is allowed a credit under section 47 of the Code for making qualified rehabilitation expenditures of at least three million dollars ($3,000,000) with respect to a certified rehabilitation of an eligible site is allowed a credit equal to a percentage of the expenditures that qualify for the federal credit. The credit may be claimed in the year in which the eligible site is placed into service. When the eligible site is placed into service in two or more phases in different years, the amount of credit that may be claimed in a year is the amount based on the qualified rehabilitation expenditures associated with the phase placed into service during that year. In order to be eligible for a credit allowed by this Article, the taxpayer must provide to the Secretary a copy of the eligibility certification and the cost certification. The amount of the credit is as follows:

(1) For an eligible site located in a development tier one or two area, determined as of the date of the eligibility certification, the amount of the credit is equal to forty percent (40%) of the qualified rehabilitation expenditures.

(2) For an eligible site located in a development tier three area, determined as of the date of the eligibility certification, the amount of the credit is equal to thirty percent (30%) of the qualified rehabilitation expenditures.

(b) Allocation. - Notwithstanding the provisions of G.S. 105-131.8 and G.S. 105-269.15, a pass-through entity that qualifies for the credit provided in this section may allocate the credit among any of its owners in its discretion as long as an owner's adjusted basis in the pass-through entity, as determined under the Code, at the end of the taxable year in which the eligible site is placed in service, is at least forty percent (40%) of the amount of credit allocated to that owner. Owners to whom a credit is allocated are allowed the credit as if they had qualified for the credit directly. A pass-through entity and its owners must include with their tax returns for every taxable year in which an allocated credit is claimed a statement of the allocation made by the pass-through entity and the allocation that would have been required under G.S. 105-131.8 or G.S. 105-269.15.

(c) Forfeiture for Change in Ownership. - If an owner of a pass-through entity that has qualified for the credit allowed under this section disposes of all or a portion of the owner's interest in the pass-through entity within five years from the date the eligible site is placed in service and the owner's interest in the pass-through entity is reduced to less than two-thirds of the owner's interest in the pass-through entity at the time the eligible site was placed in service, the owner forfeits a portion of the credit. The amount forfeited is determined by multiplying the amount of credit by the percentage reduction in ownership and then multiplying that product by the forfeiture percentage. The forfeiture percentage equals the recapture percentage found in the table in section 50(a)(1)(B) of the Code.

(d) Exceptions to Forfeiture. - Forfeiture as provided in subsection (c) of this section is not required if the change in ownership is the result of any of the following:

(1) The death of the owner.

(2) A merger, consolidation, or similar transaction requiring approval by the shareholders, partners, or members of the taxpayer under applicable State law, to the extent the taxpayer does not receive cash or tangible property in the merger, consolidation, or other similar transaction.

(e) Liability from Forfeiture. - A taxpayer or an owner of a pass-through entity that forfeits a credit under this section is liable for all past taxes avoided as a result of the credit plus interest at the rate established under G.S. 105-241.21, computed from the date the taxes would have been due if the credit had not been allowed. The past taxes and interest are due 30 days after the date the credit is forfeited. A taxpayer or owner of a pass-through entity that fails to pay the taxes and interest by the due date is subject to the penalties provided in G.S. 105-236. (2006-40, s. 1; 2006-252, s. 2.23; 2006-259, s. 47.5; 2007-491, s. 44(1)a; 2008-107, s. 28.4(b).)

§ 105-129.72. (See note for repeal) Credit for nonincome-producing rehabilitated mill property.

(a) Credit. - A taxpayer who is not allowed a federal income tax credit under section 47 of the Code and who makes rehabilitation expenses of at least three million dollars ($3,000,000) with respect to a certified rehabilitation of an eligible site is allowed a credit equal to a percentage of the rehabilitation expenses. The entire credit may not be taken for the taxable year in which the property is placed in service, but must be taken in five equal installments beginning with the taxable year in which the property is placed in service. When the eligible site is placed into service in two or more phases in different years, the amount of credit that may be claimed in a year is the amount based on the rehabilitation expenses associated with the phase placed into service during that year. In order to be eligible for a credit allowed by this Article, the taxpayer must provide to the Secretary a copy of the eligibility certification and the cost certification. For an eligible site located in a development tier one or two area, determined as of the date of the eligibility certification, the amount of the credit is equal to forty percent (40%) of the rehabilitation expenses. No credit is allowed for a site located in a development tier three area.

(b) Allocation. - Notwithstanding the provisions of G.S. 105-131.8 and G.S. 105-269.15, a pass-through entity that qualifies for the credit provided in this section may allocate the credit among any of its owners in its discretion as long as an owner's adjusted basis in the pass-through entity, as determined under the Code, at the end of the taxable year in which the eligible site is placed in service, is at least forty percent (40%) of the amount of credit allocated to that owner. Owners to whom a credit is allocated are allowed the credit as if they had qualified for the credit directly. A pass-through entity and its owners must include with their tax returns for every taxable year in which an allocated credit is claimed a statement of the allocation made by the pass-through entity and the allocation that would have been required under G.S. 105-131.8 or G.S. 105-269.15.

(c) Forfeiture for Change in Ownership. - If an owner of a pass-through entity that has qualified for the credit allowed under this section disposes of all or a portion of the owner's interest in the pass-through entity within five years from the date the eligible site is placed in service and the owner's interest in the pass-through entity is reduced to less than two-thirds of the owner's interest in the pass-through entity at the time the eligible site was placed in service, the owner forfeits a portion of the credit. The amount forfeited is determined by multiplying the amount of credit by the percentage reduction in ownership and then multiplying that product by the forfeiture percentage. The forfeiture percentage equals the recapture percentage found in the table in section 50(a)(1)(B) of the Code. The remaining allocable credit is allocated equally among the five years in which the credit is claimed.

(d) Exceptions to Forfeiture. - Forfeiture as provided in subsection (c) of this section is not required if the change in ownership is the result of any of the following:

(1) The death of the owner.

(2) A merger, consolidation, or similar transaction requiring approval by the shareholders, partners, or members of the taxpayer under applicable State law, to the extent the taxpayer does not receive cash or tangible property in the merger, consolidation, or other similar transaction.

(e) Liability from Forfeiture. - A taxpayer or an owner of a pass-through entity that forfeits a credit under this section is liable for all past taxes avoided as a result of the credit plus interest at the rate established under G.S. 105-241.21, computed from the date the taxes would have been due if the credit had not been allowed. The past taxes and interest are due 30 days after the date the credit is forfeited. A taxpayer or owner of a pass-through entity that fails to pay the taxes and interest by the due date is subject to the penalties provided in G.S. 105-236. (2006-40, s. 1; 2006-252, s. 2.24; 2007-491, s. 44(1)a; 2008-107, s. 28.4(c).)

§ 105-129.73. (See note for repeal) Tax credited; cap.

(a) Taxes Credited. - The credits allowed by this Article may be claimed against the franchise tax imposed under Article 3 of this Chapter, the income taxes imposed under Article 4 of this Chapter, or the gross premiums tax imposed under Article 8B of this Chapter. The taxpayer may take the credits allowed by this Article against only one of the taxes against which it is allowed. The taxpayer must elect the tax against which a credit will be claimed when filing the return on which it is claimed. This election is binding. Any carryforwards of the credit must be claimed against the same tax.

(b) Cap. - A credit allowed under this Article may not exceed the amount of the tax against which it is claimed for the taxable year reduced by the sum of all credits allowed, except payment of tax made by or on behalf of the taxpayer. Any unused portion of the credit may be carried forward for the succeeding nine years. (2006-40, s. 1.)

§ 105-129.74. (See note for repeal) Coordination with Article 3D of this Chapter.

A taxpayer that claims a credit under this Article may not also claim a credit under Article 3D of this Chapter with respect to the same activity. The rules and fee schedule adopted under G.S. 105-129.36A apply to this Article. (2006-40, s. 1.)

§ 105-129.75. Sunset.

This Article expires January 1, 2015, for rehabilitation projects for which an application for an eligibility certification is submitted on or after that date. (2006-40, s. 1; 2008-107, s. 28.4(d); 2010-31, s. 31.5(a); 2012-36, s. 12(b).)

§ 105-129.75A. (See note for repeal) Report.

The Department must include in the economic incentives report required by G.S. 105-256 the following information itemized by taxpayer:

(1)   The number of taxpayers that took the credits allowed in this Article.

(2)   The amount of rehabilitation expenses and qualified rehabilitation expenditures with respect to which credits were taken.

(3)   The total cost to the General Fund of the credits taken. (2010-166, s. 1.8.)

Article 3I.

§ 105-129.76. Reserved for future codification purposes.

§ 105-129.77. Reserved for future codification purposes.

Article 3I.

§ 105-129.78. Reserved for future codification purposes.

§ 105-129.79. Reserved for future codification purposes.

Article 3J.

Tax Credits for Growing Businesses.

(See G.S. 105-129.82(a) for repeal of Article.)

§ 105-129.80. (See notes) Legislative findings.

The General Assembly finds that:

(1)   It is the policy of the State of North Carolina to stimulate economic activity and to create new jobs for the citizens of the State by encouraging and promoting the expansion of existing business and industry within the State and by recruiting and attracting new business and industry to the State.

(2)   Both short-term and long-term economic trends at the State, national, and international levels have made the successful implementation of the State's economic development policy and programs both more critical and more challenging, and the decline in the State's traditional industries, and the resulting adverse impact upon the State and its citizens, have been exacerbated in recent years by adverse national and State economic trends that contribute to the reduction in the State's industrial base and that inhibit the State's ability to sustain or attract new and expanding businesses.

(3)   The economic condition of the State is not static, and recent changes in the State's economic condition have created economic distress that requires a reevaluation of certain existing State programs and the enactment of a new program as provided in this Article that is designed to stimulate new economic activity and to create new jobs within the State.

(4)   The enactment of this Article is necessary to stimulate the economy and create new jobs in North Carolina, and this Article will promote the general welfare and confer, as its primary purpose and effect, benefits on citizens throughout the State through the creation of new jobs, an enlargement of the

overall tax base, an expansion and diversification of the State's industrial base, and an increase in revenue to the State and its political subdivisions.

(5) The purpose of this Article is to stimulate economic activity and to create new jobs within the State.

(6) The State is in need of a focused tax credit program that encourages and facilitates economic growth and development within the State.

(7) The resources of the State are not evenly distributed throughout the State and different communities have different abilities and needs in attracting and maintaining new and expanding business and industry. (2006-252, s. 1.1.)

§ 105-129.81. (See notes) Definitions.

The following definitions apply in this Article:

(1) Agrarian growth zone. - Defined in G.S. 143B-437.010.

(2) Air courier services. - Defined in G.S. 143B-437.01.

(3) Aircraft maintenance and repair. - The provision of specialized maintenance or repair services for commercial aircraft or the rebuilding of commercial aircraft.

(4) Business property. - Tangible personal property that is used in a business and capitalized by the taxpayer for tax purposes under the Code.

(5) Company headquarters. - Defined in G.S. 143B-437.01.

(6) Cost. - In the case of property owned by the taxpayer, cost is determined pursuant to regulations adopted under section 1012 of the Code. In the case of property the taxpayer leases from another, cost is value as determined pursuant to G.S. 105-130.4(j)(2).

(7) Customer service call center. - The provision of support service by a business to its customers by telephone or other electronic means to support products or services of the business. For the purposes of this definition, an establishment is primarily engaged in providing support services by telephone or

other electronic means only if at least sixty percent (60%) of its calls are incoming or at least sixty percent (60%) of its other electronic communications are initiated by its customers.

(8) Development tier. - The classification assigned to an area pursuant to G.S. 143B-437.08.

(9) Electronic shopping and mail order houses. - An industry in electronic shopping and mail order houses industry group 4541 as defined by NAICS.

(9a) Environmental disqualifying event. - Any of the following occurrences:

a. During the tax year in which the activity occurred for which a credit is being claimed, a civil penalty was assessed against the taxpayer by the Department of Environment and Natural Resources for failure to comply with an order issued by an agency of the Department to abate or remediate a violation of any program administered by the agency.

b. During the tax year in which the activity occurred for which a credit is being claimed or in the prior two tax years, any of the following:

1. A finding was made by the Department of Environment and Natural Resources that the taxpayer knowingly and willfully, as defined in G.S. 143-215.6B, including all limitations thereto, committed a violation of any program implemented by an agency of the Department.

2. An assessment for damages to fish or wildlife pursuant to G.S. 143-215.3(a)(7) was made against the taxpayer.

3. A judicial order for injunctive relief was issued against the taxpayer in connection with a violation of any program implemented by an agency of the Department of Environment and Natural Resources.

c. During the tax year in which the activity occurred for which the credit is being claimed or in the prior four tax years, a criminal penalty was imposed on the taxpayer in connection with a violation of any program implemented by an agency of the Department of Environment and Natural Resources.

(10) Establishment. - Defined in 29 C.F.R. § 1904.46, as it existed on January 1, 2002.

(11) Full-time job. - A position that requires at least 1,600 hours of work per year and is intended to be held by one employee during the entire year. A full-time employee is an employee who holds a full-time job.

(12) Hub. - Defined in G.S. 105-164.3.

(13) Information technology and services. - Defined in G.S. 143B-437.01.

(14) Long-term unemployed worker. - An individual that has been totally unemployed for at least the preceding 26 consecutive weeks as evidenced by records maintained by the Division of Employment Security (DES) of the Department of Commerce.

(15) Manufacturing. - Defined in G.S. 143B-437.01.

(16) Motorsports facility. - A motorsports racetrack classified in the United States racetrack national industry 711212, as defined by NAICS.

(17) Motorsports racing team. - A professional racing team primarily engaged in the research and development, design, manufacture, repair, maintenance, and operation of motor vehicles used in live motorsports racing events before a paying audience.

(18) NAICS. - Defined in G.S. 105-228.90.

(19) New job. - A full-time job that represents a net increase in the number of the taxpayer's employees statewide. A new employee is an employee who holds a new job. The term does not include a job currently located in this State that is transferred to the business from a related member of the business.

(20) Overdue tax debt. - Defined in G.S. 105-243.1.

(20a) (Effective for taxable years beginning on or after January 1, 2013) Port enhancement zone. - Defined in G.S. 143B-437.013.

(21) Purchase. - Defined in section 179 of the Code.

(22) Related member. - Defined in G.S. 105-130.7A.

(23) Research and development. - An industry in scientific research and development services industry group 5417 as defined by NAICS.

(24) Urban progress zone. - The classification assigned to an area pursuant to G.S. 143B-437.09.

(25) Warehousing. - Defined in G.S. 143B-437.01.

(26) Wholesale trade. - Defined in G.S. 143B-437.01. (2006-252, s. 1.1; 2007-484, s. 33(b); 2010-147, s. 1.3; 2011-302, s. 6; 2011-330, s. 31(b); 2011-401, s. 5.1; 2012-79, s. 2.4; 2013-360, s. 15.18(b).)

§ 105-129.82. (See notes) Sunset; studies.

(a) Sunset. - This Article is repealed effective for business activities that occur on or after January 1, 2014.

(b) Equity Study. - The Department of Commerce shall study the effect of the tax incentives provided in this Article on tax equity. This study shall include the following:

(1) Reexamining the formula in G.S. 143B-437.08 used to define development tiers, to include consideration of alternative measures for more equitable treatment of counties in similar economic circumstances.

(2) Considering whether the assignment of tiers and the applicable thresholds are equitable for smaller counties.

(3) Compiling any available data on whether expanding North Carolina businesses receive fewer benefits than out-of-State businesses that locate to North Carolina.

(c) Impact Study. - The Department of Commerce shall study the effectiveness of the tax incentives provided in this Article. This study shall include:

(1) Studying the distribution of tax incentives across new and expanding businesses and industries.

(2) Examining data on economic recruitment for the period from 2005 through the most recent year for which data are available by county, by industry

type, by size of investment, and by number of jobs, and other relevant information to determine the pattern of business locations and expansions before and after the enactment of this Article.

(3) Measuring the direct costs and benefits of the tax incentives.

(4) Compiling available information on the current use of incentives by other states and whether that use is increasing or declining.

(d) Report. - The Department of Commerce shall report the results of these studies and its recommendations to the General Assembly biennially with the first report due by June 1, 2009. (2006-252, s. 1.1; 2010-147, s. 1.1; 2012-36, s. 5.)

§ 105-129.83. (See note for repeal) Eligibility; forfeiture.

(a) Eligible Business. - A taxpayer is eligible for a credit under this Article only with respect to activities occurring at an establishment whose primary activity is listed in this subsection. The primary activity of an establishment is determined based on the establishment's principal product or group of products produced or distributed, or services rendered.

(1) Air courier services hub.

(2) Aircraft maintenance and repair.

(3) Company headquarters, but only if the additional eligibility requirements of subsection (b) of this section are satisfied.

(4) Customer service call centers.

(5) Electronic shopping and mail order houses.

(6) Information technology and services.

(7) Manufacturing.

(8) Motorsports facility.

(9) Motorsports racing team.

(10) Research and development.

(11) Warehousing.

(12) Wholesale trade.

(b) Company Headquarters Eligibility. - A taxpayer is eligible for a credit under this Article with respect to a company headquarters only if the taxpayer creates at least 75 new jobs at the company headquarters within a 24-month period. A taxpayer that meets this job creation requirement is eligible for credits under this Article with respect to the company headquarters for three taxable years beginning with the year in which the job creation requirement is satisfied. A taxpayer that creates an additional 75 new jobs at the company headquarters in a 24-month period during a three-year eligibility period does not qualify for any extended eligibility period. However, a taxpayer that creates an additional 75 new jobs at the company headquarters in a 24-month period after the completion of a three-year eligibility period is eligible for credits with respect to the company headquarters for an additional three taxable years beginning in the year in which the additional job creation requirement is satisfied.

(c) (Effective for taxable years beginning before January 1, 2013) Wage Standard. - A taxpayer is eligible for a credit under this Article in a development tier two or three area only if the taxpayer satisfies a wage standard. The taxpayer is not required to satisfy a wage standard if the activity occurs in a development tier one area. Jobs that are located within an urban progress zone or an agrarian growth zone but not in a development tier one area satisfy the wage standard if they pay an average weekly wage that is at least equal to ninety percent (90%) of the lesser of the average wage for all insured private employers in the State and the average wage for all insured private employers in the county. All other jobs satisfy the wage standard if they pay an average weekly wage that is at least equal to the lesser of one hundred ten percent (110%) of the average wage for all insured private employers in the State and ninety percent (90%) of the average wage for all insured private employers in the county. The Department of Commerce shall annually publish the wage standard for each county.

In making the wage calculation, the taxpayer shall include any jobs that were filled for at least 1,600 hours during the calendar year the taxpayer engages in the activity that qualifies for the credit even if those jobs are not filled at the time the taxpayer claims the credit. For a taxpayer with a taxable year other than a calendar year, the taxpayer shall use the wage standard for the calendar year in which the taxable year begins. Only full-time jobs are included when making the wage calculation.

(c) (Effective for taxable years beginning on or after January 1, 2013) Wage Standard. - A taxpayer is eligible for a credit under this Article in a development tier two or three area only if the taxpayer satisfies a wage standard. The taxpayer is not required to satisfy a wage standard if the activity occurs in a development tier one area. Jobs that are located within an urban progress zone, a port enhancement zone, or an agrarian growth zone but not in a development tier one area satisfy the wage standard if they pay an average weekly wage that is at least equal to ninety percent (90%) of the lesser of the average wage for all insured private employers in the State and the average wage for all insured private employers in the county. All other jobs satisfy the wage standard if they pay an average weekly wage that is at least equal to the lesser of one hundred ten percent (110%) of the average wage for all insured private employers in the State and ninety percent (90%) of the average wage for all insured private employers in the county. The Department of Commerce shall annually publish the wage standard for each county.

In making the wage calculation, the taxpayer shall include any jobs that were filled for at least 1,600 hours during the calendar year the taxpayer engages in the activity that qualifies for the credit even if those jobs are not filled at the time the taxpayer claims the credit. For a taxpayer with a taxable year other than a calendar year, the taxpayer shall use the wage standard for the calendar year in which the taxable year begins. Only full-time jobs are included when making the wage calculation.

(d) Health Insurance. - A taxpayer is eligible for a credit under this Article only if the taxpayer provides health insurance for all of the full-time jobs at the establishment with respect to which the credit is claimed when the taxpayer engages in the activity that qualifies for the credit. For the purposes of this subsection, a taxpayer provides health insurance if it pays at least fifty percent (50%) of the premiums for health care coverage that equals or exceeds the minimum provisions of the basic health care plan of coverage recommended by the Small Employer Carrier Committee pursuant to G.S. 58-50-125.

Each year that a taxpayer claims a credit or carryforward of a credit allowed under this Article, the taxpayer shall provide with the tax return the taxpayer's certification that the taxpayer continues to provide health insurance for all the jobs at the establishment with respect to which the credit was claimed. If the taxpayer ceases to provide health insurance for the jobs during a taxable year, the credit expires, and the taxpayer may not take any remaining installment or carryforward of the credit.

(e)   Environmental Impact. - A taxpayer is eligible for a credit allowed under this Article only if the taxpayer certifies that, at the time the taxpayer claims the credit, there has not been a final determination unfavorable to the taxpayer with respect to an environmental disqualifying event. For the purposes of this section, a "final determination unfavorable to the taxpayer" occurs when there is no further opportunity for the taxpayer to seek administrative or judicial appeal, review, certiorari, or rehearing of the environmental disqualifying event and the disqualifying event has not been reversed or withdrawn. No later than January 31 of each year, the Secretary of Environment and Natural Resources shall provide an annual report to the Department listing all environmental disqualifying events for which a final determination unfavorable to the taxpayer was made in the prior calendar year and shall provide the name of the taxpayer involved and the date that the disqualifying event occurred.

(f)   Safety and Health Programs. - A taxpayer is eligible for a credit allowed under this Article only if the taxpayer certifies that, as of the time the taxpayer claims the credit, at the establishment with respect to which the credit is claimed, the taxpayer has no citations under the Occupational Safety and Health Act that have become a final order within the past three years for willful serious violations or for failing to abate serious violations. For the purposes of this subsection, "serious violation" has the same meaning as in G.S. 95-127. The Commissioner of Labor shall notify the Department of Revenue annually of all employers who have had these citations become final orders within the past three years.

(g)   Overdue Tax Debts. - A taxpayer is not eligible for a credit allowed under this Article if, at the time the taxpayer claims the credit or an installment or carryforward of the credit, the taxpayer has received a notice of an overdue tax debt and that overdue tax debt has not been satisfied or otherwise resolved.

(h)   Expiration. - If, during the period that installments of a credit under this Article accrue, the taxpayer is no longer engaged in one of the types of business described in subsection (a) of this section at the establishment for which the credit was claimed, the credit expires. If, during the period that installments of a credit under this Article accrue, the number of jobs of an eligible company headquarters falls below the minimum number required under subsection (b) of this section, any credit associated with that company headquarters expires. When a credit expires, the taxpayer may not take any remaining installments of the credit. The taxpayer may, however, take the portion of an installment that accrued in a previous year and was carried forward to the extent permitted under G.S. 105-129.84. A change in the development tier designation of the location of an establishment does not result in expiration of a credit under this Article.

(i)   Forfeiture. - A taxpayer forfeits a credit allowed under this Article if the taxpayer was not eligible for the credit for the calendar year in which the taxpayer engaged in the activity for which the credit was claimed. A taxpayer forfeits a credit previously allowed under this Article if a final determination unfavorable to the taxpayer with respect to an environmental disqualifying event is made that is applicable to the year in which the activity occurred for which the credit was claimed. In addition, a taxpayer forfeits a credit for investment in real property under G.S. 105-129.89 if the taxpayer fails to timely create the number of required new jobs or to timely make the required level of investment under G.S. 105-129.89(b). A taxpayer that forfeits a credit under this Article is liable for all past taxes avoided as a result of the credit plus interest at the rate established under G.S. 105-241.21, computed from the date the taxes would have been due if the credit had not been allowed. The past taxes and interest are due 30 days after the date the credit is forfeited; a taxpayer that fails to pay the past taxes and interest by the due date is subject to the penalties provided in G.S. 105-236.

(j)   Change in Ownership of Business. - As used in this subsection, the term "business" means a taxpayer or an establishment. The sale, merger, consolidation, conversion, acquisition, or bankruptcy of a business, or any transaction by which an existing business reformulates itself as another business, does not create new eligibility in a succeeding business with respect to credits for which the predecessor was not eligible under this Article. A successor business may, however, take any credit or carried-over portion of a credit that its predecessor could have taken if it had a tax liability. The acquisition of a business is a new investment that creates new eligibility in the acquiring taxpayer under this Article if any of the following conditions are met:

(1)   The business closed before it was acquired.

(2)   The business was required to file a notice of plant closing or mass layoff under the federal Worker Adjustment and Retraining Notification Act, 29 U.S.C. § 2101, before it was acquired.

(3) The business was acquired by its employees directly or indirectly through an acquisition company under an employee stock option transaction or another similar mechanism. For the purpose of this subdivision, "acquired" means that as part of the initial purchase of a business by the employees, the purchase included an agreement for the employees through the employee stock option transaction or another similar mechanism to obtain one of the following:

a. Ownership of more than fifty percent (50%) of the business.

b. Ownership of not less than forty percent (40%) of the business within seven years if the business has tangible assets with a net book value in excess of one hundred million dollars ($100,000,000) and has the majority of its operations located in a development tier one area.

(k) Advisory Ruling. - A taxpayer may request in writing from the Secretary of Revenue specific advice regarding eligibility for a credit under this Article. G.S. 105-264 governs the effect of this advice. A taxpayer may not legally rely upon advice offered by any other State or local government official or employee acting in an official capacity regarding eligibility for a credit under this Article.

(l) (Effective for taxable years beginning before January 1, 2013) Planned Expansion. - A taxpayer that signs a letter of commitment with the Department of Commerce, after the Department has calculated the development tier designations for the next year but before the beginning of that year, to undertake specific activities at a specific site within the next two years may calculate the credit for which it qualifies based on the establishment's development tier designation and urban progress zone or agrarian growth zone designation in the year in which the letter of commitment was signed by the taxpayer. If the taxpayer does not engage in the activities within the two-year period, the taxpayer does not qualify for the credit; however, if the taxpayer later engages in the activities, the taxpayer qualifies for the credit based on the development tier and urban progress zone or agrarian growth zone designations in effect at that time.

(l) (Effective for taxable years beginning on or after January 1, 2013) Planned Expansion. - A taxpayer that signs a letter of commitment with the Department of Commerce, after the Department has calculated the development tier designations for the next year but before the beginning of that year, to undertake specific activities at a specific site within the next two years may calculate the credit for which it qualifies based on the establishment's development tier designation and urban progress zone, port enhancement zone, or agrarian growth zone designation in the year in which the letter of commitment was signed by the taxpayer. If the taxpayer does not engage in the activities within the two-year period, the taxpayer does not qualify for the credit; however, if the taxpayer later engages in the activities, the taxpayer qualifies for the credit based on the development tier and urban progress zone, port enhancement zone, or agrarian growth zone designations in effect at that time.

(m) Qualified Capital Intensive Corporations. - A corporation that is a qualified capital intensive corporation under G.S. 105-130.4(s1) is not eligible for any credit under this Article with respect to the facility that satisfies the condition of subdivision (2) of that subsection. (2006-252, s. 1.1; 2007-491, s. 44(1)a; 2009-54, s. 3; 2010-147, s. 1.4; 2011-302, s. 7.)

§ 105-129.84. (See notes) Tax election; cap; carryforwards; limitations.

(a) Tax Election. - The credits provided in this Article are allowed against the franchise tax levied in Article 3 of this Chapter, the income taxes levied in Article 4 of this Chapter, and the gross premiums tax levied in Article 8B of this Chapter. The taxpayer may divide a credit between the taxes against which it is allowed. Carryforwards of a credit may be divided between the taxes against which it is allowed without regard to the original election regarding the division of the credit.

(b) Cap. - The credits allowed under this Article may not exceed fifty percent (50%) of the cumulative amount of taxes against which they may be claimed for the taxable year, reduced by the sum of all other credits allowed against those taxes, except tax payments made by or on behalf of the taxpayer. This limitation applies to the cumulative amount of credit, including carryforwards, claimed by the taxpayer under this Article for the taxable year.

(c) Carryforward. - Unless a longer carryforward period applies, any unused portion of a credit allowed under G.S. 105-129.87 or G.S. 105-129.88 may be carried forward for the succeeding five years, and any unused portion of a credit allowed under G.S. 105-129.89 may be carried forward for the succeeding 15 years. If the Secretary of Commerce makes a written determination that the taxpayer is expected to purchase or lease, and place in service in connection with an eligible business within a two-year period, at least one hundred fifty million dollars ($150,000,000) worth of business and real property, any unused portion of a credit under this Article with respect to the establishment that satisfies that condition may be carried forward for the succeeding 20 years. If the taxpayer does not make the required level of investment, the taxpayer shall apply the standard carryforward period rather than the 20-year carryforward period.

(d) Statute of Limitations. - Notwithstanding Article 9 of this Chapter, a taxpayer shall claim a credit under this Article within six months after the date set by statute for the filing of the return, including any extensions of that date.

(e) Credit Treated as Tax Payment. - The owner of a pass-through entity that claims a credit under this Article may treat some or all of the credit claimed as a tax payment made by or on behalf of the taxpayer. A credit claimed that is treated as a tax payment is subject to all provisions of this section. A credit claimed that is treated as a tax payment does not accrue interest under G.S. 105-241.21 if the payment is determined to be an overpayment. A taxpayer that elects to have a credit claimed under this Article treated as a tax payment must make this election when the return is filed. (2006-252, s. 1.1; 2011-297, s. 4; 2013-414, s. 4.)

§ 105-129.85. (See notes) Fees and reports.

(a) Fee. - When filing a return for a taxable year in which the taxpayer engaged in activity for which the taxpayer is eligible for a credit under this Article, the taxpayer shall pay the Department of Revenue a fee of five hundred dollars ($500.00) for each type of credit the taxpayer claims or intends to claim with respect to an establishment. The fee is due at the time the return is due for the taxable year in which the taxpayer engaged in the activity for which the taxpayer is eligible for a credit. No credit is allowed under this Article for a taxable year until all outstanding fees have been paid. Fees collected under this section shall be credited to the General Fund.

(b) Report. - The Department must include in the economic incentives report required by G.S. 105-256 the following information itemized by credit and by taxpayer:

(1) The number and amount of credits generated and taken for each credit allowed in this Article.

(2)   The number and development tier area of new jobs with respect to which credits were generated and to which credits were taken.

(3)   The cost and development tier area of business property with respect to which credits were generated and to which credits were taken.

(4)   The cost and development tier area of real property investment with respect to which credits were generated and to which credits were taken. (2006-252, s. 1.1; 2010-166, s. 1.9.)

§ 105-129.86. (See notes) Substantiation.

(a)   Records. - To claim a credit allowed by this Article, the taxpayer shall provide any information required by the Secretary of Revenue. Every taxpayer claiming a credit under this Article shall maintain and make available for inspection by the Secretary of Revenue any records the Secretary considers necessary to determine and verify the amount of the credit to which the taxpayer is entitled. The burden of proving eligibility for the credit and the amount of the credit shall rest upon the taxpayer, and no credit shall be allowed to a taxpayer that fails to maintain adequate records or to make them available for inspection.

(b)   Documentation. - Each taxpayer shall provide with the tax return qualifying information for each credit claimed under this Article. The qualifying information shall be in the form prescribed by the Secretary and shall be signed and affirmed by the individual who signs the taxpayer's tax return. The information required by this subsection is information demonstrating that the taxpayer has met the conditions for qualifying for a credit and any carryforwards and includes the following:

(1)   The physical location of the jobs and investment with respect to which the credit is claimed, including the street address and the development tier designation of the establishment.

(2)   The type of business with respect to which the credit is claimed and the average weekly wage at the establishment with respect to which the credit is claimed.

(3)   Any other qualifying information related to a specific credit allowed under this Article. (2006-252, s. 1.1.)

§ 105-129.87. (Effective for taxable years beginning before January 1, 2013 — See notes) Credit for creating jobs.

(a) Credit. - A taxpayer that meets the eligibility requirements set out in G.S. 105-129.83 and satisfies the threshold requirement for new job creation in this State under subsection (b) of this section during the taxable year is allowed a credit for creating jobs. The amount of the credit for each new job created is set out in the table below and is based on the development tier designation of the county in which the job is located. If the job is located in an urban progress zone or an agrarian growth zone, the amount of the credit is increased by one thousand dollars ($1,000) per job. In addition, if a job located in an urban progress zone or an agrarian growth zone is filled by a resident of that zone or by a long-term unemployed worker, the amount of the credit is increased by an additional two thousand dollars ($2,000) per job.

Area Development Tier	Amount of Credit
Tier One	$12,500
Tier Two	5,000
Tier Three	750

(b) Threshold. - The applicable threshold is the appropriate amount set out in the following table based on the development tier designation of the county where the new jobs are created during the taxable year. If the taxpayer creates new jobs at more than one eligible establishment in a county during the taxable year, the threshold applies to the aggregate number of new jobs created at all eligible establishments within the county during that year. If the taxpayer creates new jobs at eligible establishments in different counties during the taxable year, the threshold applies separately to the aggregate number of new jobs created at eligible establishments in each county. If the taxpayer creates new jobs in an urban progress zone or an agrarian growth zone, the applicable threshold is the one for a development tier one area. New jobs created in an urban progress zone or an agrarian growth zone are not aggregated with jobs created at any other eligible establishments regardless of county.

Area Development Tier	Threshold
Tier One	5

Tier Two   10

Tier Three   15

(c)   Calculation. - A job is located in a county, an urban progress zone, or an agrarian growth zone if more than fifty percent (50%) of the employee's duties are performed in the county or the zone. The number of new jobs a taxpayer creates during the taxable year is determined by subtracting the average number of full-time employees the taxpayer had in this State during the 12-month period preceding the beginning of the taxable year from the average number of full-time employees the taxpayer has in this State during the taxable year.

(d)   Installments. - The credit may not be taken in the taxable year in which the new jobs are created. Instead, the credit shall be taken in equal installments over the four years following the taxable year in which the new jobs were created and is conditional upon the continued maintenance of those jobs by the taxpayer. If, in one of the four years in which the installment of a credit accrues, a job is no longer filled, the credit with respect to that job expires, and the taxpayer may not take any remaining installment of the credit with respect to that job. If, in one of the years in which the installment of a credit accrues, the number of the taxpayer's full-time employees falls below the sum of the applicable threshold and the number of full-time employees the taxpayer had in the year before the year in which the taxpayer qualified for the credit, the credits with respect to all of the new jobs expire, and the taxpayer may not take any remaining installments of the credits. When a credit expires under this subsection, the taxpayer may, however, take the portion of an installment that accrued in a previous year and was carried forward to the extent permitted under G.S. 105-129.84.

(e)   Transferred Jobs. - Jobs transferred from one area in the State to another area in the State are not considered new jobs for purposes of this section. Jobs that were located in this State and that are transferred to the taxpayer from a related member of the taxpayer are not considered new jobs for purposes of this section. If, in one of the four years in which the installment of a credit accrues, the job with respect to which the credit was claimed is moved to an area in a higher-numbered development tier or out of an urban progress zone or an agrarian growth zone, the remaining installments of the credit are allowed only to the extent they would have been allowed if the job was initially created in the area to which it was moved. If, in one of the years in which the installment of a credit accrues, the job with respect to which the credit was claimed is moved to an area in a lower-numbered development tier or an urban progress zone or an agrarian growth zone, the remaining installments of the credit shall be calculated as if the job had been created initially in the area to which it was moved.

(f) Wage Standard. - For the purposes of this section, a taxpayer satisfies the wage standard requirement of G.S. 105-129.83 only if the taxpayer satisfies the requirement with respect to both the new jobs, considered collectively, for which a credit is claimed and all of the jobs at the establishment, considered collectively, with respect to which a credit is claimed.

(g) No Double Credit. - A taxpayer may not claim a credit under this section with respect to jobs for which a taxpayer claims a credit under G.S. 105-129.8. (2006-252, s. 1.1; 2007-527, s. 6.)

§ 105-129.87. (Effective for taxable years beginning on or after January 1, 2013 - See notes for repeal) Credit for creating jobs.

(a) Credit. - A taxpayer that meets the eligibility requirements set out in G.S. 105-129.83 and satisfies the threshold requirement for new job creation in this State under subsection (b) of this section during the taxable year is allowed a credit for creating jobs. The amount of the credit for each new job created is set out in the table below and is based on the development tier designation of the county in which the job is located. If the job is located in an urban progress zone, a port enhancement zone, or an agrarian growth zone, the amount of the credit is increased by one thousand dollars ($1,000) per job. In addition, if a job located in an urban progress zone, a port enhancement zone, or an agrarian growth zone is filled by a resident of that zone or by a long-term unemployed worker, the amount of the credit is increased by an additional two thousand dollars ($2,000) per job.

Area Development Tier	Amount of Credit
Tier One	$12,500
Tier Two	5,000
Tier Three	750

(b) Threshold. - The applicable threshold is the appropriate amount set out in the following table based on the development tier designation of the county where the new jobs are created during the taxable year. If the taxpayer creates new jobs at more than one eligible establishment in a county during the taxable year, the threshold applies to the aggregate number of new jobs created at all eligible establishments within the county during that year. If the taxpayer creates new jobs at eligible establishments in different counties during the taxable year, the threshold applies separately to the aggregate number of new jobs created at eligible establishments in each county. If the taxpayer creates new jobs in an urban progress zone, a port enhancement zone, or an agrarian growth zone, the applicable threshold is the one for a development tier one area. New jobs created in an urban progress zone, a port enhancement zone, or an agrarian growth zone are not aggregated with jobs created at any other eligible establishments regardless of county.

Area Development Tier	Threshold
Tier One	5
Tier Two	10
Tier Three	15

(c) Calculation. - A job is located in a county, an urban progress zone, a port enhancement zone, or an agrarian growth zone if more than fifty percent (50%) of the employee's duties are performed in the county or the zone. The number of new jobs a taxpayer creates during the taxable year is determined by subtracting the average number of full-time employees the taxpayer had in this State during the 12-month period preceding the beginning of the taxable year from the average number of full-time employees the taxpayer has in this State during the taxable year.

(d) Installments. - The credit may not be taken in the taxable year in which the new jobs are created. Instead, the credit shall be taken in equal installments over the four years following the taxable year in which the new jobs were created and is conditional upon the continued maintenance of those jobs by the taxpayer. If, in one of the four years in which the installment of a credit accrues, a job is no longer filled, the credit with respect to that job expires, and the taxpayer may not take any remaining installment of the credit with respect to that job. If, in one of the years in which the installment of a credit accrues, the number of the taxpayer's full-time employees falls below the sum of the applicable threshold and the number of full-time employees the taxpayer had in the year before the year in which the taxpayer qualified for the credit, the credits with respect to all of the new jobs expire, and the taxpayer may not take any remaining installments of the credits. When a credit expires under this subsection, the taxpayer may, however, take the portion of an installment that accrued in a previous year and was carried forward to the extent permitted under G.S. 105-129.84.

(e) Transferred Jobs. - Jobs transferred from one area in the State to another area in the State are not considered new jobs for purposes of this section. Jobs that were located in this State and that are transferred to the taxpayer from a related member of the taxpayer are not considered new jobs for purposes of this section. If, in one of the four years in which the installment of a credit accrues, the job with respect to which the credit was claimed is moved to an area in a higher-numbered development tier or out of an urban progress zone, a port enhancement zone, or an agrarian growth zone, the remaining installments of the credit are allowed only to the extent they would have been allowed if the job was initially created in the area to which it was moved. If, in one of the years in which the installment of a credit accrues, the job with respect to which the credit was claimed is moved to an area in a lower-numbered development tier or an urban progress zone, a port enhancement zone, or an agrarian growth zone, the remaining installments of the credit shall be calculated as if the job had been created initially in the area to which it was moved.

(f) Wage Standard. - For the purposes of this section, a taxpayer satisfies the wage standard requirement of G.S. 105-129.83 only if the taxpayer satisfies the requirement with respect to both the new jobs, considered collectively, for which a credit is claimed and all of the jobs at the establishment, considered collectively, with respect to which a credit is claimed.

(g) No Double Credit. - A taxpayer may not claim a credit under this section with respect to jobs for which a taxpayer claims a credit under G.S. 105-129.8. (2006-252, s. 1.1; 2007-527, s. 6; 2011-302, s. 8.)

§ 105-129.88. (Effective for taxable years beginning before January 1, 2013 — See notes) Credit for investing in business property.

(a) General Credit. - A taxpayer that meets the eligibility requirements set out in G.S. 105-129.83 and that has purchased or leased business property and placed it in service in this State during the taxable year and that has satisfied the threshold requirements of subsection (c) of this section is allowed a credit equal to the applicable percentage of the excess of the eligible investment amount over the applicable threshold. If the taxpayer places business property in service in an urban progress zone or an agrarian growth zone, the applicable percentage is the one for a development tier one area. Business property is eligible if it is not leased to another party. The credit may not be taken for the taxable year in which the business property is placed in service but shall be taken in equal installments over the four years following the taxable year in which it is placed in service. The applicable percentage is as follows:

Area Development Tier	Applicable Percentage
Tier One	7%
Tier Two	5%
Tier Three	3.5%

(b) Eligible Investment Amount. - The eligible investment amount is the lesser of (i) the cost of the eligible business property and (ii) the amount by which the cost of all of the taxpayer's eligible business property that is in service in this State on the last day of the taxable year exceeds the cost of all of the taxpayer's eligible business property that was in service in this State on the last day of the base year. The base year is that year, of the three immediately preceding taxable years, in which the taxpayer had the most eligible business property in service in this State.

(c) Threshold. - The applicable threshold is the appropriate amount set out in the following table based on the development tier where the eligible business property is placed in service during the taxable year. If the taxpayer places business property in service in an urban progress zone or an agrarian growth zone, the applicable threshold is the one for a development tier one area. Business property placed in service in an urban progress zone or an agrarian growth zone is not aggregated with business property placed in service at any other eligible establishments regardless of county. If the taxpayer places eligible business property in service at more than one establishment in a county during the taxable year, the threshold applies to the aggregate amount of eligible business property placed in service during the taxable year at all establishments in the county. If the taxpayer places eligible business property in service at establishments in different counties, the threshold applies separately to the aggregate amount of eligible business property placed in service in each county. If the taxpayer places eligible business property in service at an establishment over the course of a two-year period, the applicable threshold for the second taxable year is reduced by the eligible investment amount for the previous taxable year.

Area Development Tier	Threshold
Tier One	$ -0-
Tier Two	1,000,000
Tier Three	2,000,000

(d) Expiration. - As used in this subsection, the term "disposed of" means disposed of, taken out of service, or moved out of State. If, in one of the four years in which the installment of a credit accrues, the business property with respect to which the credit was claimed is disposed of, the credit expires, and the taxpayer may not take any remaining installment of the credit for that business property unless the cost of that business property is offset in the same taxable year by the taxpayer's new investment in eligible business property placed in service in the same county, as provided in this subsection. If, during the taxable year, the taxpayer disposed of the business property for which installments remain, there has been a net reduction in the cost of all the taxpayer's eligible business property that are in service in the same county as the business property that was disposed of, and the amount of this reduction is greater than twenty percent (20%) of the cost of the business property that was disposed of, then the credit for the business property that was disposed of expires. If the amount of the net reduction is equal to twenty percent (20%) or less of the cost of the business property that was disposed of, or if there is no net reduction, then the credit does not expire. In determining the amount of any net reduction during the taxable year, the cost of business property the taxpayer placed in service during the taxable year and for which the taxpayer claims a credit under Article 3A or Article 3B of this Chapter may not be included in the cost of all the taxpayer's eligible business property that is in service. If in a single taxable year business property with respect to two or more credits in the same county are disposed of, the net reduction in the cost of all the taxpayer's eligible business property that is in service in the same county is compared to the total cost of all the business property for which credits expired in order to determine whether the remaining installments of the credits are forfeited.

The expiration of a credit does not prevent the taxpayer from taking the portion of an installment that accrued in a previous year and was carried forward to the extent permitted under G.S. 105-129.84.

(e) Transferred Property. - If, in one of the four years in which the installment of a credit accrues, the business property with respect to which the credit was claimed is moved to a county in a higher-numbered development tier or out of an urban progress zone or an agrarian growth zone, the remaining installments of the credit are allowed only to the extent they would have been allowed if the business property had been placed in service initially in the area to which it was moved. If, in one of the four years in which the installment of a credit accrues, the business property with respect to which a credit was claimed is moved to a county in a lower-numbered development tier or an urban progress zone or an agrarian growth zone, the remaining installments of the credit shall be calculated as if the business property had been placed in service initially in the area to which it was moved.

(f) Wage Standard. - For the purposes of this section, a taxpayer satisfies the wage standard requirement of G.S. 105-129.83 only if the taxpayer satisfies the requirement with respect to all of the jobs at the establishment, considered collectively, with respect to which a credit is claimed.

(g) No Double Credit. - A taxpayer may not claim a credit under this section with respect to business property for which the taxpayer claims a credit under G.S. 105-129.9 or G.S. 105-129.9A. (2006-252, s. 1.1; 2007-527, ss. 7, 8.)

§ 105-129.88. (Effective for taxable years beginning on or after January 1, 2013 - See notes for repeal) Credit for investing in business property.

(a) General Credit. - A taxpayer that meets the eligibility requirements set out in G.S. 105-129.83 and that has purchased or leased business property and placed it in service in this State during the taxable year and that has satisfied the threshold requirements of subsection (c) of this section is allowed a credit equal to the applicable percentage of the excess of the eligible investment amount over the applicable threshold. If the taxpayer places business property in service in an urban progress zone, a port enhancement zone, or an agrarian growth zone, the applicable percentage is the one for a development tier one area. Business property is eligible if it is not leased to another party. The credit may not be taken for the taxable year in which the business property is placed in service but shall be taken in equal installments over the four years following the taxable year in which it is placed in service. The applicable percentage is as follows:

Area Development Tier	Applicable Percentage
Tier One	7%
Tier Two	5%
Tier Three	3.5%

(b)　Eligible Investment Amount. - The eligible investment amount is the lesser of (i) the cost of the eligible business property and (ii) the amount by which the cost of all of the taxpayer's eligible business property that is in service in this State on the last day of the taxable year exceeds the cost of all of the taxpayer's eligible business property that was in service in this State on the last day of the base year. The base year is that year, of the three immediately preceding taxable years, in which the taxpayer had the most eligible business property in service in this State.

(c)　Threshold. - The applicable threshold is the appropriate amount set out in the following table based on the development tier where the eligible business property is placed in service during the taxable year. If the taxpayer places business property in service in an urban progress zone, a port enhancement zone, or an agrarian growth zone, the applicable threshold is the one for a development tier one area. Business property placed in service in an urban progress zone, a port enhancement zone, or an agrarian growth zone is not aggregated with business property placed in service at any other eligible establishments regardless of county. If the taxpayer places eligible business property in service at more than one establishment in a county during the taxable year, the threshold applies to the aggregate amount of eligible business property placed in service during the taxable year at all establishments in the county. If the taxpayer places eligible business property in service at establishments in different counties, the threshold applies separately to the aggregate amount of eligible business property placed in service in each county. If the taxpayer places eligible business property in service at an establishment over the course of a two-year period, the applicable threshold for the second taxable year is reduced by the eligible investment amount for the previous taxable year.

Area Development Tier	Threshold
Tier One	$ -0-
Tier Two	1,000,000
Tier Three	2,000,000

(d) Expiration. - As used in this subsection, the term "disposed of" means disposed of, taken out of service, or moved out of State. If, in one of the four years in which the installment of a credit accrues, the business property with respect to which the credit was claimed is disposed of, the credit expires, and the taxpayer may not take any remaining installment of the credit for that business property unless the cost of that business property is offset in the same taxable year by the taxpayer's new investment in eligible business property placed in service in the same county, as provided in this subsection. If, during the taxable year, the taxpayer disposed of the business property for which installments remain, there has been a net reduction in the cost of all the taxpayer's eligible business property that are in service in the same county as the business property that was disposed of, and the amount of this reduction is greater than twenty percent (20%) of the cost of the business property that was disposed of, then the credit for the business property that was disposed of expires. If the amount of the net reduction is equal to twenty percent (20%) or less of the cost of the business property that was disposed of, or if there is no net reduction, then the credit does not expire. In determining the amount of any net reduction during the taxable year, the cost of business property the taxpayer placed in service during the taxable year and for which the taxpayer claims a credit under Article 3A or Article 3B of this Chapter may not be included in the cost of all the taxpayer's eligible business property that is in service. If in a single taxable year business property with respect to two or more credits in the same county are disposed of, the net reduction in the cost of all the taxpayer's eligible business property that is in service in the same county is compared to the total cost of all the business property for which credits expired in order to determine whether the remaining installments of the credits are forfeited.

The expiration of a credit does not prevent the taxpayer from taking the portion of an installment that accrued in a previous year and was carried forward to the extent permitted under G.S. 105-129.84.

(e) Transferred Property. - If, in one of the four years in which the installment of a credit accrues, the business property with respect to which the credit was claimed is moved to a county in a higher-numbered development tier or out of an urban progress zone, a port enhancement zone, or an agrarian growth zone, the remaining installments of the credit are allowed only to the extent they would have been allowed if the business property had been placed in service initially in the area to which it was moved. If, in one of the four years in which the installment of a credit accrues, the business property with respect to which a credit was claimed is moved to a county in a lower-numbered development tier or an urban progress zone, a port enhancement zone, or an agrarian growth zone, the remaining installments of the credit shall be calculated as if the business property had been placed in service initially in the area to which it was moved.

(f) Wage Standard. - For the purposes of this section, a taxpayer satisfies the wage standard requirement of G.S. 105-129.83 only if the taxpayer satisfies the requirement with respect to all of the jobs at the establishment, considered collectively, with respect to which a credit is claimed.

(g) No Double Credit. - A taxpayer may not claim a credit under this section with respect to business property for which the taxpayer claims a credit under G.S. 105-129.9 or G.S. 105-129.9A. (2006-252, s. 1.1; 2007-527, ss. 7, 8; 2011-302, s. 9.)

§ 105-129.89. (See notes) Credit for investment in real property.

(a) Credit. - If a taxpayer that has purchased or leased real property in a development tier one area begins to use the property in an eligible business during the taxable year, the taxpayer is allowed a credit equal to thirty percent (30%) of the eligible investment amount if all of the eligibility requirements of G.S. 105-129.83 and of subsection (b) of this section are met. For the purposes of this section, property is located in a development tier one area if the area the property is located in was a development tier one area at the time the taxpayer made a written application for the determination required under subsection (b) of this section. The eligible investment amount is the lesser of (i) the cost of the property and (ii) the amount by which the cost of all of the real property the taxpayer is using in this State in an eligible business on the last day of the taxable year exceeds the cost of all of the real property the taxpayer was using in this State in an eligible business on the last day of the base year. The base year is that year, of the three immediately preceding taxable years, in which the taxpayer was using the most real property in this State in an eligible business. In the case of property that is leased, the cost of the property is not determined as provided in G.S. 105-129.81 but is considered to be the taxpayer's lease payments over a seven-year period, plus any expenditures made by the taxpayer to improve the property before it is used by the taxpayer if the expenditures are not reimbursed or credited by the lessor. The entire credit may not be taken for the taxable year in which the property is first used in an eligible business but shall be taken in equal installments over the seven years following the taxable year in which the property is first used in an eligible business. When part of the property is first used in an eligible business in one year and part is first used in an eligible business in a later year, separate credits may be claimed for the amount of property first used in an eligible business in each year. The basis in any real property for which a credit is allowed under this section shall be reduced by the amount of credit allowable.

(b)   Determination by the Secretary of Commerce. - A taxpayer is eligible for the credit allowed under this section with respect to an establishment only if the Secretary of Commerce makes a written determination that the taxpayer is expected to purchase or lease and use in an eligible business at that establishment within a three-year period at least ten million dollars ($10,000,000) of real property and that the establishment that is the subject of the credit will create at least 200 new jobs within two years of the time that the property is first used in an eligible business. If the taxpayer fails to timely make the required level of investment or fails to timely create the required number of new jobs, the taxpayer forfeits the credit as provided in G.S. 105-129.83.

(c)   Mixed Use Property. - If the taxpayer uses only part of the property in an eligible business, the amount of the credit allowed under this section is reduced by multiplying it by a fraction, the numerator of which is the square footage of the property used in an eligible business and the denominator of which is the total square footage of the property.

(d)   Expiration. - If, in one of the seven years in which the installment of a credit accrues, the property with respect to which the credit was claimed is no longer used in an eligible business, the credit expires, and the taxpayer may not take any remaining installment of the credit. If, in one of the seven years in which the installment of a credit accrues, part of the property with respect to which the credit was claimed is no longer used in an eligible business, the remaining installments of the credit shall be reduced by multiplying it by the fraction described in subsection (c) of this section. If, in one of the years in which the installment of a credit accrues and by which the taxpayer is required to have created 200 new jobs at the property, the total number of employees the taxpayer employs at the property with respect to which the credit is claimed is less than 200, the credit expires, and the taxpayer may not take any remaining installment of the credit.

In each of these cases, the taxpayer may nonetheless take the portion of an installment that accrued in a previous year and was carried forward to the extent permitted under G.S. 105-129.84.

(e) No Double Credit. - A taxpayer may not claim a credit under this section with respect to real property for which a credit is claimed under G.S. 105-129.12 or G.S. 105-129.12A. (2006-252, s. 1.1.)

§ 105-129.90. Reserved for future codification purposes.

§ 105-129.91. Reserved for future codification purposes.

§ 105-129.92. Reserved for future codification purposes.

§ 105-129.93. Reserved for future codification purposes.

§ 105-129.94. Reserved for future codification purposes.

Article 3K.

Tax Incentives for Railroad Intermodal Facilities.

(Repealed for taxable years beginning on or after January 1, 2038. See G.S. 105-129.99.)

§ 105-129.95. (Repealed for taxable years beginning on or after January 1, 2038 - see note) Definitions.

The following definitions apply in this Article:

(1) Costs of construction. - The costs of acquiring and improving land, constructing buildings and other structures, equipping the facility, and constructing and equipping rail tracks to the railroad intermodal facility that are

necessary to access and support facility operations. In the case of property owned or leased by the taxpayer, cost is determined pursuant to regulations adopted under section 1012 of the Code.

(2) Eligible railroad intermodal facility. - A railroad intermodal facility whose costs of construction exceed thirty million dollars ($30,000,000).

(3) Intermodal facility. - A facility where freight is transferred from one mode of transportation to another.

(4) Railroad intermodal facility. - An intermodal facility whose primary purpose is to transfer freight between a railroad and another mode of transportation. (2007-323, s. 31.23(a); 2007-345, s. 14.7(a).)

§ 105-129.96. (Repealed for taxable years beginning on or after January 1, 2038 - see note) Credit for constructing a railroad intermodal facility.

(a) Credit. - A taxpayer that constructs or leases an eligible railroad intermodal facility in this State and places it in service during the taxable year is allowed a tax credit equal to fifty percent (50%) of all amounts payable by the taxpayer towards the costs of construction or under the lease.

(b) Taxes Credited. - The credit provided in this section is allowed against the franchise tax levied in Article 3 of this Chapter or the income taxes levied in Article 4 of this Chapter. The taxpayer must elect the tax against which a credit will be claimed when filing the return on which the first installment of the credit is claimed. This election is binding. The credit may not exceed fifty percent (50%) of the tax against which it is applied. Any unused portion of a credit may be carried forward for the succeeding 10 years. Any carryforwards of a credit must be claimed against the same tax. (2007-323, s. 31.23(a).)

§ 105-129.97. (Repealed for taxable years beginning on or after January 1, 2038 - see note) Substantiation.

To claim a credit allowed by this Article, the taxpayer must provide any information required by the Secretary. Each taxpayer claiming a credit under this Article must maintain and make available for inspection by the Secretary any records the Secretary considers necessary to determine and verify the amount of the credit to which the taxpayer is entitled. The burden of proving eligibility for a credit and the amount of the credit rests upon the taxpayer, and no credit may be allowed to a taxpayer that fails to maintain adequate records or to make them available for inspection. (2007-323, s. 31.23(a).)

§ 105-129.98. (Repealed for taxable years beginning on or after January 1, 2038 - see note) Report.

The Department must include in the economic incentives report required by G.S. 105-256 the following information itemized by taxpayer:

(1)   The number of taxpayers that claimed a credit allowed in this Article.

(2)   The amount of each credit claimed and the taxes against which it was applied.

(3)   The total cost to the General Fund of the credits claimed. (2007-323, s. 31.23(a); 2010-166, s. 1.10.)

§ 105-129.99. Sunset.

This Article is repealed effective for taxable years beginning on or after January 1, 2038. (2007-323, s. 31.23(a).)

Article 4.

Income Tax.

Part 1. Corporation Income Tax.

§ 105-130. Short title.

This Part of the income tax Article shall be known and may be cited as the Corporation Income Tax Act. (1939, c. 158, s. 300; 1967, c. 1110, s. 3; 1998-98, ss. 42, 61, 68.)

§ 105-130.1. Purpose.

The general purpose of this Part is to impose a tax for the use of the State government upon the net income of every domestic corporation and of every foreign corporation doing business in this State.

The tax imposed upon the net income of corporations in this Part is in addition to all other taxes imposed under this Subchapter. (1939, c. 158, s. 301; 1967, c. 1110, s. 3; 1998-98, s. 69.)

§ 105-130.2. Definitions.

The following definitions apply in this Part:

(1)   Affiliate. - A corporation is an affiliate of another corporation when both are directly or indirectly controlled by the same parent corporation or by the same or associated financial interests by stock ownership, interlocking directors, or by any other means whatsoever, whether the control is direct or through one or more subsidiary, affiliated, or controlled corporations.

(2)   Code. - Defined in G.S. 105-228.90.

(3)   Corporation. - A joint-stock company or association, an insurance company, a domestic corporation, a foreign corporation, or a limited liability company.

(4)   C Corporation. - A corporation that is not an S Corporation.

(5)   Department. - The Department of Revenue.

(6)   Domestic corporation. - A corporation organized under the laws of this State.

(7) Fiscal year. - An income year, ending on the last day of any month other than December. A corporation that pursuant to the provisions of the Code has elected to compute its federal income tax liability on the basis of an annual period varying from 52 to 53 weeks shall compute its taxable income under this Part on the basis of the same period used by the corporation in computing its federal income tax liability for the income year.

(8) Foreign corporation. - Any corporation other than a domestic corporation.

(9) Gross income. - Defined in section 61 of the Code.

(10) Income year. - The calendar year or the fiscal year upon the basis of which the net income is computed under this Part. If no fiscal year has been established, the income year is the calendar year. In the case of a return made for a fractional part of a year under the provisions of this Part or under rules adopted by the Secretary, the income year is the period for which the return is made.

(11) Limited liability company. - Either a domestic limited liability company organized under Chapter 57D of the General Statutes or a foreign limited liability company authorized by that Chapter to transact business in this State that is classified for federal income tax purposes as a corporation. As applied to a limited liability company that is a corporation under this Part, the term "shareholder" means a member of the limited liability company and the term "corporate officer" means a member or manager of the limited liability company.

(12) Parent. - A corporation is a parent of another corporation when, directly or indirectly, it controls the other corporation by stock ownership, interlocking directors, or by any other means whatsoever exercised by the same or associated financial interests, whether the control is direct or through one or more subsidiary, affiliated, or controlled corporations.

(13) S Corporation. - Defined in G.S. 105-131(b).

(14) Secretary. - The Secretary of Revenue.

(15) State net income. - The taxpayer's federal taxable income as determined under the Code, adjusted as provided in G.S. 105-130.5 and, in the case of a corporation that has income from business activity that is taxable both

within and without this State, allocated and apportioned to this State as provided in G.S. 105-130.4.

(16) Subsidiary. - A corporation is a subsidiary of another corporation when, directly or indirectly, it is subject to control by the other corporation by stock ownership, interlocking directors, or by any other means whatsoever exercised by the same or associated financial interest, whether the control is direct or through one or more subsidiary, affiliated, or controlled corporations.

(17) Taxable year. - Income year.

(18) Taxpayer. - A corporation subject to the tax imposed by this Part. (1939, c. 158, s. 302; 1941, c. 50, s. 5; 1955, c. 1331, s. 2; 1957, c. 1340, s. 4; 1963, c. 1169, s. 2; 1967, c. 1110, s. 3; 1973, c. 476, s. 193; 1983, c. 713, ss. 68, 82; 1985, c. 656, s. 7; 1985 (Reg. Sess., 1986), c. 853, s. 1; 1987, c. 778, s. 1; 1987 (Reg. Sess., 1988), c. 1015, s. 3; 1989, c. 36, s. 3; 1989 (Reg. Sess., 1990), c. 981, s. 3; 1991, c. 689, s. 257; 1991 (Reg. Sess., 1992), c. 922, s. 4; 1993, c. 12, s. 5; c. 354, s. 12; 1995, c. 17, s. 3; 1998-98, s. 69; 2006-162, s. 3(a); 2012-79, s. 1.14(b); 2013-157, s. 27.)

§ 105-130.3. (Effective for taxable years beginning before January 1, 2014) Corporations.

A tax is imposed on the State net income of every C Corporation doing business in this State. An S Corporation is not subject to the tax levied in this section. The tax is a percentage of the taxpayer's State net income computed as follows:

Income Years Beginning	Tax
In 1997	7.5%
In 1998	7.25%
In 1999	7%
After 1999	6.9%.

(1939, c. 158, s. 311; 1941, c. 50, s. 5; 1943, c. 400, s. 4; 1945, c. 752, s. 3; 1953, c. 1302, s. 4; 1955, c. 1350, s. 18; 1957, c. 1340, s. 4; 1959, c. 1259, s. 4;

1963, c. 1169, s. 2; c. 1186; 1967, c. 1110, s. 3; 1973, c. 1287, s. 4; 1975, c. 275, s. 4; 1977, c. 657, s. 4; 1979, c. 179, s. 2; 1981, c. 15; 1983, c. 713, s. 69; 1987, c. 622, s. 8; 1987 (Reg. Sess., 1988), c. 1089, s. 5; 1989, c. 728, s. 1.33; 1991, c. 689, s. 258; 1996, 2nd Ex. Sess., c. 13, s. 2.1.)

§ 105-130.3. (Effective for taxable years beginning on or after January 1, 2014, and before January 1, 2015) Corporations.

A tax is imposed on the State net income of every C Corporation doing business in this State at the rate of six percent (6%). An S Corporation is not subject to the tax levied in this section. (1939, c. 158, s. 311; 1941, c. 50, s. 5; 1943, c. 400, s. 4; 1945, c. 752, s. 3; 1953, c. 1302, s. 4; 1955, c. 1350, s. 18; 1957, c. 1340, s. 4; 1959, c. 1259, s. 4; 1963, c. 1169, s. 2; c. 1186; 1967, c. 1110, s. 3; 1973, c. 1287, s. 4; 1975, c. 275, s. 4; 1977, c. 657, s. 4; 1979, c. 179, s. 2; 1981, c. 15; 1983, c. 713, s. 69; 1987, c. 622, s. 8; 1987 (Reg. Sess., 1988), c. 1089, s. 5; 1989, c. 728, s. 1.33; 1991, c. 689, s. 258; 1996, 2nd Ex. Sess., c. 13, s. 2.1; 2013-316, s. 2.1(a).)

§ 105-130.3. (Effective for taxable years beginning on or after January 1, 2015) Corporations.

A tax is imposed on the State net income of every C Corporation doing business in this State at the rate of five percent (5%). An S Corporation is not subject to the tax levied in this section. (1939, c. 158, s. 311; 1941, c. 50, s. 5; 1943, c. 400, s. 4; 1945, c. 752, s. 3; 1953, c. 1302, s. 4; 1955, c. 1350, s. 18; 1957, c. 1340, s. 4; 1959, c. 1259, s. 4; 1963, c. 1169, s. 2; c. 1186; 1967, c. 1110, s. 3; 1973, c. 1287, s. 4; 1975, c. 275, s. 4; 1977, c. 657, s. 4; 1979, c. 179, s. 2; 1981, c. 15; 1983, c. 713, s. 69; 1987, c. 622, s. 8; 1987 (Reg. Sess., 1988), c. 1089, s. 5; 1989, c. 728, s. 1.33; 1991, c. 689, s. 258; 1996, 2nd Ex. Sess., c. 13, s. 2.1; 2013-316, ss. 2.1(a), 2.2(a).)

§ 105-130.3A: Expired.

§ 105-130.3B. (Effective for taxable years beginning on or after January 1, 2009, and expiring for taxable years beginning on or after January 1, 2011) Income tax surtax.

(a) Surtax. - An income tax surtax is imposed on a taxpayer equal to three percent (3%) of the tax payable by the taxpayer under G.S. 105-130.3 for the taxable year. This tax is in addition to the tax imposed by G.S. 105-130.3 and is due at the time prescribed in G.S. 105-130.17 for filing a corporate income tax return.

(b) Sunset. - This section expires for taxable years beginning on or after January 1, 2011. (2009-451, s. 27A.1(a).)

§ 105-130.3C. Rate reduction trigger.

If the amount of net General Fund tax collected in fiscal year 2014-2015 or fiscal year 2015-2016 exceeds the anticipated General Fund tax collections for that fiscal year, the rate of tax set in G.S. 105-130.3 may be decreased in accordance with this section effective for the taxable year that begins on the following January 1. The amount of net General Fund tax collected for a fiscal year is the amount reported by the State Controller in the State's Comprehensive Annual Financial Report, required to be prepared under G.S. 143B-426.39. The Secretary must monitor the net General Fund tax collections and notify taxpayers if the rate decreases under this section. The rate is decreased by one percent (1%) if net General Fund tax collections for fiscal year 2014-2015 exceed twenty billion two hundred million dollars ($20,200,000,000). The rate is decreased by one percent (1%) if net General Fund tax collections for fiscal year 2015-2016 exceed twenty billion nine hundred seventy-five million dollars ($20,975,000,000). Effective for taxable years beginning on or after January 1, 2017, the rate of tax set in G.S. 105-130.3 is the rate determined in accordance with this section. (2013-316, s. 2.2(b).)

§ 105-130.4. Allocation and apportionment of income for corporations.

(a) As used in this section, unless the context otherwise requires:

(1) "Apportionable income" means all income that is apportionable under the United States Constitution.

(2) "Commercial domicile" means the principal place from which the trade or business of the taxpayer is directed or managed.

(3) "Compensation" means wages, salaries, commissions and any other form of remuneration paid to employees for personal services.

(4) "Excluded corporation" means any corporation engaged in business as a building or construction contractor, a securities dealer, or a loan company or a corporation that receives more than fifty percent (50%) of its ordinary gross income from intangible property.

(5) "Nonapportionable income" means all income other than apportionable income.

(6) "Public utility" means any corporation that is subject to control of one or more of the following entities: the North Carolina Utilities Commission, the Federal Communications Commission, the Interstate Commerce Commission, the Federal Energy Regulatory Commission, or the Federal Aviation Agency; and that owns or operates for public use any plant, equipment, property, franchise, or license for the transmission of communications, the transportation of goods or persons, or the production, storage, transmission, sale, delivery or furnishing of electricity, water, steam, oil, oil products, or gas. The term also includes a motor carrier of property whose principal business activity is transporting property by motor vehicle for hire over the public highways of this State.

(7) "Sales" means all gross receipts of the corporation except for the following receipts:

a. Receipts from a casual sale of property.

b. Receipts allocated under subsections (c) through (h) of this section.

c. Receipts exempt from taxation.

d. The portion of receipts realized from the sale or maturity of securities or other obligations that represents a return of principal.

(8) "Casual sale of property" means the sale of any property which was not purchased, produced or acquired primarily for sale in the corporation's regular trade or business.

(9) "State" means any state of the United States, the District of Columbia, the Commonwealth of Puerto Rico, any territory or possession of the United States, and any foreign country or political subdivision thereof.

(b) A corporation having income from business activity which is taxable both within and without this State shall allocate and apportion its net income or net loss as provided in this section. For purposes of allocation and apportionment, a corporation is taxable in another state if (i) the corporation's business activity in that state subjects it to a net income tax or a tax measured by net income, or (ii) that state has jurisdiction based on the corporation's business activity in that state to subject the corporation to a tax measured by net income regardless whether that state exercises its jurisdiction. For purposes of this section, "business activity" includes any activity by a corporation that would establish a taxable nexus pursuant to 15 United States Code section 381.

(c) Rents and royalties from real or tangible personal property, gains and losses, interest, dividends, patent and copyright royalties and other kinds of income, to the extent that they constitute nonapportionable income, less related expenses shall be allocated as provided in subsections (d) through (h) of this section.

(d) (1) Net rents and royalties from real property located in this State are allocable to this State.

(2) Net rents and royalties from tangible personal property are allocable to this State:

a. If and to the extent that the property is utilized in this State, or

b. In their entirety if the corporation's commercial domicile is in this State and the corporation is not organized under the laws of, or is not taxable in, the state in which the property is utilized.

(3) The extent of utilization of tangible personal property in a state is determined by multiplying the rents and royalties by a fraction, the numerator of which is the number of days of physical location of the property in the state during the rental or royalty period in the income year and the denominator of

which is the number of days of physical location of the property everywhere during all rental or royalty periods in the income year. If the physical location of the property during the rental or royalty period is unknown or unascertainable by the corporation, tangible personal property is utilized in the state in which the property was located at the time the rental or royalty payer obtained possession.

(e) (1) Gains and losses from sales or other disposition of real property located in this State are allocable to this State.

(2) Gains and losses from sales or other disposition of tangible personal property are allocable to this State if

a. The property had a situs in this State at the time of the sale, or

b. The corporation's commercial domicile is in this State and the corporation is not taxable in the state in which the property has a situs.

(3) Gains and losses from sales or other disposition of intangible personal property are allocable to this State if the corporation's commercial domicile is in this State.

(f) Interest and net dividends are allocable to this State if the corporation's commercial domicile is in this State. For purposes of this section, the term "net dividends" means gross dividend income received less related expenses.

(g) (1) Royalties or similar income received from the use of patents, copyrights, secret processes and other similar intangible property are allocable to this State:

a. If and to the extent that the patent, copyright, secret process or other similar intangible property is utilized in this State, or

b. If and to the extent that the patent, copyright, secret process or other similar intangible property is utilized in a state in which the taxpayer is not taxable and the taxpayer's commercial domicile is in this State.

(2) A patent, secret process or other similar intangible property is utilized in a state to the extent that it is employed in production, fabrication, manufacturing, processing, or other use in the state or to the extent that a patented product is produced in the state. If the basis of receipts from such intangible property does not permit allocation to states or if the accounting procedures do not reflect

states of utilization, the intangible property is utilized in the state in which the taxpayer's commercial domicile is located.

(3) A copyright is utilized in a state to the extent that printing or other publication originates in the state. If the basis of receipts from copyright royalties does not permit allocation to states or if the accounting procedures do not reflect states of utilization, the copyright is utilized in the state in which the taxpayer's commercial domicile is located.

(h) The income less related expenses from any other activities producing nonapportionable income or investments not otherwise specified in this section is allocable to this State if the business situs of the activities or investments is located in this State.

(i) All apportionable income of corporations other than public utilities, excluded corporations, and qualified capital intensive corporations shall be apportioned to this State by multiplying the income by a fraction, the numerator of which is the property factor plus the payroll factor plus twice the sales factor, and the denominator of which is four. If the sales factor does not exist, the denominator of the fraction is the number of existing factors and if the sales factor exists but the payroll factor or the property factor does not exist, the denominator of the fraction is the number of existing factors plus one.

(j) (1) The property factor is a fraction, the numerator of which is the average value of the corporation's real and tangible personal property owned or rented and used in this State during the income year and the denominator of which is the average value of all the corporation's real and tangible personal property owned or rented and used during the income year.

(2) Property owned by the corporation is valued at its original cost. Property rented by the corporation is valued at eight times the net annual rental rate. Net annual rental rate is the annual rental rate paid by the corporation less any annual rental rate received by the corporation from subrentals except that subrentals shall not be deducted when they constitute apportionable income. Any property under construction and any property the income from which constitutes nonapportionable income shall be excluded in the computation of the property factor.

(3) The average value of property shall be determined by averaging the values at the beginning and end of the income year, but in all cases the Secretary of Revenue may require the averaging of monthly or other periodic

values during the income year if reasonably required to reflect properly the average value of the corporation's property. A corporation that ceases its operations in this State before the end of its income year because of its intention to dissolve or to relinquish its certificate of authority, or because of a merger, conversion, or consolidation, or for any other reason whatsoever shall use the real estate and tangible personal property values as of the first day of the income year and the last day of its operations in this State in determining the average value of property, but the Secretary may require averaging of monthly or other periodic values during the income year if reasonably required to reflect properly the average value of the corporation's property.

(k)	(1)	The payroll factor is a fraction, the numerator of which is the total amount paid in this State during the income year by the corporation as compensation, and the denominator of which is the total compensation paid everywhere during the income year. All compensation paid to general executive officers and all compensation paid in connection with nonapportionable income shall be excluded in computing the payroll factor. General executive officers shall include the chairman of the board, president, vice-presidents, secretary, treasurer, comptroller, and any other officers serving in similar capacities.

(2)	Compensation is paid in this State if:

a.	The individual's service is performed entirely within the State; or

b.	The individual's service is performed both within and without the State, but the service performed without the State is incidental to the individual's service within the State; or

c.	Some of the service is performed in this State and (i) the base of operations or, if there is no base of operations, the place from which the service is directed or controlled is in this State, or (ii) the base of operations or the place from which the service is directed or controlled is not in any state in which some part of the service is performed, but the individual's residence is in this State.

(l)	(1)	The sales factor is a fraction, the numerator of which is the total sales of the corporation in this State during the income year, and the denominator of which is the total sales of the corporation everywhere during the income year. Notwithstanding any other provision under this Part, the receipts from any casual sale of property shall be excluded from both the numerator and the denominator of the sales factor. Where a corporation is not taxable in another state on its apportionable income but is taxable in another state only because of nonapportionable income, all sales shall be treated as having been made in this State.

(2) Sales of tangible personal property are in this State if the property is received in this State by the purchaser. In the case of delivery of goods by common carrier or by other means of transportation, including transportation by the purchaser, the place at which the goods are ultimately received after all transportation has been completed shall be considered as the place at which the goods are received by the purchaser. Direct delivery into this State by the taxpayer to a person or firm designated by a purchaser from within or without the State shall constitute delivery to the purchaser in this State.

(3) Other sales are in this State if:

a. The receipts are from real or tangible personal property located in this State; or

b. The receipts are from intangible property and are received from sources within this State; or

c. The receipts are from services and the income-producing activities are in this State.

(m) All apportionable income of a railroad company shall be apportioned to this State by multiplying the income by a fraction, the numerator of which is the "railway operating revenue" from business done within this State and the denominator of which is the "total railway operating revenue" from all business done by the company as shown by its records kept in accordance with the standard classification of accounts prescribed by the Interstate Commerce Commission.

"Railway operating revenue" from business done within this State shall mean "railway operating revenue" from business wholly within this State, plus the equal mileage proportion within this State of each item of "railway operating revenue" received from the interstate business of the company. "Equal mileage proportion" shall mean the proportion which the distance of movement of property and passengers over lines in this State bears to the total distance of movement of property and passengers over lines of the company receiving such revenue. "Interstate business" shall mean "railway operating revenue" from the interstate transportation of persons or property into, out of, or through this State. If the Secretary of Revenue finds, with respect to any particular company, that its accounting records are not kept so as to reflect with exact accuracy such division of revenue by State lines as to each transaction involving interstate revenue, the Secretary of Revenue may adopt such regulations, based upon averages, as will approximate with reasonable accuracy the proportion of interstate revenue actually earned upon lines in this State. Provided, that where a railroad is being operated by a partnership which is treated as a corporation for income tax purposes and pays a net income tax to this State, or if located in another state would be so treated and so pay as if located in this State, each partner's share of the net profits shall be considered as dividends paid by a corporation for purposes of this Part and shall be so treated for inclusion in gross income, deductibility, and separate allocation of dividend income.

(n) All apportionable income of a telephone company shall be apportioned to this State by multiplying the income by a fraction, the numerator of which is gross operating revenue from local service in this State plus gross operating revenue from toll services performed wholly within this State plus the proportion of revenue from interstate toll services attributable to this State as shown by the records of the company plus the gross operating revenue in North Carolina from other service less the uncollectible revenue in this State, and the denominator of which is the total gross operating revenue from all business done by the company everywhere less total uncollectible revenue. Provided, that where a telephone company is required to keep its records in accordance with the standard classification of accounts prescribed by the Federal Communications Commission the amounts in such accounts shall be used in computing the apportionment fraction as provided in this subsection.

(o) All apportionable income of a motor carrier of property shall be apportioned by multiplying the income by a fraction, the numerator of which is the number of vehicle miles in this State and the denominator of which is the total number of vehicle miles of the company everywhere. The words "vehicle miles" shall mean miles traveled by vehicles owned or operated by the company hauling property for a charge or traveling on a scheduled route.

(p) All apportionable income of a motor carrier of passengers shall be apportioned by multiplying the income by a fraction, the numerator of which is the number of vehicle miles in this State and the denominator of which is the total number of vehicle miles of the company everywhere. The words "vehicle miles" shall mean miles traveled by vehicles owned or operated by the company carrying passengers for a fare or traveling on a scheduled route.

(q) All apportionable income of a telegraph company shall be apportioned by multiplying the income by a fraction, the numerator of which is the property factor plus the payroll factor plus the sales factor and the denominator of which is three.

The property factor shall be as defined in subsection (j) of this section, the payroll factor shall be as defined in subsection (k) of this section, and the sales factor shall be as defined in subsection (l) of this section.

(r) All apportionable income of an excluded corporation and of all other public utilities shall be apportioned by multiplying the income by the sales factor as determined under subsection (l) of this section.

(s) All apportionable income of an air or water transportation corporation shall be apportioned by a fraction, the numerator of which is the corporation's revenue ton miles in this State and the denominator of which is the corporation's revenue ton miles everywhere. The term "revenue ton mile" means one ton of passengers, freight, mail, or other cargo carried one mile. In making this computation, a passenger is considered to weigh two hundred pounds.

(s1) (Effective for taxable years beginning on or after January 1, 2010; see Editor's note for contingent repeal) All apportionable income of a qualified capital intensive corporation shall be apportioned by multiplying the income by the sales factor as determined under subsection (l) of this section. A "qualified capital intensive corporation" is a corporation that satisfies all of the conditions of this subsection. A corporation that is subject to this subsection must list on its return the property, payroll, and sales factors it used in determining whether it is a qualified capital intensive corporation. If the corporation fails to invest one billion dollars ($1,000,000,000) in private funds within nine years as required by subdivision (2) of this subsection, the benefit of this subsection expires and the corporation must apportion income as it would otherwise be required to do under this section absent this subsection. The conditions are:

(1) The corporation's property factor as a percentage of the sum of the factors in the formula set out in subsection (i) of this section, including the doubling of the sales factor, exceeds seventy-five percent (75%) or the corporation's average property factor for the preceding three years as a percentage of the average sum of the factors in the formula set out in subsection (i) of this section, including the doubling of the sales factors, for the preceding three years exceeds seventy-five percent (75%).

(2) The Secretary of Commerce makes a written determination that the corporation has invested or is expected to invest at least one billion dollars ($1,000,000,000) in private funds to construct a facility in this State within nine years after the time that construction begins. For the purposes of this subsection, costs of construction include costs of acquiring and improving land for the facility, costs for renovations or repairs to existing buildings, and costs of equipping or reequipping the facility.

(3) The corporation maintains the average number of employees it has at the facility during the first two years after the facility is placed in service for the remainder of time in which the corporation must complete the investment required under subdivision (2) of this subsection.

(4) The facility that satisfies the condition of subdivision (2) of this subsection is located in a county that was designated as a development tier one or two area at the time construction of the facility began.

(5) The corporation satisfies a wage standard at the facility that satisfies the condition of subdivision (2) of this subsection. For the purposes of this subdivision, the wage standard that must be satisfied is the one established under G.S. 105-129.83(c).

(6) The corporation provides health insurance for all of its full-time employees at the facility that satisfies the condition of subdivision (2) of this subsection. For the purposes of this subdivision, a company provides health insurance if it satisfies the provisions of G.S. 105-129.83(d).

(t) Repealed by Session Laws 2007-491, s. 2, effective January 1, 2008. For applicability, see Editor's note.

(t1) Alternative Apportionment Method. - A corporation that believes the statutory apportionment method that otherwise applies to it under this section subjects a greater portion of its income to tax than is attributable to its business in this State may make a written request to the Secretary for permission to use an alternative method. The request must set out the reasons for the corporation's belief and propose an alternative method.

The statutory apportionment method that otherwise applies to a corporation under this section is presumed to be the best method of determining the portion of the corporation's income that is attributable to its business in this State. A corporation has the burden of establishing by clear, cogent, and convincing proof that the proposed alternative method is a better method of determining the amount of the corporation's income attributable to the corporation's business in this State.

The Secretary must issue a written decision on a corporation's request for an alternative apportionment method. If the decision grants the request, it must describe the alternative method the corporation is authorized to use and state the tax years to which the alternative method applies. A decision may apply to no more than three tax years. A corporation may renew a request to use an alternative apportionment method by following the procedure in this subsection. A decision of the Secretary on a request for an alternative apportionment method is final and is not subject to administrative or judicial review. A corporation authorized to use an alternative method may apportion its income in accordance with the alternative method or the statutory method. A corporation may not use an alternative apportionment method except upon written order of the Secretary, and any return in which any alternative apportionment method, other than the method prescribed by statute, is used without permission of the Secretary is not a lawful return.

(t2)   Repealed by Session Laws 2011-330, s. 5, effective June 27, 2011. (1939, c. 158, s. 311; 1941, c. 50, s. 5; 1943, c. 400, s. 4; 1945, c. 752, s. 3; 1953, c. 1302, s. 4; 1955, c. 1350, s. 18; 1957, c. 1340, s. 4; 1959, c. 1259, s. 4; 1963, c. 1169, s. 2; c. 1186; 1967, c. 1110, s. 3; 1973, c. 476, s. 193; c. 1287, s. 4; 1981 (Reg. Sess., 1982), c. 1212; 1987, c. 804, s. 2; 1987 (Reg. Sess., 1988), c. 994, s. 1; 1993, c. 532, s. 12; 1995, c. 350, s. 3; 1996, 2nd Ex. Sess., c. 14, s. 5; 1998-98, s. 69; 1999-369, s. 5.4; 2000-126, s. 5; 2001-327, s. 1(c); 2002-126, s. 30G.1(a); 2003-349, ss. 1.2, 1.3; 2003-416, ss. 5(a)-5(h); 2004-170, s. 15; 2005-435, s. 53; 2007-491, ss. 2, 12; 2009-54, ss. 1, 2, 6; 2009-445, ss. 4, 5; 2010-89, s. 2(a), (b); 2011-330, s. 5; 2013-414, s. 2(b).)

§ 105-130.5. Adjustments to federal taxable income in determining State net income.

(a)   The following additions to federal taxable income shall be made in determining State net income:

(1)   Taxes based on or measured by net income by whatever name called and excess profits taxes.

(2) Interest paid in connection with income exempt from taxation under this Part.

(3) The contributions deduction allowed by the Code.

(4) Interest income earned on bonds and other obligations of other states or their political subdivisions, less allowable amortization on any bond acquired on or after January 1, 1963.

(5) The amount by which gains have been offset by the capital loss carryover allowed under the Code. All gains recognized on the sale or other disposition of assets must be included in determining State net income or loss in the year of disposition.

(6) Any amount allowed as a net operating loss deduction under the Code.

(7) Repealed by Session Laws 2001-327, s. 3(a), effective for taxable years beginning on or after January 1, 2001.

(8) Repealed by Session Laws 1987, c. 778, s. 2.

(9) Payments to or charges by a parent, subsidiary or affiliated corporation in excess of fair compensation in all intercompany transactions of any kind whatsoever pursuant to the Revenue Laws of this State.

(10) The total amounts allowed under this Chapter during the taxable year as a credit against the taxpayer's income tax. This subdivision does not apply to a credit allowed under G.S. 105-130.47. A corporation that apportions part of its income to this State shall make the addition required by this subdivision after it determines the amount of its income that is apportioned and allocated to this State and shall not apply to a credit taken under this Chapter the apportionment factor used by it in determining the amount of its apportioned income.

(11) The amount by which the percentage depletion allowance allowed by sections 613 and 613A of the Code for mines, oil and gas wells, and other natural deposits exceeds the cost depletion allowance for these items under the Code, except as otherwise provided herein. This subdivision does not apply to depletion deductions for clay, gravel, phosphate rock, lime, shells, stone, sand, feldspar, gemstones, mica, talc, lithium compounds, tungsten, coal, peat, olivine, pyrophyllite, and other solid minerals or rare earths extracted from the soil or waters of this State. Corporations required to apportion income to North

Carolina shall first add to federal taxable income the amount of all percentage depletion in excess of cost depletion that was subtracted from the corporation's gross income in computing its federal income taxes and shall then subtract from the taxable income apportioned to North Carolina the amount by which the percentage depletion allowance allowed by sections 613 and 613A of the Code for solid minerals or rare earths extracted from the soil or waters of this State exceeds the cost depletion allowance for these items.

(12) The amount allowed under the Code for depreciation or as an expense in lieu of depreciation for a utility plant acquired by a natural gas local distribution company, to the extent the plant is included in the company's rate base at zero cost in accordance with G.S. 62-158.

(13) Repealed by Session Laws 2001-427, s. 4(b), effective for taxable years beginning on or after January 1, 2002.

(14) Royalty payments required to be added by G.S. 105-130.7A, to the extent deducted in calculating federal taxable income.

(15) through (15b) Repealed by Session Laws 2013-414, s. 34(a), effective August 23, 2013.

(16) The amount excluded from gross income under Subchapter R of Chapter 1 of the Code.

(17) The amount excluded from gross income under section 199 of the Code.

(18) Repealed by Session Laws 2006-220, s. 1, effective for taxable years beginning on and after January 1, 2007.

(19) The dividend paid deduction allowed under the Code to a captive REIT, as defined in G.S. 105-130.12.

(20) The amount of a donation made to a nonprofit organization or a unit of State or local government for which a credit is claimed under G.S. 105-129.16H.

(21) The amount of income deferred under section 108(i)(1) of the Code from the discharge of indebtedness in connection with a reacquisition of an applicable debt instrument.

(22) The amount allowed as a deduction under section 163(e)(5)(F) of the Code for an original issue discount on an applicable high yield discount obligation.

(23), (23a) Repealed by Session Laws 2013-414, s. 34(a), effective August 23, 2013.

(24) The amount required to be added under G.S. 105-130.5B when the State decouples from federal accelerated depreciation and expensing.

(b) The following deductions from federal taxable income shall be made in determining State net income:

(1) Interest upon the obligations of the United States or its possessions, to the extent included in federal taxable income: Provided, interest upon the obligations of the United States shall not be an allowable deduction unless interest upon obligations of the State of North Carolina or any of its political subdivisions is exempt from income taxes imposed by the United States.

(1a) Interest upon the obligations of any of the following, net of related expenses, to the extent included in federal taxable income:

a. This State, a political subdivision of this State, or a commission, an authority, or another agency of this State or of a political subdivision of this State.

b. A nonprofit educational institution organized or chartered under the laws of this State.

(2) Payments received from a parent, subsidiary or affiliated corporation in excess of fair compensation in intercompany transactions which in the determination of the net income or net loss of such corporation were not allowed as a deduction under the Revenue Laws of this State.

(3) Repealed by Session Laws 2003-349, s. 1.1, effective January 1, 2003.

(3a) Dividends treated as received from sources outside the United States as determined under section 862 of the Code, net of related expenses, to the extent included in federal taxable income. Notwithstanding the proviso in subdivision (c)(3) of this section, the netting of related expenses shall be calculated in accordance with subdivision (c)(3) of this section and G.S. 105-130.6A.

(3b)   Any amount included in federal taxable income under section 78 or section 951 of the Code, net of related expenses.

(4)   Losses in the nature of net economic losses sustained by the corporation in any or all of the 15 preceding years pursuant to the provisions of G.S. 105-130.8. A corporation required to allocate and apportion its net income under the provisions of G.S. 105-130.4 shall deduct its allocable net economic loss only from total income allocable to this State pursuant to the provisions of G.S. 105-130.8.

(5)   Contributions or gifts made by any corporation within the income year to the extent provided under G.S. 105-130.9.

(6)   Amortization in excess of depreciation allowed under the Code on the cost of any sewage or waste treatment plant, and facilities or equipment used for purposes of recycling or resource recovery of or from solid waste, or for purposes of reducing the volume of hazardous waste generated as provided in G.S. 105-130.10.

(7)   Depreciation of emergency facilities acquired prior to January 1, 1955. Any corporation shall be permitted to depreciate any emergency facility, as such is defined in section 168 of the Code, over its useful life, provided such facility was acquired prior to January 1, 1955, and no amortization has been claimed on such facility for State income tax purposes.

(8)   The amount of losses realized on the sale or other disposition of assets not allowed under section 1211(a) of the Code. All losses recognized on the sale or other disposition of assets must be included in determining State net income or loss in the year of disposition.

(9)   With respect to a shareholder of a regulated investment company, the portion of undistributed capital gains of such regulated investment company included in such shareholder's federal taxable income and on which the federal tax paid by the regulated investment company is allowed as a credit or refund to the shareholder under section 852 of the Code.

(10)   Repealed by Session Laws 1987, c. 778, s. 2.

(11) If a deduction for an ordinary and necessary business expense was required to be reduced or was not allowed under the Code because the corporation claimed a federal tax credit against its federal income tax liability for the income year in lieu of a deduction, the amount by which the deduction was reduced and the amount of the deduction that was disallowed. This deduction is allowed only to the extent that a similar credit is not allowed by this Chapter for the amount.

(12) Reasonable expenses, in excess of deductions allowed under the Code, paid for reforestation and cultivation of commercially grown trees; provided, that this deduction shall be allowed only to those corporations in which the real owners of all the shares of such corporation are natural persons actively engaged in the commercial growing of trees, or the spouse, siblings, or parents of such persons. Provided, further, that in no case shall a corporation be allowed a deduction for the same reforestation or cultivation expenditure more than once.

(13) The eligible income of an international banking facility to the extent included in determining federal taxable income, determined as follows:

a. "International banking facility" shall have the same meaning as is set forth in the laws of the United States or regulations of the board of governors of the federal reserve system.

b. The eligible income of an international banking facility for the taxable year shall be an amount obtained by multiplying State taxable income as determined under G.S. 105-130.3 (determined without regard to eligible income of an international banking facility and allocation and apportionment, if applicable) for such year by a fraction, the denominator of which shall be the gross receipts for such year derived by the bank from all sources, and the numerator of which shall be the adjusted gross receipts for such year derived by the international banking facility from:

1. Making, arranging for, placing or servicing loans to foreign persons substantially all the proceeds of which are for use outside the United States;

2. Making or placing deposits with foreign persons which are banks or foreign branches of banks (including foreign subsidiaries or foreign branches of the taxpayer) or with other international banking facilities; or

3. Entering into foreign exchange trading or hedging transactions related to any of the transactions described in this paragraph.

c. The adjusted gross receipts shall be determined by multiplying the gross receipts of the international banking facility by a fraction the numerator of which is the average amount for the taxable year of all assets of the international banking facility which are employed outside the United States and the denominator of which is the average amount for the taxable year of all assets of the international banking facility.

d. For the purposes of this subsection the term "foreign person" means:

1. An individual who is not a resident of the United States;

2. A foreign corporation, a foreign partnership or a foreign trust, as defined in section 7701 of the Code, other than a domestic branch thereof;

3. A foreign branch of a domestic corporation (including the taxpayer);

4. A foreign government or an international organization or an agency of either, or

5. An international banking facility.

For purposes of this paragraph, the terms "foreign" and "domestic" shall have the same meaning as set forth in section 7701 of the Code.

(14) The amount by which the basis of a depreciable asset is required to be reduced under the Code for federal tax purposes because of a tax credit allowed against the corporation's federal income tax liability or because of a grant allowed under section 1603 of the American Recovery and Reinvestment Tax Act of 2009, P.L. 111-3. This deduction may be claimed only in the year in which the Code requires that the asset's basis be reduced. In computing gain or loss on the asset's disposition, this deduction shall be considered as depreciation.

(15) The amount paid during the income year, pursuant to 7 U.S.C. § 1445-2, as marketing assessments on tobacco grown by the corporation in North Carolina.

(16) The amount of natural gas expansion surcharges collected by a natural gas local distribution company under G.S. 62-158.

(17) To the extent included in federal taxable income, 911 charges imposed under G.S. 62A-43 and remitted to the 911 Fund under that section.

(18) Interest, investment earnings, and gains of a trust, the settlors of which are two or more manufacturers that signed a settlement agreement with this State to settle existing and potential claims of the State against the manufacturers for damages attributable to a product of the manufacturers, if the trust meets all of the following conditions:

a. The purpose of the trust is to address adverse economic consequences resulting from a decline in demand of the manufactured product potentially expected to occur because of market restrictions and other provisions in the settlement agreement.

b. A court of this State approves and retains jurisdiction over the trust.

c. Certain portions of the distributions from the trust are made in accordance with certifications that meet the criteria in the agreement creating the trust and are provided by a nonprofit entity, the governing board of which includes State officials.

(19) To the extent included in federal taxable income, the amount paid to the taxpayer during the taxable year from the Hurricane Floyd Reserve Fund in the Office of State Budget and Management for hurricane relief or assistance, but not including payments for goods or services provided by the taxpayer.

(20) Royalty payments received from a related member who added the payments to income under G.S. 105-130.7A for the same taxable year.

(21) through (21b) Repealed by Session Laws 2013-414, s. 34(a), effective August 23, 2013.

(22) To the extent included in federal taxable income, the amount paid to the taxpayer during the taxable year from the Disaster Relief Reserve Fund in the Office of State Budget and Management for hurricane relief or assistance, but not including payments for goods or services provided by the taxpayer.

(23) A dividend received from a captive REIT, as defined in G.S. 105-130.12.

(24) (Expiring for taxable years beginning on or after January 1, 2015) Five percent (5%) of the gross purchase price of a qualified sale of a manufactured home community. A qualified sale is a transfer of land comprising a manufactured home community in a single purchase to a group composed of a majority of the manufactured home community leaseholders or to a nonprofit organization that represents such a group. To be eligible for this deduction, a taxpayer must give notice of the sale to the North Carolina Housing Finance Agency under G.S. 42-14.3.

(25) The amount added to federal taxable income as deferred income under section 108(i)(1) of the Code. This deduction applies to taxable years beginning on or after January 1, 2014.

(26), (26a) Repealed by Session Laws 2013-414, s. 34(a), effective August 23, 2013.

(27) The amount allowed as a deduction under G.S. 105-130.5B as a result of an add-back for federal accelerated depreciation and expensing.

(c) The following other adjustments to federal taxable income shall be made in determining State net income:

(1) In determining State net income, no deduction shall be allowed for annual amortization of bond premiums applicable to any bond acquired prior to January 1, 1963. The amount of premium paid on any such bond shall be deductible only in the year of sale or other disposition.

(2) Federal taxable income must be increased or decreased to account for any difference in the amount of depreciation, amortization, or gains or losses applicable to property which has been depreciated or amortized by use of a different basis or rate for State income tax purposes than used for federal income tax purposes prior to the effective date of this Part.

(3) No deduction is allowed for any direct or indirect expenses related to income not taxed under this Part; provided, no adjustment shall be made under this subsection for adjustments addressed in G.S. 105-130.5(a) and (b). G.S. 105-130.6A applies to the adjustment for expenses related to dividends received that are not taxed under this Part.

(4) The taxpayer shall add to federal taxable income the amount of any recovery during the taxable year not included in federal taxable income, to the extent the taxpayer's deduction of the recovered amount in a prior taxable year reduced the taxpayer's tax imposed by this Part but, due to differences between the Code and this Part, did not reduce the amount of the taxpayer's tax imposed by the Code. The taxpayer may deduct from federal taxable income the amount of any recovery during the taxable year included in federal taxable income under section 111 of the Code, to the extent the taxpayer's deduction of the recovered amount in a prior taxable year reduced the taxpayer's tax imposed by the Code but, due to differences between the Code and this Part, did not reduce the amount of the taxpayer's tax imposed by this Part.

(5) A savings and loan association may deduct interest earned on deposits at the Federal Home Loan Bank of Atlanta, or its successor, to the extent included in federal taxable income.

(d) Repealed by Session Laws 1987, c. 778, s. 3.

(e) Notwithstanding any other provision of this section, any recapture of depreciation required under the Code must be included in a corporation's State net income to the extent required for federal income tax purposes.

(f) Expired. (1967, c. 1110, s. 3; 1969, cc. 1113, 1124; 1971, c. 820, s. 1; c. 1206, s. 1; 1973, c. 1287, s. 4; 1975, c. 764, s. 4; 1977, 2nd Sess., c. 1200, s. 1; 1979, c. 179, s. 2; c. 801, s. 32; 1981, c. 704, s. 20; c. 855, s. 1; 1983, c. 61; c. 713, ss. 70-73, 82, 83; 1985, c. 720, s. 1; c. 791, s. 43; 1985 (Reg. Sess., 1986), c. 825; 1987, c. 89; c. 637, s. 1; c. 778, ss. 2, 3; c. 804, s. 3; 1991, c. 598, ss. 3, 10; 1991 (Reg. Sess., 1992), c. 857, s. 1; 1993 (Reg. Sess., 1994), c. 745, ss. 4, 5; 1995, c. 509, s. 50; 1996, 2nd Ex. Sess., c. 14, ss. 4, 10; 1997-439, s. 1; 1998-98, ss. 1(c), 4, 69; 1998-158, s. 5; 1998-171, s. 7; 1999-333, s. 2; 1999-337, s. 1; 1999-463, Ex. Sess., s. 4.6(b); 2000-140, s. 93.1(a); 2000-173, s. 19(c); 2001-327, ss. 1(d), (e), 3(a), (b); 2001-424, s. 12.2(b); 2001-427, ss. 4(b), 10(a); 2002-72, s. 14; 2002-126, ss. 30C.2(a), 30C.2(c); 2002-136, ss. 1, 4; 2003-284, s. 37A.3; 2003-349, s. 1.1; 2005-1, s. 5.7(b); 2005-276, ss. 35.1(b), 39.1(e); 2006-220, s. 1; 2007-323, ss. 31.18(a), (b); 2007-383, s. 5; 2007-397, s. 13(b); 2008-107, ss. 28.1(c), (d), (g), 28.25(b), 28.27(a); 2008-134, s. 2(b); 2009-451, s. 27A.6(c), (d); 2010-89, s. 1; 2011-5, ss. 2(a), (b), 3(a), (b); 2011-330, s. 11; 2012-79, s. 1.1; 2013-10, ss. 2(a), (b), 3(a), (b); 2013-414, s. 34(a).)

§ 105-130.5A. Secretary's authority to adjust net income or require a combined return.

(a) Notice. - When the Secretary has reason to believe that any corporation so conducts its trade or business in such manner as to fail to accurately report its State net income properly attributable to its business carried on in the State through the use of transactions that lack economic substance or are not at fair market value between members of an affiliated group of entities, the Secretary may, upon written notice to the corporation, require any information reasonably necessary to determine whether the corporation's intercompany transactions have economic substance and are at fair market value and for the accurate computation of the corporation's State net income properly attributable to its business carried on in the State. The corporation must provide the information requested within 90 days of the date of the notice.

(b) Adjust Net Income. - If upon review of the information provided, the Secretary finds as a fact that the corporation's intercompany transactions lack economic substance or are not at fair market value, the Secretary may redetermine the State net income of the corporation properly attributable to its business carried on in the State under this section by (i) adding back, eliminating, or otherwise adjusting intercompany transactions to accurately compute the corporation's State net income properly attributable to its business carried on in the State, or, if such adjustments are not adequate under the circumstances to redetermine State net income, (ii) requiring the corporation to file a return that reflects the net income on a combined basis of all members of its affiliated group that are conducting a unitary business. The Secretary shall consider and be authorized to use any reasonable method proposed by the corporation for redetermining its State net income attributable to its business carried on in the State. In determining whether the corporation's intercompany transactions lack economic substance or are not at fair market value, the Secretary shall consider each taxable year separately.

(c) Voluntary Redetermination. - In addition to the authority granted under subsection (b) of this section, if the Secretary has reason to believe that any corporation's State net income properly attributable to its business carried on in this State is not accurately reported on a separate return required by this Part because of intercompany transactions, without making a finding that those transactions lack economic substance or are not at fair market value, the Secretary and the corporation may jointly determine and agree to an alternative filing methodology that accurately reports State net income. The Secretary is authorized to allow any reasonable method for redetermining the corporation's State net income attributable to its business carried on in this State.

(d) Combined Return. - If the Secretary finds as a fact that a combined return is required, the Secretary may, upon written notice to the corporation, require the corporation to submit the combined return, and the corporation shall submit the combined return within 90 days of the date of the notice. The submission by the corporation of the combined return required by the Secretary shall not be deemed to be a return or construed as an agreement by the corporation that an assessment based on the combined return is correct or that additional tax is due by the Secretary's deadline for submitting the combined return. The Secretary or the corporation may propose a combination of fewer than all members of the unitary group, and the Secretary shall be authorized to consider whether such proposed combination is a reasonable means of redetermining State net income; provided, however, the Secretary shall not require a combination of fewer than all members of the unitary group without the consent of the corporation.

(e) Written Statement of Findings. - If the Secretary makes an adjustment or requires a combined return under this section, the Secretary shall provide the corporation with a written statement containing detail of the facts, circumstances, and reasons for which the Secretary has found as a fact that the corporation did not accurately report its State net income properly attributable to its business carried on in the State and the Secretary's proposed method for computation of the corporation's State net income no later than 90 days following the issuance of a proposed assessment as provided in this section.

(f) Members of Affiliated Group. - The Secretary may require a combined return under this section regardless of whether the members of the affiliated group are or are not doing business in this State.

(g) Economic Substance. - A transaction has economic substance if (i) the transaction, or the series of transactions of which the transaction is a part, has one or more reasonable business purposes other than the creation of State income tax benefits and (ii) the transaction, or the series of transactions of which the transaction is a part, has economic effects beyond the creation of State income tax benefits. In determining whether a transaction has economic substance, all of the following apply:

(1) Reasonable business purposes and economic effects include, but are not limited to, any material benefit from the transaction other than State income tax benefits not allowable under subdivision (3) of this subsection.

(2) In determining whether to require a combined return, whether the transaction has economic effects beyond the creation of State income tax benefits may be satisfied by demonstrating material business activity of the entities involved in the transaction.

(3) If State income tax benefits resulting from a transaction, or a series of transactions of which the transaction is a part, are consistent with legislative intent, such State income tax benefits shall be considered in determining whether such transaction has business purpose and economic substance.

(4) Centralized cash management of an affiliated group as defined in subsection (j) of this section shall not constitute evidence of an absence of economic substance.

(5) Achieving a financial accounting benefit shall not be taken into account as a reasonable business purpose for entering into a transaction if the origin of such financial accounting benefit is a reduction of State income tax.

(h) Allocation of Income and Deductions. - In determining whether transactions between members of the affiliated group of entities are not at fair market value, the Secretary shall apply the standards contained in the regulations adopted under section 482 of the Code.

(i) Apportionment. - If the Secretary requires a combined return under this section, the combined State net income of the corporation and the members of the affiliated group of entities shall be apportioned to this State by use of an apportionment formula that accurately reports the State net income properly attributable to the corporation's business carried on in the State and which fairly reflects the apportionment formula in G.S. 105-130.4 applicable to the corporation and each member of the affiliated group included in the combined return.

(j) Affiliated Group Defined. - For purposes of this section, an affiliated group is a group of two or more corporations or noncorporate entities in which more than fifty percent (50%) of the voting stock of each member corporation or ownership interest of each member noncorporate entity is directly or indirectly owned or controlled by a common owner or owners, either corporate or noncorporate, or by one or more of the member corporations or noncorporate entities. Nothing in this subsection shall be construed to limit or negate the Secretary's authority to add back, eliminate, or otherwise adjust intercompany transactions involving the listed entities to accurately compute the corporation's State net income properly attributable to its business carried on in the State, as provided in subsection (b) of this section.

The following entities shall not be included in a combined return:

(1)   A corporation not required to file a federal income tax return.

(2)   An insurance company, other than a captive insurance company, (i) which is subject to tax under Article 8B of this Chapter, (ii) whose premiums are subject to tax under Article 21 of Chapter 58 or a similar tax in another state, (iii) which is licensed as a reinsurance company, (iv) which is a life insurance company as defined in Section 816 of the Code, or (v) which is an insurance company subject to tax imposed by Section 831 of the Code. A "captive insurance company" means an insurer that is part of an affiliated group where the insurer receives more than fifty percent (50%) of its net written premiums or other amounts received as compensation for insurance from members of the affiliated group.

(3)   A corporation exempt from taxation under section 501 of the Code.

(4)   An S corporation.

(5)   A foreign corporation as defined in section 7701 of the Code, other than a domestic branch thereof.

(6)   A partnership, limited liability company, or other entity not taxed as a corporation.

(7)   A corporation with at least eighty percent (80%) of its gross income from all sources in the tax year being active foreign business income as defined in section 861(c)(1)(B) of the Code in effect as of July 1, 2009.

(k)   Proposed Assessment or Refund. - If the Secretary redetermines the State net income of the corporation in accordance with this section by adjusting the State net income of the corporation or requiring a combined return, the Secretary shall issue a proposed assessment or refund upon making such redetermination. The procedures for a proposed assessment or a refund in

Article 9 of Chapter 105 shall be applicable to proposed assessments and refunds made under this section.

(l) Penalties. - If a combined return required by this section is not timely submitted by a corporation, then the corporation is subject to the penalties provided in G.S. 105-236(a)(3). Penalties shall not be imposed on an assessment under this section except as expressly authorized in this section and in G.S. 105-236(a)(5)f.

(m) Advice. - A corporation may request in writing from the Secretary specific advice regarding whether a redetermination of the corporation's State net income or a combined return would be required under this section under certain facts and circumstances. The Secretary may request information from the taxpayer that is required to provide the specific advice. The Secretary shall provide the specific advice within 120 days of the receipt of the requested information from the taxpayer. G.S. 105-264 governs the effect of this advice.

(n) Extension. - The Secretary and the taxpayer may extend any time limit contained in this section by mutual agreement.

(o) Other Tax Adjustments. - Nothing in this section shall be construed to limit or negate the Secretary's authority to make tax adjustments as otherwise permitted by law, except that the Secretary shall not make adjustments pursuant to this section that limit a corporation's options for reporting royalty payments under G.S. 105-130.7A.

(p) Appeals. - If the corporation appeals a final determination by the Department under this section to the Office of Administrative Hearings in a contested tax case, the administrative law judge shall review de novo (i) whether the separate income tax returns submitted by the taxpayer fail to report State net income properly attributable to its business carried on in this State through the use of intercompany transactions that lack economic substance or are not at fair market value between members of an affiliated group of entities; (ii) whether the Department's means of determining the corporation's State net income under this section is an appropriate means of determining the corporation's State net income properly attributable to this State; and (iii) if a combined return is required by the Department, whether adjustments other than requiring the corporation to file a return on a combined basis are adequate under the circumstances to redetermine State net income. (2011-390, s. 2; 2011-411, s. 8(a), (b).)

§ 105-130.5B. Adjustments when State decouples from federal accelerated depreciation and expensing.

(a)   Special Accelerated Depreciation. - A taxpayer who takes a special accelerated depreciation deduction for property under section 168(k) or 168(n) of the Code must add to the taxpayer's federal taxable income eighty-five percent (85%) of the amount taken for that year under those Code provisions. A taxpayer is allowed to deduct twenty percent (20%) of the add-back in each of the first five taxable years following the year the taxpayer is required to include the add-back in income.

(b)   2009 Depreciation Exception. - A taxpayer who placed property in service during the 2009 taxable year and whose North Carolina taxable income for the 2009 taxable year reflected a special accelerated depreciation deduction allowed for the property under section 168(k) of the Code must add eighty-five percent (85%) of the amount of the special accelerated depreciation deduction to its federal taxable income for the 2010 taxable year. A taxpayer is allowed to deduct this add-back under subsection (a) of this section as if it were for property placed in service in 2010.

(c)   Section 179 Expense. - For purposes of this subdivision, the definition of section 179 property has the same meaning as under section 179 of the Code as of January 2, 2013. A taxpayer who places section 179 property in service during a taxable year listed in the table below must add to the taxpayer's federal taxable income eighty-five percent (85%) of the amount by which the taxpayer's expense deduction under section 179 of the Code exceeds the dollar and investment limitation listed in the table below for the taxable year.

A taxpayer is allowed to deduct twenty percent (20%) of the add-back in each of the first five taxable years following the year the taxpayer is required to include the add-back in income.

Taxable Year of 85% Add-Back	Dollar Limitation	Investment Limitation
2010	$250,000	$800,000
2011	$250,000	$800,000
2012	$250,000	$800,000

2013 $25,000 $125,000

(d)   Asset Basis. - The adjustments made in this section do not result in a difference in basis of the affected assets for State and federal income tax purposes, except as modified in subsection (e) of this section.

(e)   Bonus Asset Basis. - In the event of an actual or deemed transfer of an asset occurring on or after January 1, 2013, wherein the tax basis of the asset carries over from the transferor to the transferee for federal income tax purposes, the transferee must add any remaining deductions allowed under subsection (a) of this section to the basis of the transferred asset and depreciate the adjusted basis over any remaining life of the asset. Notwithstanding the provisions of subsection (a) of this section, the transferor is not allowed any remaining future bonus depreciation deductions associated with the transferred asset.

(f)   Prior Transactions. - For any transaction meeting the requirements of subsection (e) of this section prior to January 1, 2013, the transferor and transferee can make an election to make the basis adjustment allowed in that subsection on the transferee's 2013 tax return, to the extent that the transferor has not taken the bonus depreciation deduction on a prior return and provided that the transferor certifies in writing to the transferee that the transferor will not take any remaining deductions allowed under subsection (a) of this section for tax years beginning on or after January 1, 2013, for depreciation associated with the transferred asset. (2013-414, s. 34(b).)

§ 105-130.6. (Repealed effective for taxable years beginning on or after January 1, 2012) Subsidiary and affiliated corporations.

The net income of a corporation doing business in this State that is a parent, subsidiary, or affiliate of another corporation shall be determined by eliminating all payments to or charges by the parent, subsidiary, or affiliated corporation in excess of fair compensation in all intercompany transactions of any kind whatsoever. If the Secretary finds as a fact that a report by a corporation does not disclose the true earnings of the corporation on its business carried on in this State, the Secretary may require the corporation to file a consolidated return of the entire operations of the parent corporation and of its subsidiaries and affiliates, including its own operations and income. The Secretary shall determine the true amount of net income earned by such corporation in this

State. The combined net income of the corporation and of its parent, subsidiaries, and affiliates shall be apportioned to this State by use of the applicable apportionment formula required to be used by the corporation under G.S. 105-130.4. The return shall include in the apportionment formula the property, payrolls, and sales of all corporations for which the return is made. For the purposes of this section, a corporation is considered a subsidiary of another corporation when, directly or indirectly, it is subject to control by the other corporation by stock ownership, interlocking directors, or by any other means whatsoever exercised by the same or associated financial interests, whether the control is direct or through one or more subsidiary, affiliated, or controlled corporations. A corporation is considered an affiliate of another corporation when both are directly or indirectly controlled by the same parent corporation or by the same or associated financial interests by stock ownership, interlocking directors, or by any other means whatsoever, whether the control is direct or through one or more subsidiary, affiliated, or controlled corporations. The secretary may require a consolidated return under this section regardless of whether the parent or controlling corporation or interests or its subsidiaries or affiliates, other than the taxpayer, are or are not doing business in this State.

If a consolidated return required by this section is not filed within 60 days after it is demanded, then the corporation is subject to the penalties provided in G.S. 105-230 and G.S. 105-236.

The parent, subsidiary, or affiliated corporation must incorporate in its return required under this section information needed to determine the net income taxable under this Part, and must furnish any additional information the Secretary requires. If the return does not contain the information required or the additional information requested is not furnished within 30 days after it is demanded, the corporation is subject to the penalties provided in G.S. 105-230 and G.S. 105-236.

If the Secretary finds that the determination of the income of a parent, subsidiary, or affiliated corporation under a consolidated return will produce a greater or lesser figure than the amount of income earned in this State, the Secretary may readjust the determination by reasonable methods of computation to make it conform to the amount of income earned in this State. If the corporation contends the figure produced is greater than the earnings in this State, it must file with the Secretary within 30 days after notice of the determination a statement of its objections and of an alternative method of determination. The Secretary must consider the statement in determining the income earned in this State. The findings and conclusions of the Secretary shall be presumed to be correct and shall not be set aside unless shown to be plainly wrong.

In order to provide clarity for taxpayers, the Secretary may adopt rules in accordance with G.S. 105-262 that describe facts and circumstances under which the Secretary will require a corporation to file a consolidated or combined return. The adoption of these rules does not limit the Secretary's authority to require a consolidated or combined return under sets of facts and circumstances not described in the rules when the Secretary finds as a fact that a report by a corporation does not disclose the true earnings of the corporation on its business carried on in this State. (1939, c. 158, s. 3181/2; 1941, c. 50, s. 5; 1943, c. 400, s. 4; 1945, c. 708, s. 4; 1959, c. 1259, ss. 4, 8; 1967, c. 1110, s. 3; 1971, c. 1223, s. 1; 1973, c. 476, s. 193; 1998-98, s. 69; 1998-212, s. 29A.14(f); 2010-31, s. 31.10(d); 2011-390, s. 1; 2011-411, s. 8(b).)

§ 105-130.6A. Adjustment for expenses related to dividends.

(a) Definitions. - The definitions in G.S. 105-130.2 govern the determination of whether a corporation is a subsidiary or an affiliate of another corporation. In addition, the following definitions apply in this section:

(1) Affiliated group. - A group that includes a corporation, all other corporations that are affiliates or subsidiaries of that corporation, and all other corporations that are affiliates or subsidiaries of another corporation in the group.

(2) Bank holding company. - A holding company with an affiliate that is subject to the privilege tax on banks levied in G.S. 105-102.3.

(3) Dividends. - Dividends received that are not taxed under this Part.

(4) (Effective until July 1, 2014) Electric power holding company. - A holding company with an affiliate or a subsidiary that is subject to the franchise tax on electric power companies levied in G.S. 105-116.

(4) (Effective July 1, 2014) Electric power holding company. - A holding company with an affiliate or a subsidiary that is engaged in the business of producing electric power.

(5) Expense adjustment. - The adjustment required by G.S. 105-130.5(c)(3) for expenses related to dividends not taxed under this Part.

(6) Holding company. - Defined in G.S. 105-120.2.

(b) General Rule. - For corporations other than bank holding companies and electric power holding companies, the adjustment under G.S. 105-130.5(c)(3) for expenses related to dividends not taxed under this Part may not exceed an amount equal to fifteen percent (15%) of the dividends.

(c) Bank Holding Companies. - For bank holding companies the adjustment under G.S. 105-130.5(c)(3) for expenses related to dividends not taxed under this Part may not exceed an amount equal to twenty percent (20%) of the dividends.

(d) Electric Power Holding Companies. - For electric power holding companies, the adjustment under G.S. 105-130.5(c)(3) for expenses related to dividends not taxed under this Part may not exceed an amount equal to fifteen percent (15%) of its total interest expenses.

(e) Cap for Bank Holding Companies. - After calculating the expense adjustment as provided in subsection (c) of this section, each bank holding company must calculate the amount of additional tax that results from the expense adjustments for the holding company and for every corporation in the holding company's affiliated group for the taxable year. If the expense adjustments result in additional tax exceeding eleven million dollars ($11,000,000) for a taxable year for the affiliated group, the affiliated group may reduce the amount of the expense adjustment so that the resulting additional tax does not exceed this maximum. This maximum applies once to each affiliated group each taxable year, whether or not the group includes more than one bank holding company.

The members of the affiliated group may allocate this reduction among themselves in their discretion. In order to take this reduction, each member of the affiliated group that is required to file a return under this Part and that has dividends for the taxable year must provide a schedule with its return that lists every member of the group that has dividends, the amount of the dividends, and whether the member is a bank holding company. In addition, the schedule must show the expense adjustments for those members whose additional tax as a result of the expense adjustment constitutes the maximum amount. In addition, each member must provide any other documentation required by the Secretary.

If the expense adjustment for an affiliated group is reduced under this subsection, and the return of a member of the group is later changed in a manner that reduces below the maximum the amount of additional tax for the group resulting from the expense adjustment, the Secretary may increase the expense adjustment for any member of the group in order to increase to the maximum the amount of additional tax for the group resulting from the expense adjustment. In this situation, the amount of the increase is considered a forfeited tax benefit with respect to the affiliated group for the purposes of G.S. 105-241.8. The date of the forfeiture is the date of the change that triggers the Secretary's authority to increase the expense adjustment. Any member whose expense adjustment the Secretary increases is liable for interest on the amount of the increase at the rate established under G.S. G.S. 105-241.21 computed from the date the taxes would have been due if the expense adjustment had been calculated correctly on the original return. The amount of the increase and the interest are due 60 days after the date of the forfeiture. A taxpayer that fails to pay the amount of the increase and interest by the due date is subject to the penalties provided in G.S. 105-236.

(f) Credits for Bank Holding Companies. - If the affiliated group of which a bank holding company is a member is eligible for the reduction provided in subsection (e) of this section for a taxable year, the affiliated group is also eligible for a credit equal to two million dollars ($2,000,000). If the affiliated group of which a bank holding company is a member is not eligible for the reduction provided in subsection (e) of this section for a taxable year, the affiliated group is eligible for a credit equal to the amount of additional tax that results from its expense adjustments in excess of the amount of additional tax that would result from the expense adjustments if the expense adjustment of any bank holding company in the group were equal to fifteen percent (15%) of the holding company's dividends for that taxable year.

A credit allowed by this subsection may be taken in four equal, annual installments beginning with the later of the following taxable year or the taxpayer's taxable year beginning in 2003. The members of the affiliated group may allocate a credit allowed by this subsection among themselves in their discretion.

(g) Credit for Electric Power Holding Companies. - After calculating the adjustment for expenses related to dividends under G.S. 105-130.5(c)(3), each electric power holding company must calculate the amount of additional tax under this Part that results from the expense adjustment for the taxable year.

The electric power holding company is allowed a credit for the following taxable year equal to one-half of this amount of additional tax.

As an alternative to taking this credit against its own tax liability, an electric power holding company may elect to allocate the credit among the members of its affiliated group. In this case, the credit must be taken in four equal installments beginning in the later of the following taxable year or the taxable year for which the taxpayer's final return is due in 2004.

(h)   Limitation on Credits. - The credits provided in this section are allowed against the tax levied in this Part and the franchise tax levied in Article 3 of this Chapter. A taxpayer may claim a credit against only one of the taxes against which it is allowed. Each taxpayer must elect the tax against which the credit will be taken when filing the return on which the first installment of the credit is claimed. This election is binding. All installments and carryforwards of the credit must be taken against the same tax.

In order for a member of an affiliated group to take a credit, each member of the affiliated group that is required to file a return under this Part or under Article 3 of this Chapter must attach a schedule to its return that shows for every member of the group the amount of the credit taken by it, the tax against which it is taken, and the amount of the resulting tax. In addition, each member must provide any other documentation required by the Secretary.

A credit allowed in this section may not exceed the amount of tax against which it is taken for the taxable year reduced by the sum of all credits allowable, except tax payments made by or on behalf of the taxpayer. Any unused portion of the credit may be carried forward to succeeding taxable years. (2002-136, s. 2; 2007-491, s. 13; 2013-316, s. 4.1(b); 2013-414, s. 36.)

§ 105-130.7: Repealed by Session Laws 2003-349, s. 1.1, effective January 1, 2003.

§ 105-130.7A. Royalty income reporting option.

(a)   Purpose. - Royalty payments received for the use of intangible property in this State are income derived from doing business in this State. This section provides taxpayers with an option concerning the method by which these royalties can be reported for taxation when the recipient and the payer are related members. As provided in this section, these royalty payments can be either (i) deducted by the payer and included in the income of the recipient, or (ii) added back to the income of the payer and excluded from the income of the recipient.

(b) Definitions. - The following definitions apply in this section:

(1) Component member. - Defined in section 1563(b) of the Code.

(1a) Intangible property. - Copyrights, patents, and trademarks.

(2) North Carolina royalty. - An amount charged that is for, related to, or in connection with the use in this State of intangible property. The term includes royalty and technical fees, licensing fees, and other similar charges.

(3) Own. - To own directly, indirectly, beneficially, or constructively. The attribution rules of section 318 of the Code apply in determining ownership under this section.

(4) Related entity. - Any of the following:

a. A stockholder who is an individual, or a member of the stockholder's family enumerated in section 318 of the Code, if the stockholder and the members of the stockholder's family own in the aggregate at least eighty percent (80%) of the value of the taxpayer's outstanding stock.

b. A stockholder, or a stockholder's partnership, limited liability company, estate, trust, or corporation, if the stockholder and the stockholder's partnerships, limited liability companies, estates, trusts, and corporations own in the aggregate at least fifty percent (50%) of the value of the taxpayer's outstanding stock.

c. A corporation, or a party related to the corporation in a manner that would require an attribution of stock from the corporation to the party or from the party to the corporation under the attribution rules of section 318 of the Code, if the taxpayer owns at least eighty percent (80%) of the value of the corporation's outstanding stock.

(5) Related member. - A person that, with respect to the taxpayer during any part of the taxable year, is one or more of the following:

a. A related entity.

b. A component member.

c. A person to or from whom there would be attribution of stock ownership in accordance with section 1563(e) of the Code if the phrase "5 percent or more" were replaced by "twenty percent (20%) or more" each place it appears in that section.

(6) Royalty payment. - Either of the following:

a. Expenses, losses, and costs paid, accrued, or incurred for North Carolina royalties, to the extent the amounts are allowed as deductions or costs in determining taxable income before operating loss deduction and special deductions for the taxable year under the Code.

b. Amounts directly or indirectly allowed as deductions under section 163 of the Code, to the extent the amounts are paid, accrued, or incurred for a time price differential charged for the late payment of any expenses, losses, or costs described in this subdivision.

(7) Trademark. - A trademark, trade name, service mark, or other similar type of intangible asset.

(8) Use. - Use of intangible property includes direct or indirect maintenance, management, ownership, sale, exchange, or disposition of the intangible property.

(c) Election. - For the purpose of computing its State net income, a taxpayer must add royalty payments made to, or in connection with transactions with, a related member during the taxable year. This addition is not required for an amount of royalty payments that meets any of the following conditions:

(1) The related member includes the amount as income on a return filed under this Part for the same taxable year that the amount is deducted by the taxpayer, and the related member does not elect to deduct the amount pursuant to G.S. 105-130.5(b)(20).

(2) The taxpayer can establish that the related member during the same taxable year directly or indirectly paid, accrued, or incurred the amount to a person who is not a related member.

(3) The taxpayer can establish that the related member to whom the amount was paid is organized under the laws of a country other than the United States, the country has a comprehensive income tax treaty with the United States, and the country imposes a tax on the royalty income of the related member at a rate that equals or exceeds the rate set in G.S. 105-130.3.

(d) Indirect Transactions. - For the purpose of this section, an indirect transaction or relationship has the same effect as if it were direct. (2001-327, s. 1(b); 2003-416, s. 15; 2006-66, s. 24A.3(a); 2006-196, s. 10.)

§ 105-130.8. Net economic loss.

(a) Net economic losses sustained by a corporation in any or all of the 15 preceding income years shall be allowed as a deduction to the corporation subject to the following limitations:

(1) The purpose in allowing the deduction of a net economic loss of a prior year is to grant some measure of relief to the corporation that has incurred economic misfortune or is otherwise materially affected by strict adherence to the annual accounting rule in the determination of net income. The deduction allowed in this section does not authorize the carrying forward of any particular items or category of loss except to the extent that the loss results in the impairment of the net economic situation of the corporation so as to result in a net economic loss as defined in this section.

(2) The net economic loss for any year means the amount by which allowable deductions for the year other than prior year losses exceed income from all sources in the year including any income not taxable under this Part.

(3) Any net economic loss of prior years brought forward and claimed as a deduction in any income year may be deducted from net income of the year only to the extent that the loss carried forward from the prior years exceeds any income not taxable under this Part received in the same year in which the deduction is claimed, except that in the case of a corporation required to allocate and apportion to North Carolina its net income, only that proportionate part of the net economic loss of a prior year shall be deductible from total income allocable to this State as would be determined by the use of the allocation and apportionment provisions of G.S. 105-130.4 for the year of the loss.

(4)   A net economic loss carried forward from any year shall first be applied to, or offset by, any income taxable or nontaxable of the next succeeding year before any portion of the loss may be carried forward to a succeeding year.

(5)   For purposes of this section, any income item deductible in determining State net income under the provisions of G.S. 105-130.5 and any nonapportionable income not allocable to this State under the provisions of G.S. 105-130.4 shall be considered as income not taxable under this Part. The amount of the income item considered income not taxable under this Part is determined after subtracting related expenses for which a deduction was allowed under this Part.

(6)   No loss shall either directly or indirectly be carried forward more than 15 years.

(b)   A corporation claiming a deduction for a loss for the current year or carried forward from a prior year must maintain and make available for inspection by the Secretary all records necessary to determine and verify the amount of the deduction. The Secretary or the taxpayer may redetermine an item originating in a taxable year that is closed under the statute of limitations for the purpose of determining the amount of net economic loss that can be carried forward to a taxable year that remains open under the statute of limitations. (1939, c. 158, s. 322; 1941, c. 50, s. 5; 1943, c. 400, s. 4; c. 668; 1945, c. 708, s. 4; c. 752, s. 3; 1947, c. 501, s. 4; c. 894; 1949, c. 392, s. 3; 1951, c. 643, s. 4; c. 937, s. 4; 1953, c. 1031, s. 1; c. 1302, s. 4; 1955, c. 1100, s. 1; c. 1331, s. 1; cc. 1332, 1342; c. 1343, s. 1; 1957, c. 1340, ss. 4, 8; 1959, c. 1259, s. 4; 1961, c. 201, s. 1; c. 1148; 1963, c. 1169, s. 2; 1965, c. 1048; 1967, c. 1110, s. 3; 1998-98, s. 69; 1998-171, ss. 6, 8; 2002-136, s. 3; 2003-416, s. 5(i).)

§ 105-130.9. Contributions.

Contributions shall be allowed as a deduction to the extent and in the manner provided as follows:

(1)   Charitable contributions as defined in section 170(c) of the Code, exclusive of contributions allowed in subdivision (2) of this section, shall be allowed as a deduction to the extent provided herein. The amount allowed as a deduction hereunder shall be limited to an amount not in excess of five percent

(5%) of the corporation's net income as computed without the benefit of this subdivision or subdivision (2) of this section. Provided, that a carryover of contributions shall not be allowed and that contributions made to North Carolina donees by corporations allocating a part of their total net income outside this State shall not be allowed under this subdivision, but shall be allowed under subdivision (3) of this section.

(2) Contributions by any corporation to the State of North Carolina, any of its institutions, instrumentalities, or agencies, any county of this State, its institutions, instrumentalities, or agencies, any municipality of this State, its institutions, instrumentalities, or agencies, and contributions or gifts by any corporation to educational institutions located within North Carolina, no part of the net earnings of which inures to the benefit of any private stockholders or dividend. For the purpose of this subdivision, the words "educational institution" shall mean only an educational institution which normally maintains a regular faculty and curriculum and normally has a regularly organized body of students in attendance at the place where the educational activities are carried on. The words "educational institution" shall be deemed to include all of such institution's departments, schools and colleges, a group of "educational institutions" and an organization (corporation, trust, foundation, association or other entity) organized and operated exclusively to receive, hold, invest and administer property and to make expenditures to or for the sole benefit of an "educational institution" or group of "educational institutions."

(3) Corporations allocating a part of their total net income outside North Carolina under the provisions of G.S. 105-130.4 shall deduct from total income allocable to North Carolina contributions made to North Carolina donees qualified under subdivisions (1) and (2) of this section or made through North Carolina offices or branches of other donees qualified under the above-mentioned subdivisions of this section; provided, such deduction for contributions made to North Carolina donees qualified under subdivision (1) of this section shall be limited in amount to five percent (5%) of the total income allocated to North Carolina as computed without the benefit of this deduction for contributions.

(4) (Effective for taxable years beginning before January 1, 2013) The amount of a contribution for which the taxpayer claimed a tax credit pursuant to G.S. 105-130.34 or G.S. 105-130.48 shall not be eligible for a deduction under this section. The amount of the credit claimed with respect to the contribution is not, however, required to be added to income under G.S. 105-130.5(a)(10).

(4)   (Effective for taxable years beginning on or after January 1, 2013) The amount of a contribution for which the taxpayer claimed a tax credit pursuant to G.S. 105-130.34 shall not be eligible for a deduction under this section. The amount of the credit claimed with respect to the contribution is not, however, required to be added to income under G.S. 105-130.5(a)(10). (1939, c. 158, s. 322; 1941, c. 50, s. 5; 1943, c. 400, s. 4; c. 668; 1945, c. 708, s. 4; c. 752, s. 3; 1947, c. 501, s. 4; c. 894; 1949, c. 392, s. 3; 1951, c. 643, s. 4; c. 937, s. 4; 1953, c. 1031, s. 1; c. 1302, s. 4; 1955, c. 1100, s. 1; c. 1331, s. 1; cc. 1332, 1342; c. 1343, s. 1; 1957, c. 1340, ss. 4, 8; 1959, c. 1259, s. 4; 1961, c. 201, s. 1; c. 1148; 1963, c. 1169, s. 2; 1965, c. 1048; 1967, c. 1110, s. 3; 1969, c. 1175, s. 1; 1973, c. 1287, s. 4; 1983, c. 713, s. 82; c. 793, s. 2; 1995, c. 370, s. 4; 2006-66, s. 24.18(b); 2011-330, s. 36.)

§ 105-130.10. Amortization of air-cleaning devices, waste treatment facilities and recycling facilities.

In lieu of any depreciation allowance, at the option of the corporation, a deduction shall be allowed for the amortization, based on a period of 60 months, of the cost of:

(1)   Any air-cleaning device, sewage or waste treatment plant, including waste lagoons, and pollution abatement equipment purchased or constructed and installed which reduces the amount of air or water pollution resulting from the emission of air contaminants or the discharge of sewage, industrial waste, or other polluting materials or substances into the outdoor atmosphere or streams, lakes, rivers, or coastal waters. The deduction provided herein shall apply also to the facilities or equipment of private or public utilities built and installed primarily for the purpose of providing sewer service to residential and outlying areas. The deduction provided for in this subdivision shall be allowed by the Secretary of Revenue only upon the condition that the corporation claiming such allowance shall furnish to the Secretary a certificate from the Department of Environment and Natural Resources or from a local air pollution control program for air-cleaning devices located in an area where the Environmental Management Commission has certified a local air pollution control program pursuant to G.S. 143-215.112 certifying that the Environmental Management Commission or local air pollution control program has found as a fact that the air-cleaning device, waste treatment plant or other pollution abatement equipment purchased or constructed and installed as above described has actually been constructed and installed and that such construction, plant or

equipment complies with the requirements of the Environmental Management Commission or local air pollution control program with respect to such devices, construction, plants or equipment, that such device, plant or equipment is being effectively operated in accordance with the terms and conditions set forth in the permit, certificate of approval, or other document of approval issued by the Environmental Management Commission or local air pollution control program, and that the primary purpose thereof is to reduce air or water pollution resulting from the emission of air contaminants or the discharge of sewage and waste and not merely incidental to other purposes and functions.

(2)   Purchasing and installing equipment or constructing facilities for the purpose of recycling or resource recovering of or from solid waste, or for the purpose of reducing the volume of hazardous waste generated. The deduction provided for in this subdivision shall be allowed by the Secretary of Revenue only upon the condition that the corporation claiming such allowance shall furnish to the Secretary a certificate from the Department of Environment and Natural Resources certifying that the Department of Environment and Natural Resources has found as a fact that the equipment or facility has actually been purchased, installed or constructed, that it is in conformance with all rules and regulations of the Department of Environment and Natural Resources, and that recycling or resource recovering is the primary purpose of the facility or equipment. (1939, c. 158, s. 322; 1941, c. 50, s. 5; 1943, c. 400, s. 4; c. 668; 1945, c. 708, s. 4; c. 752, s. 3; 1947, c. 501, s. 4; c. 894; 1949, c. 392, s. 3; 1951, c. 643, s. 4; c. 937, s. 4; 1953, c. 1031, s. 1; c. 1302, s. 4; 1955, c. 1100, s. 1; c. 1331, s. 1; cc. 1332, 1342; c. 1343, s. 1; 1957, c. 1340, ss. 4, 8; 1959, c. 1259, s. 4; 1961, c. 201, s. 1; c. 1148; 1963, c. 1169, s. 2; 1965, c. 1048; 1967, c. 1110, s. 3; 1969, c. 817; 1973, c. 476, s. 193; c. 1262, s. 23; 1975, c. 764, s. 3; 1977, c. 771, s. 4; 1981, c. 704, s. 19; 1987, c. 804, s. 4; 1989, c. 148, s. 2; c. 727, ss. 218(40), 219(28); 1997-443, s. 11A.119(a).)

§ 105-130.10A. Amortization of equipment mandated by OSHA.

(a)   In lieu of any depreciation allowance, at the option of the corporation, a deduction shall be allowed for the amortization, based on a period of 60 months, of the cost of any equipment mandated by the Occupational Safety and Health Act (OSHA), including the cost of planning, acquiring, constructing, modifying, and installing said equipment.

(b) For the purposes of this section and G.S. 105-147(13)d, the term "equipment mandated by the Occupational Safety and Health Act" is any tangible personal property and other buildings and structural components of buildings, which is acquired, constructed, reconstructed, modified, or erected after January 1, 1979; and which the taxpayer must acquire, construct, install, or make available in order to comply with the occupational safety and health standards adopted and promulgated by the United States Secretary of Labor or the Commissioner of Labor of North Carolina, and the term "occupational safety and health standards" includes but is not limited to interim federal standards, consensus standards, any proprietary standards or permanent standards, as well as temporary emergency standards which may be adopted by the United States Secretary of Labor, promulgated as provided by the Occupational Safety and Health Act of 1970, (Public Law 91-596, 91st Congress, Act of December 29, 1970, 84 Stat. 1950) and which standards or regulations are published in the Code of Federal Regulations or otherwise properly promulgated under the Occupational Safety and Health Act of 1970 or any alternative rule, regulation or standard promulgated by the Commissioner of Labor of North Carolina as provided in G.S. 95-131. (1979, c. 776, s. 1.)

§ 105-130.11. Conditional and other exemptions.

(a) Exempt Organizations. - Except as provided in subsections (b) and (c), the following organizations and any organization that is exempt from federal income tax under the Code are exempt from the tax imposed under this Part.

(1) Fraternal beneficiary societies, orders or associations

a. Operating under the lodge system or for the exclusive benefit of the members of a fraternity itself operating under the lodge system, and

b. Providing for the payment of life, sick, accident, or other benefits to the members of such society, order or association, or their dependents.

(2) Cooperative banks without capital stock organized and operated for mutual purposes and without profit; and electric and telephone membership corporations organized under Chapter 117 of the General Statutes.

(3) Cemetery corporations and corporations organized for religious, charitable, scientific, literary, or educational purposes, or for the prevention of cruelty to children or animals, no part of the net earnings of which inures to the benefit of any private stockholder or individual.

(4) Business leagues, chambers of commerce, merchants' associations, or boards of trade not organized for profit, and no part of the net earnings of which inures to the benefit of any private stockholder or individual.

(5) Civic leagues or organizations not organized for profit, but operated exclusively for the promotion of social welfare.

(6) Clubs organized and operated exclusively for pleasure, recreation, and other nonprofitable purposes, no part of the net earnings of which inures to the benefit of any private stockholder or member.

(7) Farmers' or other mutual hail, cyclone, or fire insurance companies, mutual ditch or irrigation companies, mutual or cooperative telephone companies, or like organizations of a purely local character the income of which consists solely of assessments, dues, and fees collected from members for the sole purpose of meeting expenses.

(8) Farmers', fruit growers', or like organizations organized and operated as sales agents for the purpose of marketing the products of members and turning back to them the proceeds of sales, less the necessary selling expenses, on the basis of the quantity of product furnished by them.

(9) Mutual associations formed under G.S. 54-111 through 54-128 to conduct agricultural business on the mutual plan and marketing associations organized under G.S. 54-129 through 54-158.

Nothing in this subdivision shall be construed to exempt any cooperative, mutual association, or other organization from an income tax on net income that has not been refunded to patrons on a patronage basis and distributed either in cash, stock, or certificates, or in some other manner that discloses the amount of each patron's refund. Provided, in arriving at net income for purposes of this subdivision, no deduction shall be allowed for dividends paid on capital stock. Patronage refunds made after the close of the taxable year and on or before the fifteenth day of the ninth month following the close of the taxable year are considered as to be made on the last day of the taxable year to the extent the allocations are attributable to income derived before the close of the year; provided, that no stabilization or marketing organization that handles agricultural products for sale for producers on a pool basis is considered to have realized any net income or profit in the disposition of a pool or any part of a pool until all of the products in that pool have been sold and the pool has been closed; provided, further, that a pool is not considered closed until the expiration of at least 90 days after the sale of the last remaining product in that pool. These cooperatives and other organizations shall file an annual information return with the Secretary on forms to be furnished by the Secretary and shall include the names and addresses of all persons, patrons, or shareholders whose patronage refunds amount to ten dollars ($10.00) or more.

(10) Insurance companies paying the tax on gross premiums as specified in G.S. 105-228.5.

(11) Corporations or organizations, such as condominium associations, homeowner associations, or cooperative housing corporations not organized for profit, the membership of which is limited to the owners or occupants of residential units in the condominium, housing development, or cooperative housing corporation, and operated exclusively for the management, operation, preservation, maintenance, or landscaping of the common areas and facilities owned by the corporation or organization or its members situated contiguous to the houses, apartments, or other dwellings or for the management, operation, preservation, maintenance, and repair of the houses, apartments, or other dwellings owned by the corporation or organization or its members, but only if no part of the net earnings of the corporation or organization inures (other than through the performance of related services for the members of such corporation or organization) to the benefit of any member of such corporation or organization or other person.

(b) Unrelated Business Income. - Except as provided in this subsection, an organization described in subdivision (a)(1), (3), (4), (5), (6), (7), (8), or (9) of this section and any organization exempt from federal income tax under the Code is subject to the tax provided in G.S. 105-130.3 on its unrelated business taxable income, as defined in section 512 of the Code, adjusted as provided in G.S. 105-130.5. The tax does not apply, however, to net income derived from any of the following:

(1) Research performed by a college, university, or hospital.

(2) Research performed for the United States or its instrumentality or for a state or its political subdivision.

(3) Research performed by an organization operated primarily to carry on fundamental research, the results of which are freely available to the general public.

(c) Homeowner Association Income. - An organization described in subdivision (a)(11) of this section is subject to the tax provided in G.S. 105-130.3 on its gross income other than membership income less the deductions allowed by this Article that are directly connected with the production of the gross income other than membership income. The term "membership income" means the gross income from assessments, fees, charges, or similar amounts received from members of the organization for expenditure in the preservation, maintenance, and management of the common areas and facilities of or the residential units in the condominium or housing development.

(d) Real Estate Mortgage Investment Conduits. - An entity that qualifies as a real estate mortgage investment conduit, as defined in section 860D of the Code, is exempt from the tax imposed under this Part, except that any net income derived from a prohibited transaction, as defined in section 860F of the Code, is taxable to the real estate mortgage investment conduit under G.S. 105-130.3 and G.S. 105-130.3A, subject to the adjustments provided in G.S. 105-130.5. This subsection does not exempt the holders of a regular or residual interest in a real estate mortgage investment conduit as defined in section 860G of the Code from any tax on the income from that interest. (1939, c. 158, s. 314; 1945, c. 708, s. 4; c. 752, s. 3; 1949, c. 392, s. 3; 1951, c. 937, s. 1; 1955, c. 1313, s. 1; 1957, c. 1340, s. 4; 1959, c. 1259, s. 4; 1963, c. 1169, s. 2; 1967, c. 1110, s. 3; 1973, c. 476, s. 193; c. 1053, s. 4; 1975, c. 19, s. 28; c. 591, s. 2; 1981, c. 450, s. 2; 1983, c. 28, s. 1; c. 31; 1985 (Reg. Sess., 1986), c. 826, s. 5; 1991 (Reg. Sess., 1992), c. 921, s. 1; 1993, c. 494, s. 2; 1998-98, ss. 1(b), 69.)

§ 105-130.12. Real estate investment trusts.

(a) Definitions. - The following definitions apply in this section:

(1) Captive REIT. - A REIT whose shares or certificates of beneficial interest are not regularly traded on an established securities market and are owned or controlled, at any time during the last half of the tax year, by a person that is subject to tax under this Part and is not a REIT or a listed Australian property trust.

(2) Own or control. - To own or control directly, indirectly, beneficially, or constructively more than fifty percent (50%) of the voting power or value of an entity. The attribution rules of section 318 of the Code, as modified by section 856(d)(5) of the Code, apply in determining ownership and control.

(3) REIT. - A trust or another entity that qualifies as a real estate investment trust under section 856 of the Code.

(b) Tax. - The income of a REIT is taxable under this Part in accordance with the Code, unless the REIT is a captive REIT. A captive REIT is required to add to its federal taxable income the amount of a dividend paid deduction allowed under the Code, as provided in G.S. 105-130.5. (1963, c. 1169, s. 2; 1967, c. 110, s. 3; 1971, c. 820, s. 2; 1973, c. 476, s. 193; 1983, c. 713, s. 74; 1998-98, s. 69; 2007-323, s. 31.18(c).)

§ 105-130.13: Repealed by Session Laws 1987 (Regular Session, 1988), c. 1089, s. 2; as amended by Session Laws 1989, c. 728, s. 1.33.

§ 105-130.14. Corporations filing consolidated returns for federal income tax purposes.

Any corporation electing or required to file a consolidated income tax return with the Internal Revenue Service must determine its State net income as if the corporation had filed a separate federal return and shall not file a consolidated or combined return with the Secretary unless one of the following applies:

(1) The corporation is specifically directed in writing by the Secretary under G.S. 105-130.5A to file a consolidated or combined return.

(2) Repealed by Session Laws 2012-79, s. 1.14(c), effective June 26, 2012.

(3) Pursuant to a written request from the corporation under G.S. 105-130.5A, the Secretary has provided written advice to the corporation stating that the Secretary will allow a consolidated or combined return under the facts and circumstances set out in the request and the corporation files a consolidated or combined return in accordance with that written advice. (1967, c. 1110, s. 3; 1973, c. 476, s. 193; 2010-31, s. 31.10(e); 2012-79, s. 1.14(c).)

§ 105-130.15. Basis of return of net income.

(a) (Effective for taxable years beginning before January 1, 2012) The net income of a corporation shall be computed in accordance with the method of accounting it regularly employs in keeping its books. The method must be consistent with respect to both income and deductions. If this method does not clearly reflect the income, the computation shall be made in accordance with a method that, in the Secretary's opinion, does clearly reflect the income, but shall follow as nearly as practicable the federal practice, unless contrary to the context and intent of this Part.

The Secretary may adopt the rules and regulations and any guidelines administered or established by the Internal Revenue Service unless contrary to any provisions of this Part.

(a) (Effective for taxable years beginning on or after January 1, 2012) The net income of a corporation shall be computed in accordance with the method of accounting it regularly employs in keeping its books. The method must be consistent with respect to both income and deductions and shall follow as nearly as practicable the federal practice, unless contrary to the context and intent of this Part.

The Secretary may adopt the rules and regulations and any guidelines administered or established by the Internal Revenue Service unless contrary to any provisions of this Part.

(b) Change of Income Year. -

(1) A corporation may change the income year upon which it reports for income tax purposes without prior approval by the Secretary of Revenue if such change in income year has been approved by or is acceptable to the Federal Commissioner of Internal Revenue and is used for filing income tax returns under the provisions of the Code.

If a corporation desires to make a change in its income year other than as provided above, it may make such change in its income year with the approval of the Secretary of Revenue, provided such approval is requested at least 30 days prior to the end of its new income year.

A corporation which has changed its income year without requesting the approval of the Secretary of Revenue as provided in the first paragraph of this subdivision shall submit to the Secretary of Revenue notification of any change in the income year after the change has been approved by the Federal Commissioner of Internal Revenue or his agent where application for permission to change is required by the Federal Commissioner of Internal Revenue with such notification stating that such approval has been received. Where application for change of the income year is not required by the Federal Commissioner of Internal Revenue, notification of the change of income year shall be submitted to the Secretary of Revenue with the short period return.

(2) A return for a period of less than 12 months (referred to in this subsection as "short period") shall be made when the corporation changes its income year. In such a case, the return shall be made for the short period beginning on the day after the close of the former taxable year and ending at the close of the day before the day designated as the first day of the new taxable year, except that a corporation changing to, or from, a taxable year varying from 52 to 53 weeks shall not be required to file a short period return if such change results in a short period of 359 days or more, or less than seven days. Short period income tax returns shall be filed within the same period following the end of such short period as is required for full year returns under the provisions of G.S. 105-130.17.

(c) Any foreign corporation not domesticated in this State shall not use the installment method of reporting income to this State unless such corporation files a bond with the Secretary of Revenue in such amount and with such sureties as the Secretary shall deem necessary to secure the payment of any taxes which were deferred with respect to any installment transaction.

(d) Notwithstanding any other provision of this Part, any corporation which uses the installment method of reporting income to this State and which is planning to withdraw from this State, merge, or consolidate its business, or terminate its business in this State by any other means whatsoever, shall be required to make a report for income tax purposes, to the Secretary of Revenue, of any unrealized or unreported income from installment sales made while doing business in this State and to pay any tax which may be due on such income. The manner and form for making such report and paying the tax shall be as prescribed by the Secretary. (1939, c. 158, s. 318; 1943, c. 400, s. 4; 1945, c. 708, s. 4; 1949, c. 392, s. 3; 1955, c. 1313, s. 1; 1957, c. 1340, s. 4; 1963, c. 1169, s. 2; 1967, c. 1110, s. 3; 1973, c. 476, s. 193; 1983, c. 713, s. 82; 1998-98, s. 69; 2000-140, s. 64(a); 2011-390, s. 3; 2011-411, s. 8(b).)

§ 105-130.16. (Effective for taxable years beginning before January 1, 2012) Returns.

(a) Return. - Every corporation doing business in this State must file with the Secretary an income tax return showing specifically the items of gross income and the deductions allowed by this Part and any other facts the Secretary requires to make any computation required by this Part. The return of a corporation must be signed by its president, vice-president, treasurer, or chief financial officer. The officer signing the return must furnish an affirmation verifying the return. The affirmation must be in the form required by the Secretary.

(b) Correction of Distortions. - When the Secretary has reason to believe that any corporation so conducts its trade or business in such manner as to either directly or indirectly distort its true net income and the net income properly attributable to the State, whether by the arbitrary shifting of income, through price fixing, charges for service, or otherwise, whereby the net income is arbitrarily assigned to one or another unit in a group of taxpayers carrying on business under a substantially common control, the Secretary may require any facts the Secretary considers necessary for the proper computation of the entire net income and the net income properly attributable to the State, and in determining these computations, the Secretary must have regard to the fair profit that would normally arise from the conduct of the trade or business.

(c) Other Corrections. - When any corporation liable to taxation under this Part conducts its business in such a manner as to either directly or indirectly benefit the members or stockholders thereof or any person interested in the business by selling its products or goods or commodities in which it deals at less than the fair price which might be obtained therefor, or when a corporation, a substantial portion of whose capital stock is owned either directly or indirectly by another corporation, acquires and disposes of the products of the corporation so owning a substantial portion of its stock in such a manner as to create a loss or improper net income for either of the corporations, or when a corporation, owning directly or indirectly a substantial portion of the stock of another corporation, acquires and disposes of the products of the corporation of which it so owns a substantial portion of the stock in such manner as to create a loss or improper net income for either of the corporations, the Secretary may determine the amount of taxable income of the such corporations for the calendar or fiscal year, having due regard to the reasonable profits which, but for such arrangement or understanding, might or could have been obtained by the corporations liable to taxation under this Part from dealing in such products, goods or commodities. (1939, c. 158, s. 326; 1941, c. 50, s. 5; 1943, c. 400, s. 4; 1945, c. 708, s. 4; 1951, c. 643, s. 4; 1957, c. 1340, s. 4; 1967, c. 1110, s. 3;

1973, c. 476, s. 193; 1998-98, s. 69; 1999-337, s. 22; 2008-134, s. 4(a); 2009-445, s. 6.)

§ 105-130.16. (Effective for taxable years beginning on or after January 1, 2012) Returns.

(a) Every corporation doing business in this State must file with the Secretary an income tax return showing specifically the items of gross income and the deductions allowed by this Part and any other facts the Secretary requires to make any computation required by this Part. The return of a corporation must be signed by its president, vice-president, treasurer, or chief financial officer. The officer signing the return must furnish an affirmation verifying the return. The affirmation must be in the form required by the Secretary.

(b), (c) Repealed by Session Laws 2011-390, s. 4, as amended by Session Laws 2011-411, s. 8(b), effective for taxable years beginning on or after January 1, 2012. (1939, c. 158, s. 326; 1941, c. 50, s. 5; 1943, c. 400, s. 4; 1945, c. 708, s. 4; 1951, c. 643, s. 4; 1957, c. 1340, s. 4; 1967, c. 1110, s. 3; 1973, c. 476, s. 193; 1998-98, s. 69; 1999-337, s. 22; 2008-134, s. 4(a); 2009-445, s. 6; 2011-390, s. 4; 2011-411, s. 8(b).)

§ 105-130.17. Time and place of filing returns.

(a) Returns must be filed as prescribed by the Secretary at the place prescribed by the Secretary. Returns must be in the form prescribed by the Secretary. The Secretary must furnish forms in accordance with G.S. 105-254.

(b) Except as otherwise provided in this section, the return of a corporation shall be filed on or before the fifteenth day of the fourth month following the close of its income year. An income year ending on any day other than the last day of the month shall be deemed to end on the last day of the calendar month ending nearest to the last day of a taxpayer's actual income year.

(c) In the case of mutual associations formed under G.S. 54-111 through 54-128 to conduct agricultural business on the mutual plan and marketing associations organized under G.S. 54-129 through 54-158, which are required to file under subsection (a)(9) of G.S. 105-130.11, a return made on the basis of a calendar year shall be filed on or before the fifteenth day of the September following the close of the calendar year, and a return made on the basis of a fiscal year shall be filed on or before the fifteenth day of the ninth month following the close of the fiscal year.

(d)   A taxpayer may ask the Secretary for an extension of time to file a return under G.S. 105-263.

(d1)   Organizations described in G.S. 105-130.11(a)(1), (3), (4), (5), (6), (7) and (8) that are required to file a return under G.S. 105-130.11(b) shall file a return made on the basis of a calendar year on or before the fifteenth day of May following the close of the calendar year and a return made on the basis of a fiscal year on or before the fifteenth day of the fifth month following the close of the fiscal year.

(e)   Any corporation that ceases its operations in this State before the end of its income year because of its intention to dissolve or to withdraw from this State, or because of a merger, conversion, or consolidation or for any other reason whatsoever shall file its return for the then current income year within 105 days after the date it terminates its business in this State.

(f)   Repealed by Session Laws 1998-217, s. 42, effective October 31, 1998.

(g)   A corporation that files a federal return pursuant to section 6072(c) of the Code shall file its return on or before the fifteenth day of the seventh month following the close of its income year. (1939, c. 158, s. 329; 1943, c. 400, s. 4; 1951, c. 643, s. 4; 1953, c. 1302, s. 4; 1955, c. 17, s. 1; 1957, c. 1340, s. 4; 1963, c. 1169, s. 2; 1967, c. 1110, s. 3; 1973, c. 476, s. 193; c. 1287, s. 4; 1981, c. 56; 1989 (Reg. Sess., 1990), c. 984, s. 8; 1997-300, s. 3; 1998-217, s. 42; 1999-369, s. 5.5; 2000-140, s. 64(b); 2006-18, s. 7; 2007-491, s. 14.)

§ 105-130.18: Repealed by Session Laws 2009-445, s. 7, effective August 7, 2009.

§ 105-130.19. When tax must be paid.

(a)   Except as provided in Article 4C of this Chapter, the full amount of the tax payable as shown on the return must be paid to the Secretary within the time allowed for filing the return.

(b), (c) Repealed by Session Laws 1989, c. 37, s. 1.

(d)   Repealed by Session Laws 1993, c. 450, s. 3.

(1939, c. 158, s. 332; 1943, c. 400, s. 4; 1947, c. 501, s. 4; 1951, c. 643, s. 4; 1955, c. 17, s. 2; 1959, c. 1259, s. 2; 1963, c. 1169, s. 2; 1967, c. 1110, s. 3; 1973, c. 476, s. 193; 1977, c. 1114, s. 7; 1989, c. 37, s. 1; 1989 (Reg. Sess., 1990), c. 984, s. 9; 1991 (Reg. Sess., 1992), c. 930, s. 14; 1993, c. 450, s. 3.)

§ 105-130.20. Federal corrections.

If a taxpayer's federal taxable income is corrected or otherwise determined by the federal government, the taxpayer must, within six months after being notified of the correction or final determination by the federal government, file an income tax return with the Secretary reflecting the corrected or determined taxable income. The Secretary must propose an assessment for any additional tax due from the taxpayer as provided in Article 9 of this Chapter. The Secretary must refund any overpayment of tax as provided in Article 9 of this Chapter. A taxpayer that fails to comply with this section is subject to the penalties in G.S. 105-236 and forfeits its rights to any refund due by reason of the determination. (1939, c. 158, s. 334; 1947, c. 501, s. 4; 1949, c. 392, s. 3; 1957, c. 1340, s. 14; 1963, c. 1169, s. 2; 1967, c. 1110, s. 3; 1973, c. 476, s. 193; 1993 (Reg. Sess., 1994), c. 582, s. 2; 2006-18, s. 4; 2007-491, s. 15.)

§ 105-130.21. Information at the source.

(a) Every corporation having a place of business or having one or more employees, agents or other representatives in this State, in whatever capacity acting, including lessors or mortgagors of real or personal property, or having the control, receipt, custody, disposal, or payment of interest (other than interest coupons payable to the bearer), rent, salaries, wages, premiums, annuities, compensations, remunerations, emoluments or other fixed or determinable annual or periodical gains or profits paid or payable during any year to any taxpayer, shall make complete return thereof to the Secretary of Revenue under such regulations and in such form and manner and to such extent as may be prescribed by him. The filing of any report in compliance with the provisions of this section by a foreign corporation shall not constitute an act in evidence of and shall not be deemed to be evidence that such corporation is doing business in this State.

(b) Every corporation doing business or having a place of business in this State shall file with the Secretary of Revenue, on such form and in such manner as he may prescribe, the names and addresses of all taxpayers, residents of North Carolina, to whom dividends have been paid and the amount of such dividends during the income year. (1939, c. 158, s. 328; 1945, c. 708, s. 4; 1957, c. 1340, s. 4; 1967, c. 1110, s. 3; 1973, c. 476, s. 193.)

§ 105-130.22. (Repealed effective for taxable years beginning on or after January 1, 2014) Tax credit for construction of dwelling units for handicapped persons.

There is allowed to corporate owners of multifamily rental units located in this State as a credit against the tax imposed by this Part, an amount equal to five hundred fifty dollars ($550.00) for each dwelling unit constructed by the corporate owner that conforms to Volume I-C of the North Carolina Building Code for the taxable year within which the construction of the dwelling unit is completed. The credit is allowed only for dwelling units completed during the taxable year that were required to be built in compliance with Volume I-C of the North Carolina Building Code. If the credit allowed by this section exceeds the tax imposed by this Part reduced by all other credits allowed, the excess may be carried forward for the next succeeding year. In order to secure the credit allowed by this section the corporation shall file with its income tax return a copy of the occupancy permit on the face of which is recorded by the building inspector the number of units completed during the taxable year that conform to Volume I-C of the North Carolina Building Code. After recording the number of these units on the face of the occupancy permit, the building inspector shall promptly forward a copy of the permit to the Building Accessibility Section of the Department of Insurance. (1973, c. 910, s.1; 1979, c. 803, ss.1, 2; 1981, c. 682, s. 16; 1997-6, s. 3; 1998-98, s.69; 2013-316, s. 2.1(b).)

§ 105-130.23. Repealed by Session Laws 1999-342, s. 1, effective for taxable years beginning on or after January 1, 2000.

§ 105-130.24. Repealed by Session Laws 1983 (Regular Session, 1984), c. 1004, s. 2.

§ 105-130.25. Credit against corporate income tax for construction of cogenerating power plants.

(a) Credit. - A corporation or a partnership, other than a public utility as defined in G.S. 62-3(23), that constructs a cogenerating power plant in North Carolina is allowed as a credit against the tax imposed by this Part an amount equal to ten percent (10%) of the costs paid during the taxable year to purchase and install the electrical or mechanical power generation equipment of that plant. The credit may not be taken for the year in which the costs are paid but shall be taken for the taxable year beginning during the calendar year following the calendar year in which the costs were paid. To be eligible for the credit allowed by this section, the corporation or partnership must own or control the power plant at the time of construction. The credit allowed by this section may not exceed the amount of tax imposed by this Part for the year reduced by the sum of all credits allowed, except payments of tax made by or on behalf of the taxpayer.

(b) Cogenerating Power Plant Defined. - For purposes of this section, a cogenerating power plant is a power plant that sequentially produces electrical or mechanical power and useful thermal energy using natural gas as its primary energy source.

(c) Alternative Method. - A taxpayer eligible for the credit allowed by this section may elect to treat the costs paid during an earlier year as if they were paid during the year the plant becomes operational. This election must be made on or before April 15 following the calendar year in which the plant becomes operational. The election must be in the form prescribed by the Secretary and must contain any supporting documentation the Secretary may require. An election with respect to costs paid by a partnership must be made by the partnership and is binding on any partners to whom the credit is passed through.

The costs with respect to which this election is made will be treated, for the purposes of this section, as if they had actually been paid in the year the plant becomes operational. If a taxpayer makes this election, however, the credit may not exceed one-fourth the amount of tax imposed by this Part for the year reduced by the sum of all credits allowed, except payments of tax by or on behalf of the taxpayer, but any unused portion of the credit may be carried forward for the next 10 taxable years. An election made under this subsection is irrevocable.

(d) Application. - To be eligible for the credit allowed in this section, a taxpayer must file an application for the credit with the Secretary on or before April 15 following the calendar year in which the costs were paid. The application shall be in the form prescribed by the Secretary and shall include any supporting documentation the Secretary may require. An application with respect to costs paid by a partnership must be made by the partnership on behalf of its partners.

(e) Ceiling. - The total amount of all tax credits allowed to taxpayers under this section for payments for construction and installation made in a calendar year may not exceed five million dollars ($5,000,000). The Secretary shall calculate the total amount of tax credits claimed from the applications filed pursuant to subsection (d). If the total amount of tax credits claimed for payments made in a calendar year exceeds five million dollars ($5,000,000), the Secretary shall allow a portion of the credits claimed by allocating the total allowable amount among all taxpayers claiming the credits in proportion to the size of the credit claimed by each taxpayer. In no case may the total amount of all tax credits allowed under this section for costs paid in a calendar year exceed five million dollars ($5,000,000).

If a credit claimed under this section is reduced as provided in this subsection, the Secretary shall notify the taxpayer of the amount of the reduction of the credit on or before December 31 of the year the taxpayer applied for the credit. The amount of the reduction of the credit may be carried forward and claimed for the next 10 taxable years if the taxpayer reapplies for a credit for the amount of the reduction, as provided in subsection (d). In such a reapplication, the costs for which a credit is claimed shall be considered as if they had been paid in the year preceding the reapplication. The Secretary's allocations based on applications filed pursuant to subsection (d) are final and shall not be adjusted to account for credits applied for but not claimed. (1979, c. 801, s. 34; 1993 (Reg. Sess., 1994), c. 674, ss. 1, 2, 4; 1995, c. 17, s. 2; 1998-98, s. 69.)

§ 105-130.26. Repealed by Session Laws 1999-342, s. 1, effective for taxable years beginning on or after January 1, 2000.

§ 105-130.27 Expired.

§ 105-130.27A. Repealed by Session Laws 1999-342, s. 1, effective for taxable years beginning on or after January 1, 2000.

§ 105-130.28: Repealed by Session Laws 2000-128, s. 3, effective for costs incurred during taxable years beginning on or after January 1, 2006.

§§ 105-130.29 through 105-130.33. Repealed by Session Laws 1999-342, s. 1.

§ 105-130.34. (Repealed effective for taxable years beginning on or after January 1, 2014) Credit for certain real property donations.

(a)   Any C Corporation that makes a qualified donation of an interest in real property located in North Carolina during the taxable year that is useful for (i) public beach access or use, (ii) public access to public waters or trails, (iii) fish and wildlife conservation, (iv) forestland or farmland conservation, (v) watershed protection, (vi) conservation of natural areas as that term is defined in G.S. 113A-164.3(3), (vii) conservation of natural or scenic river areas as those terms are used in G.S. 113A-34, (viii) conservation of predominantly natural parkland, or (ix) historic landscape conservation is allowed a credit against the tax imposed by this Part equal to twenty-five percent (25%) of the fair market value of the donated property interest. To be eligible for this credit, the interest in real property must be donated in perpetuity for one of the qualifying uses listed in this subsection and accepted in perpetuity for the qualifying use for which the property is donated. The person to whom the property is donated must be the State, a local government, or a body that is both organized to receive and administer lands for conservation purposes and qualified to receive charitable contributions pursuant to G.S. 105-130.9. Lands required to be dedicated pursuant to local governmental regulation or ordinance and dedications made to increase building density levels permitted under a regulation or ordinance are not eligible for this credit.

The credit allowed under this section for one or more qualified donations made in a taxable year may not exceed five hundred thousand dollars ($500,000). To support the credit allowed by this section, the taxpayer must file with the income tax return for the taxable year in which the credit is claimed the following:

(1) A certification by the Department of Environment and Natural Resources that the property donated is suitable for one or more of the valid public benefits set forth in this subsection.

(2) A self-contained appraisal report or summary appraisal report as defined in Standards Rule 2-2 in the latest edition of the Uniform Standards of Professional Appraisal Practice as promulgated by the Appraisal Foundation for the property. For fee simple absolute donations of real property, a taxpayer may submit documentation of the county's appraised value of the donated property, as adjusted by the sales assessment ratio, in lieu of an appraisal report.

(b) The credit allowed by this section may not exceed the amount of tax imposed by this Part for the taxable year reduced by the sum of all credits allowed, except payments of tax made by or on behalf of the taxpayer.

(c) Any unused portion of this credit may be carried forward for the next succeeding five years.

(d) That portion of a qualifying donation that is the basis for a credit allowed under this section is not eligible for deduction as a charitable contribution under G.S. 105-130.9. (1983, c. 793, s. 1; 1989, c. 716, s. 1; c. 727, s. 218 (41); 1997-226, s. 1; 1997-443, s. 11A.119(a); 1998-98, s. 69; 1998-212, s. 29A.13(c); 2002-72, s. 15(a); 2007-309, s. 1; 2009-445, s. 9(c); 2010-167, s. 5(a); 2013-316, s. 2.1(b).)

§ 105-130.35: Recodified as § 105-269.5 by Session Laws 1991, c. 45, s. 20.

§ 105-130.36. (Repealed effective for taxable years beginning on or after January 1, 2014) Credit for conservation tillage equipment.

(a) Any corporation that purchases conservation tillage equipment for use in a farming business, including tree farming, shall be allowed a credit against the tax imposed by this Part equal to twenty-five percent (25%) of the cost of the equipment paid during the taxable year. This credit may not exceed two thousand five hundred dollars ($2,500) for any taxable year for any taxpayer. The credit may be claimed only by the first purchaser of the equipment and may not be claimed by a corporation that purchases the equipment for resale or for use outside this State. This credit may not exceed the amount of tax imposed by this Part for the taxable year reduced by the sum of all credits allowable, except tax payments made by or on behalf of the taxpayer. If the credit allowed by this section exceeds the tax imposed under this Part, the excess may be carried forward for the succeeding five years. The basis in any equipment for which a credit is allowed under this section shall be reduced by the amount of credit allowable.

(b) As used in this section, "conservation tillage equipment" means:

(1) A planter such as a planter commonly known as a "no-till" planter designed to minimize disturbance of the soil in planting crops or trees, including equipment that may be attached to equipment already owned by the taxpayer; or,

(2) Equipment designed to minimize disturbance of the soil in reforestation site preparation, including equipment that may be attached to equipment already owned by the taxpayer; provided, however, this shall include only those items of equipment generally known as a "KG-Blade", a "drum-chopper", or a "V-Blade". (1983 (Reg. Sess., 1984), c. 969, s. 1; 1998-98, s. 88; 2013-316, s. 2.1(b).)

§ 105-130.37. (Repealed effective for taxable years beginning on or after January 1, 2014) Credit for gleaned crop.

(a) Any corporation that grows a crop and permits the gleaning of the crop during the taxable year is allowed a credit against the tax imposed by this Part equal to ten percent (10%) of the market price of the quantity of the gleaned crop. This credit may not exceed the amount of tax imposed by this Part for the taxable year reduced by the sum of all credits allowable, except tax payments made by or on behalf of the taxpayer. No deduction is allowed under G.S. 105-130.5(b)(5) for the items for which a credit is claimed under this section. Any unused portion of the credit may be carried forward for the succeeding five years.

(b) The following definitions apply to this section:

(1) "Gleaning" means the harvesting of a crop that has been donated by the grower to the nonprofit organization which will distribute the crop to individuals or other nonprofit organizations it considers appropriate recipients of the food;

(2) "Market price" means the season average price of the crop as determined by the North Carolina Crop and Livestock Reporting Service in the

Department of Agriculture and Consumer Services, or the average price of the crop in the nearest local market for the month in which the crop is gleaned if the Crop and Livestock Reporting Service does not determine the season average price for that crop; and

(3) "Nonprofit organization" means an organization to which charitable contributions are deductible from gross income under the Code. (1983 (Reg. Sess., 1984), c. 1018, s. 1; 1993 (Reg. Sess., 1994), c. 745, s. 6; 1997-261, s. 12; 1998-98, s. 89; 2013-316, s. 2.1(b).)

§ 105-130.38: Repealed by Session Laws 1996, Second Extra Session, c. 14, s. 1.

§ 105-130.39. (Repealed effective for taxable years beginning on or after January 1, 2014) Credit for certain telephone subscriber line charges.

(a) A corporation that provides local telephone service to low-income residential consumers at reduced rates pursuant to an order of the North Carolina Utilities Commission is allowed a credit against the tax imposed by this Part equal to the difference between the following:

(1) The amount of receipts the corporation would have received during the taxable year from those low-income customers had the customers been charged the regular rates for local telephone service and fees.

(2) The amount billed those low-income customers for local telephone service during the taxable year.

(b) This credit is allowed only for a reduction in local telephone service rates and fees and is not allowed for any reduction in interstate subscriber line charges. This credit may not exceed the amount of tax imposed by this Part for the taxable year reduced by the sum of all credits allowable, except tax payments made by or on behalf of the corporation. (1985, c. 694, s. 2; 1998-98, s. 90; 2013-316, s. 2.1(b).)

§ 105-130.40: Recodified as § 105-129.8 by Session Laws 1996, 2nd Extra Session, c. 13, s. 3.2.

§ 105-130.41. (Repealed effective for taxable years beginning on or after January 1, 2014) Credit for North Carolina State Ports Authority wharfage, handling, and throughput charges.

(a) Credit. - A taxpayer whose waterborne cargo is loaded onto or unloaded from an ocean carrier calling at the State-owned port terminal at Wilmington or Morehead City, without consideration of the terms under which the cargo is moved, is allowed a credit against the tax imposed by this Part. The amount of credit allowed is equal to the excess of the wharfage, handling (in or out), and throughput charges assessed on the cargo for the current taxable year over an amount equal to the average of the charges for the current taxable year and the two preceding taxable years. The credit applies to forest products, break-bulk cargo and container cargo, including less-than-container-load cargo, that is loaded onto or unloaded from an ocean carrier calling at either the Wilmington or Morehead City port terminal and to bulk cargo that is loaded onto or unloaded from an ocean carrier calling at the Morehead City port terminal. To obtain the credit, taxpayers must provide to the Secretary a statement from the State Ports Authority certifying the amount of charges for which a credit is claimed and any other information required by the Secretary.

(b) Limitations. - This credit may not exceed fifty percent (50%) of the amount of tax imposed by this Part for the taxable year reduced by the sum of all credits allowable, except tax payments made by or on behalf of the corporation. Any unused portion of the credit may be carried forward for the succeeding five years. The maximum cumulative credit that may be claimed by a corporation under this section is two million dollars ($2,000,000).

(c) Definitions. - For purposes of this section, the terms "handling" (in or out) and "wharfage" have the meanings provided in the State Ports Tariff Publications, "Wilmington Tariff, Terminal Tariff #6," and "Morehead City Tariff, Terminal Tariff #1." For purposes of this section, the term "throughput" has the same meaning as "wharfage" but applies only to bulk products, both dry and liquid.

(c1) Report. - The Department must include in the economic incentives report required by G.S. 105-256 the following information itemized by taxpayer:

(1) The number of taxpayers taking a credit allowed in this section.

(2) The total amount of charges assessed for the taxable year.

(2a) The amount of the charges attributable to imports.

(2b) The amount of the charges attributable to exports.

(3) The total cost to the General Fund of the credits taken.

(d) Sunset. - This section is repealed effective for taxable years beginning on or after January 1, 2014. (1991 (Reg. Sess., 1992), c. 977, s. 1; 1993 (Reg. Sess., 1994), c. 681, s. 1; 1995, c. 17, s. 17; c. 495, ss. 1, 3, 4; 1996, 2nd Ex. Sess., c. 18, s. 15.3(a); 1997-443, s. 29.1(a)-(c); 1998-98, s. 69; 2001-517, ss. 1, 2; 2002-99, s. 6(c); 2003-414, s. 7; 2005-429, s. 2.9; 2007-527, s. 26(a); 2008-107, s. 28.5(a), (b); 2010-166, s. 1.11.)

§ 105-130.42: Recodified as §§ 105-129.35 through 105-129.37 by Session Laws 1999-389, ss. 2-4, effective for taxable years beginning on or after January 1, 1999.

§ 105-130.43. (Repealed effective for taxable years beginning on or after January 1, 2014) Credit for savings and loan supervisory fees.

Every savings and loan association is allowed a credit against the tax imposed by this Part for a taxable year equal to the amount of supervisory fees, paid by the association during the taxable year, that were assessed by the Commissioner of Banks of the Department of Commerce for the State fiscal year beginning during that taxable year. This credit may not exceed the amount of tax imposed by this Part for the taxable year, reduced by the sum of all credits allowed against the tax, except tax payments made by or on behalf of the taxpayer. A taxpayer that claims the credit allowed under this section may not deduct the supervisory fees in determining taxable income. (1985, c. 750, s. 1; 1989, c. 76, s. 24; c. 751, s. 7(8); 1991 (Reg. Sess., 1992), c. 959, s. 22; 1998-98, s. 1(d), (e); 2001-193, s. 16; 2013-316, s. 2.1(b).)

§ 105-130.44. (Repealed effective for taxable years beginning on or after January 1, 2014) Credit for construction of poultry composting facility.

A taxpayer who constructs in this State a poultry composting facility, as defined in G.S. 106-549.51 for the composting of whole, unprocessed poultry carcasses from commercial operations in which poultry is raised or produced, is allowed as a credit against the tax imposed by this Part an amount equal to twenty-five percent (25%) of the installation, materials, and equipment costs of construction paid during the taxable year. This credit may not exceed one thousand dollars ($1,000) for any single installation. The credit allowed by this section may not exceed the amount of tax imposed by this Part the taxable year reduced by the sum of all credits allowable, except payments of tax by or on behalf of the taxpayer. The credit allowed by this section does not apply to costs paid with funds provided the taxpayer by a State or federal agency. (1998-134, s. 1; 1998-98, s. 69; 2013-316, s. 2.1(b).)

§ 105-130.45. (Repealed effective January 1, 2018) Credit for manufacturing cigarettes for exportation.

(a) Definitions. - The following definitions apply in this section:

(1) Base year exportation volume. - The number of cigarettes manufactured and exported by a corporation during the calendar year 2003.

(2) Exportation. - The shipment of cigarettes manufactured in the United States to any of the following sufficient to relieve the cigarettes in the shipment of the federal excise tax on cigarettes:

a. A foreign country.

b. A possession of the United States.

c. A commonwealth of the United States that is not a state.

(3) Successor in business. - A corporation that through amalgamation, merger, acquisition, consolidation, or other legal succession becomes invested with the rights and assumes the burdens of the predecessor corporation and continues the cigarette exportation business.

(b) Credit. - A corporation engaged in the business of manufacturing cigarettes for exportation to a foreign country and that waterborne exports cigarettes and other tobacco products through the North Carolina State Ports during the taxable year is allowed a credit against the taxes levied by this Part. The amount of credit allowed under this section is determined by comparing the exportation volume of the corporation in the year for which the credit is claimed with the corporation's base year exportation volume, rounded to the nearest whole percentage. In the case of a successor in business, the amount of credit allowed under this section is determined by comparing the exportation volume of the corporation in the year for which the credit is claimed with all of the corporation's predecessor corporations' combined base year exportation volume, rounded to the nearest whole percentage. The amount of credit allowed may not exceed six million dollars ($6,000,000) and is computed as follows:

Current Year's Exportation Volume Compared to its Base Year's Exportation Volume	Amount of Credit per Thousand Cigarettes Exported
120% or more	40¢
119% - 100%	35¢
99% - 80%	30¢
79% - 60%	25¢
59% - 50%	20¢
Less than 50%	None

(c) Cap. - The credit allowed under this section may not exceed the lesser of six million dollars ($6,000,000) or fifty percent (50%) of the amount of tax imposed by this Part for the taxable year reduced by the sum of all other credits allowable, except tax payments made by or on behalf of the taxpayer. This limitation applies to the cumulative amount of the credit allowed in any tax year, including carryforwards claimed by the taxpayer under this section for previous tax years. Any unused portion of a credit allowed in this section may be carried forward for the next succeeding ten years.

(d) Documentation of Credit. - A corporation that claims the credit under this section must include the following with its tax return:

(1) A statement of the base year exportation volume.

(2) A statement of the exportation volume on which the credit is based.

(3) A list of the corporation's export volumes shown on its monthly reports to the Alcohol and Tobacco Tax and Trade Bureau of the United States Treasury for the months in the tax year for which the credit is claimed.

(e) No Double Credit. - A taxpayer may not claim this credit and the credit allowed under G.S. 105-130.46 for the same activity.

(f) Report. - The Department must include in the economic incentives report required by G.S. 105-256 the following information itemized by taxpayer:

(1) The number of taxpayers taking a credit allowed in this section.

(2) The total amount of exports with respect to which credits were taken.

(3) The total cost to the General Fund of the credits taken. (1999-333, s. 4; 2003-435, 2nd Ex. Sess., ss. 5.1, 5.2, 5.3; 2005-429, s. 2.10; 2010-166, s. 1.12.)

§ 105-130.46. (See notes for expiration date) Credit for manufacturing cigarettes for exportation while increasing employment and utilizing State Ports.

(a) Purpose. - The credit authorized by this section is intended to enhance the economy of this State by encouraging qualifying cigarette manufacturers to increase employment in this State with the purpose of expanding this State's economy, the use of the North Carolina State Ports, and the use of other State goods and services, including tobacco.

(b) Definitions. - The following definitions apply in this section:

(1) Employment level. - The total number of full-time jobs and part-time jobs converted into full-time equivalences. A job is included in the employment level for a year only if that job is located within the State for more than six months of the year. A job is located in this State if more than fifty percent (50%) of the employee's duties are performed in this State.

(2) Exportation. - The shipment of cigarettes manufactured in the United States to a foreign country sufficient to relieve the cigarettes in the shipment of the federal excise tax on cigarettes.

(3) Full-time job. - A position that requires at least 1,600 hours of work per year and is intended to be held by one employee during the entire year.

(4) Successor in business. - A corporation that through amalgamation, merger, acquisition, consolidation, or other legal succession becomes invested with the rights and assumes the burdens of the predecessor corporation and continues the cigarette exportation business.

(c) Employment Level. - In order to be eligible for a full credit allowed under this section, the corporation must maintain an employment level in this State for the taxable year that exceeds the corporation's employment level in this State at the end of the 2004 calendar year by at least 800 full-time jobs. In the case of a successor in business, the corporation must maintain an employment level in this State for the taxable year that exceeds all its predecessor corporations' combined employment levels in this State at the end of the 2004 calendar year by at least 800 full-time jobs.

(d) Credit. - A corporation that satisfies the employment level requirement under subsection (c) of this section, is engaged in the business of manufacturing cigarettes for exportation, and exports cigarettes and other tobacco products through the North Carolina State Ports during the taxable year is allowed a credit as provided in this section. The amount of credit allowed under this section is equal to forty cents (40¢) per one thousand cigarettes exported. The amount of credit earned during the taxable year may not exceed ten million dollars ($10,000,000).

(e) Reduction of Credit. - A corporation that has previously satisfied the qualification requirements of this section but that fails to satisfy the employment level requirement in a succeeding year may still claim a partial credit for the year in which the employment level requirement is not satisfied. The partial credit allowed is equal to the credit that would otherwise be allowed under subsection

(d) of this section multiplied by a fraction. The numerator of the fraction is the number of full-time jobs by which the corporation's employment level in this State for the taxable year exceeds the corporation's employment level in this State at the end of the 2004 calendar year. The denominator of the fraction is 800. In the case of a successor in business, the numerator of the fraction is the number of full-time jobs by which the corporation's employment level in this State for the taxable year exceeds all its predecessor corporations' combined employment levels in this State at the end of the 2004 calendar year.

(f) Allocation. - The credit allowed by this section may be taken against the income taxes levied under this Part or the franchise taxes levied under Article 3 of this Chapter. When the taxpayer claims a credit under this section, the taxpayer must elect the percentage of the credit to be applied against the taxes levied under this Part with any remaining percentage to be applied against the taxes levied under Article 3 of this Chapter. This election is binding for the year in which it is made and for any carryforwards. A taxpayer may elect a different allocation for each year in which the taxpayer qualifies for a credit.

(g) Ceiling. - The total amount of credit that may be taken in a taxable year under this section may not exceed the lesser of the amount of credit which may be earned for that year under subsection (d) of this section or fifty percent (50%) of the amount of tax against which the credit is taken for the taxable year reduced by the sum of all other credits allowable, except tax payments made by or on behalf of the taxpayer. This limitation applies to the cumulative amount of the credit allowed in any tax year, including carryforwards claimed by the taxpayer under this section or G.S. 105-130.45 for previous tax years.

(h) Carryforward. - Any unused portion of a credit allowed in this section may be carried forward for the next succeeding 10 years. All carryforwards of a credit must be taken against the tax against which the credit was originally claimed. A successor in business may take the carryforwards of a predecessor corporation as if they were carryforwards of a credit allowed to the successor in business.

(i) Documentation of Credit. - A corporation that claims the credit under this section must include the following with its tax return:

(1) A statement of the exportation volume on which the credit is based.

(2) A list of the corporation's export volumes shown on its monthly reports to the Alcohol and Tobacco Tax and Trade Bureau of the United States Treasury for the months in the tax year for which the credit is claimed.

(3) Any other information required by the Department of Revenue.

(j) No Double Credit. - A taxpayer may not claim this credit and the credit allowed under G.S. 105-130.45 for the same activity.

(k) Report. - The Department must include in the economic incentives report required by G.S. 105-256 the following information itemized by taxpayer:

(1) The number of taxpayers that took the credit allowed in this section.

(2) The amount of cigarettes and other tobacco products exported through the North Carolina State Ports with respect to which credits were taken.

(3) The percentage of domestic leaf content in cigarettes produced during the previous year, as reported by the taxpayer.

(4) The total cost to the General Fund of the credits taken. (2003-435, 2nd Ex. Sess., s. 6.1; 2004-170, s. 16(a); 2010-166, s. 1.13.)

§ 105-130.47. (Repealed for qualifying expenses occurring on or after January 1, 2015) Credit for qualifying expenses of a production company.

(a) Definitions. - The following definitions apply in this section:

(1) Highly compensated individual. - An individual who directly or indirectly receives compensation in excess of one million dollars ($1,000,000) for personal services with respect to a single production. An individual receives compensation indirectly when a production company pays a personal service company or an employee leasing company that pays the individual.

(2) Live sporting event. - A scheduled sporting competition, game, or race that is not originated by a production company, but originated solely by an amateur, collegiate, or professional organization, institution, or association for live or tape-delayed television or satellite broadcast. A live sporting event does not include commercial advertising, an episodic television series, a television

pilot, a music video, a motion picture, or a documentary production in which sporting events are presented through archived historical footage or similar footage taken at least 30 days before it is used.

(3) Production company. - Defined in G.S. 105-164.3.

(4) Qualifying expenses. - The sum of the following amounts spent in this State by a production company in connection with a production, less the amount in excess of one million dollars ($1,000,000) paid to a highly compensated individual:

a. Goods and services leased or purchased. For goods with a purchase price of twenty-five thousand dollars ($25,000) or more, the amount included in qualifying expenses is the purchase price less the fair market value of the good at the time the production is completed.

b. Compensation and wages on which withholding payments are remitted to the Department of Revenue under Article 4A of this Chapter.

c. The cost of production-related insurance coverage obtained on the production. Expenses for insurance coverage purchased from a related member are not qualifying expenses.

d. Employee fringe contributions, including health, pension, and welfare contributions.

e. Per diems, stipends, and living allowances paid for work being performed in this State.

(5) Related member. - Defined in G.S. 105-130.7A.

(b) Credit. - A taxpayer that is a production company and has qualifying expenses of at least two hundred fifty thousand dollars ($250,000) with respect to a production is allowed a credit against the taxes imposed by this Part equal to twenty-five percent (25%) of the production company's qualifying expenses. For the purposes of this section, in the case of an episodic television series, an entire season of episodes is one production. The credit is computed based on all of the taxpayer's qualifying expenses incurred with respect to the production, not just the qualifying expenses incurred during the taxable year.

(b1) Repealed by Session Laws 2009-529, s. 1, effective January 1, 2011.

(c) Pass-Through Entity. - Notwithstanding the provisions of G.S. 105-131.8 and G.S. 105-269.15, a pass-through entity that qualifies for a credit provided in this section does not distribute the credit among any of its owners. The pass-through entity is considered the taxpayer for purposes of claiming a credit allowed by this section. If a return filed by a pass-through entity indicates that the entity is paying tax on behalf of the owners of the entity, a credit allowed under this section does not affect the entity's payment of tax on behalf of its owners.

(d) Return. - A taxpayer may claim a credit allowed by this section on a return filed for the taxable year in which the production activities are completed. The return must state the name of the production, a description of the production, and a detailed accounting of the qualifying expenses with respect to which a credit is claimed. The qualifying expenses are subject to audit by the Secretary before the credit is allowed.

(e) Credit Refundable. - If a credit allowed by this section exceeds the amount of tax imposed by this Part for the taxable year reduced by the sum of all credits allowable, the Secretary must refund the excess to the taxpayer. The refundable excess is governed by the provisions governing a refund of an overpayment by the taxpayer of the tax imposed in this Part. In computing the amount of tax against which multiple credits are allowed, nonrefundable credits are subtracted before refundable credits.

(f) Limitations. - The amount of credit allowed under this section with respect to a production that is a feature film may not exceed twenty million dollars ($20,000,000). No credit is allowed under this section for any production that satisfies one of the following conditions:

(1) It is political advertising.

(2) It is a television production of a news program or live sporting event.

(3) It contains material that is obscene, as defined in G.S. 14-190.1.

(4) It is a radio production.

(g) Substantiation. - A taxpayer allowed a credit under this section must maintain and make available for inspection any information or records required by the Secretary of Revenue. The taxpayer has the burden of proving eligibility for a credit and the amount of the credit. The Secretary may consult with the

North Carolina Film Office of the Department of Commerce and the regional film commissions in order to determine the amount of qualifying expenses.

(h) Report. - The Department must include in the economic incentives report required by G.S. 105-256 the following information, itemized by taxpayer:

(1) The location of sites used in a production for which a credit was taken.

(2) The qualifying expenses for which a credit was taken, classified by whether the expenses were for goods, services, or compensation paid by the production company.

(3) The number of people employed in the State with respect to credits taken.

(4) The total cost to the General Fund of the credits taken.

(i) Repealed by Session Laws 2006-220, s. 2, effective for taxable years beginning on or after January 1, 2007.

(j) NC Film Office. - To claim a credit under this section, a taxpayer must notify the Division of Tourism, Film, and Sports Development in the Department of Commerce of the taxpayer's intent to claim the production tax credit. The notification must include the title of the production, the name of the production company, a financial contact for the production company, the proposed dates on which the production company plans to begin filming the production, and any other information required by the Division. For productions that have production credits, a taxpayer claiming a credit under this section must acknowledge in the production credits both the North Carolina Film Office and the regional film office responsible for the geographic area in which the filming of the production occurred.

(k) Sunset. - This section is repealed for qualifying expenses occurring on or after January 1, 2015. (2005-276, s. 39.1(a); 2005-345, ss. 47(a), 47(b); 2006-162, s. 4(a); 2006-220, s. 2; 2007-527, s. 24; 2008-107, s. 28.24(a); 2009-445, s. 8(a); 2009-529, s. 1; 2010-147, s. 2.1; 2010-166, s. 1.14; 2012-194, s. 79.10(a).)

§ 105-130.48. (Repealed for taxable years beginning on or after January 1, 2014) Credit for recycling oyster shells.

(a) Credit. - A taxpayer who donates oyster shells to the Division of Marine Fisheries of the Department of Environment and Natural Resources is eligible for a credit against the tax imposed by this Part. The amount of the credit is equal to one dollar ($1.00) per bushel of oyster shells donated.

(b) Limitation. - The credit allowed under this section may not exceed the amount of tax imposed by this Part for the taxable year reduced by the sum of all credits allowable, except tax payment made by or on behalf of the taxpayer.

(c) Carryforward. - Any unused portion of a credit allowed in this section may be carried forward for the succeeding five years. A successor in business may take the carryforwards of a predecessor corporation as if they were carryforwards of a credit allowed to the successor in business.

(d) No Double Benefit. - No deduction is allowed under G.S. 105-130.5(b)(5) or G.S. 105-130.9 for the donation of oyster shells for which a credit is claimed under this section.

(e) Documentation of Credit. - Upon request, to support the credit allowed by this section, the taxpayer must file with its income tax return, for the taxable year in which the credit is claimed, a certification by the Department of Environment and Natural Resources stating the number of bushels of oyster shells donated by the taxpayer.

(f) Sunset. - This section is repealed effective for taxable years beginning on or after January 1, 2014. (2006-66, s. 24.18(a); 2007-527, s. 9(a); 2010-147, s. 4.1; 2011-330, s. 36; 2012-36, s. 6(a).)

Part 1A. S Corporation Income Tax.

§ 105-131. Title; definitions; interpretation.

(a) This Part of the income tax Article shall be known and may be cited as the S Corporation Income Tax Act.

(b) For the purpose of this Part, unless otherwise required by the context:

(1) "Code" has the same meaning as in G.S. 105-228.90.

(2) "C Corporation" means a corporation that is not an S Corporation and is subject to the tax levied under Part 1 of this Article.

(3) "Department" means the Department of Revenue.

(4) "Income attributable to the State" means items of income, loss, deduction, or credit of the S Corporation apportioned and allocated to this State pursuant to G.S. 105-130.4.

(5) "Income not attributable to the State" means all items of income, loss, deduction, or credit of the S Corporation other than income attributable to the State.

(6) "Post-termination transition period" means that period defined in section 1377(b)(1) of the Code.

(7) "Pro rata share" means the share determined with respect to an S Corporation shareholder for a taxable period in the manner provided in section 1377(a) of the Code.

(8) "S Corporation" means a corporation for which a valid election under section 1362(a) of the Code is in effect.

(9) "Secretary" means the Secretary of Revenue.

(10) "Taxable period" means any taxable year or portion of a taxable year during which a corporation is an S Corporation.

(c) Except as otherwise expressly provided or clearly appearing from the context, any term used in this Part shall have the same meaning as when used in a comparable context in the Code, or in any statute relating to federal income taxes, in effect during the taxable period. Due consideration shall be given in the interpretation of this Part to applicable sections of the Code in effect and to federal rulings and regulations interpreting those sections, except where the Code, ruling, or regulation conflicts with the provisions of this Part. (1987 (Reg. Sess., 1988), c. 1089, s. 1; 1989, c. 728, ss. 1.33, 1.35; 1989 (Reg. Sess., 1990), c. 981, s. 4; 1991, c. 689, s. 251; 1991 (Reg. Sess., 1992), c. 922, s. 5; 1993, c. 12, s. 6; 1998-98, ss. 43, 68-70.)

§ 105-131.1. Taxation of an S Corporation and its shareholders.

(a) An S Corporation shall not be subject to the tax levied under G.S. 105-130.3.

(b) Each shareholder's pro rata share of an S Corporation's income attributable to the State and each resident shareholder's pro rata share of income not attributable to the State, shall be taken into account by the shareholder in the manner and subject to the adjustments provided in Parts 2 and 3 of this Article and section 1366 of the Code and shall be subject to the tax levied under Parts 2 and 3 of this Article. (1987 (Reg. Sess., 1988), c. 1089, s. 1; 1989, c. 728, ss. 1.33, 1.35; 1998-98, ss. 5, 68.)

§ 105-131.2. Adjustment and characterization of income.

(a) (Effective for taxable years beginning before January 1, 2014) Adjustment. - Each shareholder's pro rata share of an S Corporation's income is subject to the adjustments provided in G.S. 105-134.6.

(a) (Effective for taxable years beginning on or after January 1, 2014) Adjustment. - Each shareholder's pro rata share of an S Corporation's income is subject to the adjustments provided in G.S. 105-153.5 and G.S. 105-153.6.

(b) Repealed by Session Laws 1989, c. 728, s. 1.35.

(c) Characterization of Income. - S Corporation items of income, loss, deduction, and credit taken into account by a shareholder pursuant to G.S. 105-131.1(b) are characterized as though received or incurred by the S Corporation and not its shareholder. (1987 (Reg. Sess., 1988), c. 1089, s. 1; 1989, c. 728, ss. 1.33, 1.35; 1993, c. 485, s. 8; 2006-17, s. 1; 2013-316, s. 1.3(a).)

§ 105-131.3. Basis and adjustments.

(a) The initial basis of a resident shareholder in the stock of an S Corporation and in any indebtedness of the corporation owed to that shareholder shall be determined, as of the later of the date the stock is acquired, the effective date of the S Corporation election, or the date the shareholder became a resident of this State, as provided under the Code.

(b) The basis of a resident shareholder in the stock and indebtedness of an S Corporation shall be adjusted in the manner and to the extent required by section 1011 of the Code except that:

(1) Any adjustments made (other than for income exempt from federal or State income taxes) pursuant to G.S. 105-131.2 shall be taken into account; and

(2) Any adjustments made pursuant to section 1367 of the Code for a taxable period during which this State did not measure S Corporation shareholder income by reference to the corporation's income shall be disregarded.

(c) The initial basis of a nonresident shareholder in the stock of an S Corporation and in any indebtedness of the corporation to that shareholder shall be zero.

(d) The basis of a nonresident shareholder in the stock and indebtedness of an S Corporation shall be adjusted as provided in section 1367 of the Code, except that adjustments to basis shall be limited to the income taken into account by the shareholder pursuant to G.S. 105-131.1(b).

(e) The basis of a shareholder in the stock of an S Corporation shall be reduced by the amount allowed as a loss or deduction pursuant to G.S. 105-131.4(c).

(f) The basis of a resident shareholder in the stock of an S Corporation shall be reduced by the amount of any cash distribution that is not taxable to the shareholder as a result of the application of G.S. 105-131.6(b).

(g) For purposes of this section, a shareholder shall be considered to have acquired stock or indebtedness received by gift at the time the donor acquired the stock or indebtedness, if the donor was a resident of this State at the time of the gift. (1987 (Reg. Sess., 1988), c. 1089, s. 1; 1989, c. 728, ss. 1.33, 1.35.)

§ 105-131.4. Carryforwards; carrybacks; loss limitation.

(a) Carryforwards and carrybacks to and from an S Corporation shall be restricted in the manner provided in section 1371(b) of the Code.

(b) The aggregate amount of losses or deductions of an S Corporation taken into account by a shareholder pursuant to G.S. 105-131.1(b) may not exceed the combined adjusted bases, determined in accordance with G.S. 105-131.3, of the shareholder in the stock and indebtedness of the S Corporation.

(c) Any loss or deduction that is disallowed for a taxable period pursuant to subsection (b) of this section shall be treated as incurred by the corporation in the succeeding taxable period with respect to that shareholder.

(d) (1) Any loss or deduction that is disallowed pursuant to subsection (b) of this section for the corporation's last taxable period as an S Corporation shall be treated as incurred by the shareholder on the last day of any post-termination transition period.

(2) The aggregate amount of losses and deductions taken into account by a shareholder pursuant to subdivision (1) of this subsection may not exceed the adjusted basis of the shareholder in the stock of the corporation (determined in accordance with G.S. 105-131.3 at the close of the last day of any post-termination transition period and without regard to this subsection).

(e) Expired. (1987 (Reg. Sess., 1988), c. 1089, s. 1; 1989, c. 728, ss. 1.33, 1.35; 1989 (Reg. Sess., 1990), c. 984, s. 1; 1991, c. 752.)

§ 105-131.5. Part-year resident shareholder.

If a shareholder of an S Corporation is both a resident and nonresident of this State during any taxable period, the shareholder's pro rata share of the S Corporation's income attributable to the State and income not attributable to the State for the taxable period shall be further prorated between the shareholder's periods of residence and nonresidence, in accordance with the number of days in each period, as provided in G.S. 105-134.5. (1987 (Reg. Sess., 1988), c. 1089, s. 1; 1989, c. 728, ss. 1.33, 1.35.)

§ 105-131.6. Distributions.

(a) Subject to the provisions of subsection (c) of this section, a distribution made by an S Corporation with respect to its stock to a resident shareholder is taxable to the shareholder as provided in Parts 2 and 3 of this Article to the extent that the distribution is characterized as a dividend or as gain from the sale or exchange of property pursuant to section 1368 of the Code.

(b) Subject to the provisions of subsection (c) of this section, any distribution of money made by a corporation with respect to its stock to a resident shareholder during a post-termination transition period is not taxable to the shareholder as provided in Parts 2 and 3 of this Article to the extent the distribution is applied against and reduces the adjusted basis of the stock of the shareholder in accordance with section 1371(e) of the Code.

(c) In applying sections 1368 and 1371(e) of the Code to any distribution referred to in this section:

(1) The term "adjusted basis of the stock" means the adjusted basis of the shareholder's stock as determined under G.S. 105-131.3.

(2) The accumulated adjustments account maintained for each resident shareholder must be equal to, and adjusted in the same manner as, the corporation's accumulated adjustments account defined in section 1368(e)(1)(A) of the Code, except that:

a. The accumulated adjustments account shall be modified in the manner provided in G.S. 105-131.3(b)(1).

b. The amount of the corporation's federal accumulated adjustments account that existed on the day this State began to measure the S Corporation shareholders' income by reference to the income of the S Corporation is ignored and is treated for purposes of this Article as additional accumulated earnings and profits of the corporation. (1987 (Reg. Sess., 1988), c. 1089, s. 1; 1989, c. 728, ss. 1.33, 1.35; 1998-98, s. 6.)

§ 105-131.7. Returns; shareholder agreements; mandatory withholding.

(a) An S Corporation incorporated or doing business in the State shall file with the Department an annual return, on a form prescribed by the Secretary, on or before the due date prescribed for the filing of C Corporation returns in G.S.

105-130.17. The return shall show the name, address, and social security or federal identification number of each shareholder, income attributable to the State and the income not attributable to the State with respect to each shareholder as defined in G.S. 105-131(4) and (5), and such other information as the Secretary may require.

(b) The Department shall permit S Corporations to file composite returns and to make composite payments of tax on behalf of some or all nonresident shareholders. The Department may permit S Corporations to file composite returns and make composite payments of tax on behalf of some or all resident shareholders.

(c) (Effective for taxable years beginning before January 1, 2014) An S Corporation shall file with the Department, on a form prescribed by the Secretary, the agreement of each nonresident shareholder of the corporation (i) to file a return and make timely payment of all taxes imposed by this State on the shareholder with respect to the income of the S Corporation, and (ii) to be subject to personal jurisdiction in this State for purposes of the collection of any unpaid income tax, together with related interest and penalties, owed by the nonresident shareholder. If the corporation fails to timely file an agreement required by this subsection on behalf of any of its nonresident shareholders, then the corporation shall at the time specified in subsection (d) of this section pay to the Department on behalf of each nonresident shareholder with respect to whom an agreement has not been timely filed an estimated amount of the tax due the State. The estimated amount of tax due the State shall be computed at the rates levied in G.S. 105-134.2(a)(3) on the shareholder's pro rata share of the S Corporation's income attributable to the State reflected on the corporation's return for the taxable period. An S Corporation may recover a payment made pursuant to the preceding sentence from the shareholder on whose behalf the payment was made.

(c) (Effective for taxable years beginning on or after January 1, 2014) An S Corporation shall file with the Department, on a form prescribed by the Secretary, the agreement of each nonresident shareholder of the corporation (i) to file a return and make timely payment of all taxes imposed by this State on the shareholder with respect to the income of the S Corporation, and (ii) to be subject to personal jurisdiction in this State for purposes of the collection of any unpaid income tax, together with related interest and penalties, owed by the nonresident shareholder. If the corporation fails to timely file an agreement required by this subsection on behalf of any of its nonresident shareholders, then the corporation shall at the time specified in subsection (d) of this section pay to the Department on behalf of each nonresident shareholder with respect to whom an agreement has not been timely filed an estimated amount of the tax due the State. The estimated amount of tax due the State shall be computed at the rate levied in G.S. 105-153.7 on the shareholder's pro rata share of the S Corporation's income attributable to the State reflected on the corporation's return for the taxable period. An S Corporation may recover a payment made pursuant to the preceding sentence from the shareholder on whose behalf the payment was made.

(d)   The agreements required to be filed pursuant to subsection (c) of this section shall be filed at the following times:

(1)   At the time the annual return is required to be filed for the first taxable period for which the S Corporation becomes subject to the provisions of this Part.

(2)   At the time the annual return is required to be filed for any taxable period in which the corporation has a nonresident shareholder on whose behalf such an agreement has not been previously filed.

(e)   Amounts paid to the Department on account of the corporation's shareholders under subsections (b) and (c) constitute payments on their behalf of the income tax imposed on them under Parts 2 and 3 of this Article for the taxable period. (1987 (Reg. Sess., 1988), c. 1089, s. 1; 1989, c. 728, ss. 1.33, 1.35; 1991, c. 689, s. 301; 1998-98, s. 7; 1999-337, s. 24; 2013-316, s. 1.3(b).)

§ 105-131.8. Tax credits.

(a)   For purposes of G.S. 105-151 and G.S. 105-160.4, each resident shareholder is considered to have paid a tax imposed on the shareholder in an amount equal to the shareholder's pro rata share of any net income tax paid by the S Corporation to a state that does not measure the income of S Corporation shareholders by the income of the S Corporation. For purposes of the preceding sentence, the term "net income tax" means any tax imposed on or measured by a corporation's net income.

(b)   Except as otherwise provided in G.S. 105-160.3, each shareholder of an S Corporation is allowed as a credit against the tax imposed by Parts 2 and 3 of this Article an amount equal to the shareholder's pro rata share of the tax credits for which the S Corporation is eligible. (1987 (Reg. Sess., 1988), c. 1089, s. 1; 1989, c. 728, ss. 1.33, 1.35; 1991, c. 45, s. 7; 1998-98, s. 8.)

§ 105-132: Recodified as § 105-135 by Session Laws 1967, c. 1110, s. 3.

Part 2. Individual Income Tax.

§ 105-133. (Recodified for taxable years beginning on or after January 1, 2014 - see editor's note) Short title.

This Part of the income tax Article shall be known as the Individual Income Tax Act. (1967, c. 1110, s. 3; 1989, c. 728, s. 1.1; 1998-98, ss. 44, 68.)

§ 105-134. (Recodified for taxable years beginning on or after January 1, 2014 - see editor's note) Purpose.

The general purpose of this Part is to impose a tax for the use of the State government upon the taxable income collectible annually:

(1)   Of every resident of this State.

(2)   Of every nonresident individual deriving income from North Carolina sources attributable to the ownership of any interest in real or tangible personal property in this State, deriving income from a business, trade, profession, or occupation carried on in this State, or deriving income from gambling activities in this State. (1939, c. 158, s. 301; 1967, c. 1110, s. 3; 1989, c. 728, s. 1.2; 1998-98, s. 69; 2005-276, s. 31.1(dd), (jj); 2005-344, s. 10.3; 2006-259, s. 8(j); 2006-264, s. 91(a).)

§ 105-134.1. (Effective for taxable years beginning before January 1, 2012) Definitions.

The following definitions apply in this Part:

(1)   Code. - Defined in G.S. 105-228.90.

(2) Department. - The Department of Revenue.

(3) Educational institution. - An educational institution that normally maintains a regular faculty and curriculum and normally has a regularly organized body of students in attendance at the place where its educational activities are carried on.

(4) Fiscal year. - Defined in section 441(e) of the Code.

(5) Gross income. - Defined in section 61 of the Code.

(6) Head of household. - Defined in section 2(b) of the Code.

(7) Individual. - A human being.

(7a) Limited liability company. - Either a domestic limited liability company organized under Chapter 57C of the General Statutes or a foreign limited liability company authorized by that Chapter to transact business in this State that is classified for federal income tax purposes as a partnership. As applied to a limited liability company that is a partnership under this Part, the term "partner" means a member of the limited liability company.

(7b) Repealed by Session Laws 1998-98, s. 9, effective August 14, 1998.

(8) Married individual. - An individual who is married and is considered married as provided in section 7703 of the Code.

(9) Nonresident individual. - An individual who is not a resident of this State.

(10) North Carolina taxable income. - Defined in G.S. 105-134.5.

(10a) Partnership. - A domestic partnership, a foreign partnership, or a limited liability company.

(11) Person. - Defined in G.S. 105-228.90.

(12) Resident. - An individual who is domiciled in this State at any time during the taxable year or who resides in this State during the taxable year for other than a temporary or transitory purpose. In the absence of convincing proof to the contrary, an individual who is present within the State for more than 183 days during the taxable year is presumed to be a resident, but the absence of

an individual from the state for more than 183 days raises no presumption that the individual is not a resident. A resident who removes from the State during a taxable year is considered a resident until he has both established a definite domicile elsewhere and abandoned any domicile in this State. The fact of marriage does not raise any presumption as to domicile or residence.

(13) Retirement benefits. - Amounts paid to a former employee or the beneficiary of a former employee under a written retirement plan established by the employer to provide payments to an employee or the beneficiary of an employee after the end of the employee's employment with the employer where the right to receive the payments is based upon the employment relationship. With respect to a self-employed individual or the beneficiary of a self-employed individual, the term means amounts paid to the individual or beneficiary of the individual under a written retirement plan established by the individual to provide payments to the individual or the beneficiary of the individual after the end of the self-employment. In addition, the term includes amounts received from an individual retirement account described in section 408 of the Code or from an individual retirement annuity described in section 408 of the Code. For the purpose of this subdivision, the term "employee" includes a volunteer worker.

(14) S Corporation. - Defined in G.S. 105-131(b).

(15) Secretary. - The Secretary of Revenue.

(16) Taxable income. - Defined in section 63 of the Code.

(17) Taxable year. - Defined in section 441(b) of the Code.

(18) Taxpayer. - An individual subject to the tax imposed by this Part.

(19) This State. - The State of North Carolina. (1989, c. 728, s. 1.4; c. 792, s. 1.2; 1989 (Reg. Sess., 1990), c. 814, s. 15; c. 981, s. 5; 1991, c. 689, s. 252; 1991 (Reg. Sess., 1992), c. 922, s. 6; 1993, c. 12, s. 7; c. 354, s. 13; 1996, 2nd Ex. Sess., c. 13, s. 8.2; 1998-98, ss. 9, 69.)

§ 105-134.1. (Effective for taxable years beginning on or after January 1, 2012 and recodified effective for taxable years beginning on or after January 1, 2014 - see editor's note) Definitions.

The following definitions apply in this Part:

(1) Adjusted gross income. - Defined in section 62 of the Code.

(1a) Code. - Defined in G.S. 105-228.90.

(2) Department. - The Department of Revenue.

(3) Educational institution. - An educational institution that normally maintains a regular faculty and curriculum and normally has a regularly organized body of students in attendance at the place where its educational activities are carried on.

(4) Fiscal year. - Defined in section 441(e) of the Code.

(5) Gross income. - Defined in section 61 of the Code.

(6) Head of household. - Defined in section 2(b) of the Code.

(7) Individual. - A human being.

(7a) Limited liability company. - Either a domestic limited liability company organized under Chapter 57C of the General Statutes or a foreign limited liability company authorized by that Chapter to transact business in this State that is classified for federal income tax purposes as a partnership. As applied to a limited liability company that is a partnership under this Part, the term "partner" means a member of the limited liability company.

(7b) Repealed by Session Laws 1998-98, s. 9, effective August 14, 1998.

(8) Married individual. - An individual who is married and is considered married as provided in section 7703 of the Code.

(9) Nonresident individual. - An individual who is not a resident of this State.

(10) North Carolina taxable income. - Defined in G.S. 105-134.5.

(10a) Partnership. - A domestic partnership, a foreign partnership, or a limited liability company.

(11) Person. - Defined in G.S. 105-228.90.

(12) Resident. - An individual who is domiciled in this State at any time during the taxable year or who resides in this State during the taxable year for other than a temporary or transitory purpose. In the absence of convincing proof to the contrary, an individual who is present within the State for more than 183 days during the taxable year is presumed to be a resident, but the absence of an individual from the state for more than 183 days raises no presumption that the individual is not a resident. A resident who removes from the State during a taxable year is considered a resident until he has both established a definite domicile elsewhere and abandoned any domicile in this State. The fact of marriage does not raise any presumption as to domicile or residence.

(13) Retirement benefits. - Amounts paid to a former employee or the beneficiary of a former employee under a written retirement plan established by the employer to provide payments to an employee or the beneficiary of an employee after the end of the employee's employment with the employer where the right to receive the payments is based upon the employment relationship. With respect to a self-employed individual or the beneficiary of a self-employed individual, the term means amounts paid to the individual or beneficiary of the individual under a written retirement plan established by the individual to provide payments to the individual or the beneficiary of the individual after the end of the self-employment. In addition, the term includes amounts received from an individual retirement account described in section 408 of the Code or from an individual retirement annuity described in section 408 of the Code. For the purpose of this subdivision, the term "employee" includes a volunteer worker.

(14) S Corporation. - Defined in G.S. 105-131(b).

(15) Secretary. - The Secretary of Revenue.

(16) Repealed by Session Laws 2011-145, s. 31A.1(a), effective for taxable years beginning on or after January 1, 2012.

(17) Taxable year. - Defined in section 441(b) of the Code.

(18) Taxpayer. - An individual subject to the tax imposed by this Part.

(19) This State. - The State of North Carolina. (1989, c. 728, s. 1.4; c. 792, s. 1.2; 1989 (Reg. Sess., 1990), c. 814, s. 15; c. 981, s. 5; 1991, c. 689, s. 252; 1991 (Reg. Sess., 1992), c. 922, s. 6; 1993, c. 12, s. 7; c. 354, s. 13; 1996, 2nd Ex. Sess., c. 13, s. 8.2; 1998-98, ss. 9, 69; 2011-145, s. 31A.1(a); 2011-330, s. 12(a).)

§ 105-134.2. (Repealed effective for taxable years beginning on or after January 1, 2014 - see note) Individual income tax imposed.

(a) A tax is imposed upon the North Carolina taxable income of every individual. The tax shall be levied, collected, and paid annually and shall be computed at the following percentages of the taxpayer's North Carolina taxable income.

(1) For married individuals who file a joint return under G.S. 105-152 and for surviving spouses, as defined in section 2(a) of the Code:

Rate	Over	Up To
6%	-0-	$21,250
7%	$21,250	$100,000
7.75%	$100,000	NA

(2) For heads of households, as defined in section 2(b) of the Code:

Rate	Over	Up To
6%	-0-	$17,000
7%	$17,000	$80,000
7.75%	$80,000	NA

(3) For unmarried individuals other than surviving spouses and heads of households:

Rate	Over	Up To
6%	-0-	$12,750
7%	$12,750	$60,000
7.75%	$60,000	NA

(4) For married individuals who do not file a joint return under G.S. 105-152:

Rate	Over	Up To
6%	-0-	$10,625
7%	$10,625	$50,000
7.75%	$50,000	NA

(b) In lieu of the tax imposed by subsection (a) of this section, there is imposed for each taxable year upon the North Carolina taxable income of every individual a tax determined under tables, applicable to the taxable year, which may be prescribed by the Secretary. The amounts of the tax determined under the tables shall be computed on the basis of the rates prescribed by subsection (a) of this section. This subsection does not apply to an individual filing a return under section 443(a)(1) of the Code for a period of less than 12 months on account of a change in the individual's annual accounting period, or to an estate or trust. The tax imposed by this subsection shall be treated as the tax imposed by subsection (a) of this section. (1989, c. 728, s. 1.4; 1989 (Reg. Sess., 1990), c. 814, s. 16; 1991, c. 45, s. 8; c. 689, s. 300; 1991 (Reg. Sess., 1992), c. 930, s. 15; 2001-424, s. 34.18(a); 2003-284, s. 39.1(a); 2003-284, ss. 39.1, 39.2; 2005-276, s. 36.1(a); 2006-66, ss. 24.2(a)-(c); 2013-316, ss. 1.1(a), (b); 2013-414, s. 1(e).)

§ 105-134.2A. (Effective for taxable years beginning on or after January 1, 2009, and expiring for taxable years beginning on or after January 1, 2011) Income tax surtax.

(a) Surtax. - An income tax surtax is imposed on a taxpayer equal to a percentage of the tax payable by the taxpayer under G.S. 105-134.2 for the taxable year. This tax is in addition to the tax imposed by G.S. 105-134.2 and is due at the time prescribed in G.S. 105-155 for filing an individual income tax return. The surtax is imposed at the following percentage rates and applies to the tax payable on the taxpayer's North Carolina taxable income:

Filing Status Percentage	Over	Up To
Married, filing jointly or surviving spouse 0%	$ 0	$100,000
2%	$100,000	$250,000
3%	$250,000	NA
Head of household 0%	$ 0	$ 80,000
2%	$ 80,000	$200,000
3%	$200,000	NA
Single 0%	$ 0	$ 60,000
2%	$ 60,000	$150,000

3%	$150,000	NA
Married, filing separately 0%	$ 0	$ 50,000
2%	$ 50,000	$125,000
3%.	$125,000	NA

(b) Sunset. - This section expires for taxable years beginning on or after January 1, 2011. (2009-451, s. 27A.1(b).)

§ 105-134.3. (Repealed effective for taxable years beginning on or after January 1, 2014 - see note) Year of assessment.

The tax imposed by this Part shall be assessed, collected, and paid in the taxable year following the taxable year for which the assessment is made, except as provided to the contrary in Article 4A of this Chapter. (1989, c. 728, s. 1.4; 1998-98, s. 69; 2013-316, s. 1.1(b).)

§ 105-134.4. (Repealed effective for taxable years beginning on or after January 1, 2012) Taxable year.

A taxpayer shall compute North Carolina taxable income on the basis of the taxable year used in computing the taxpayer's income tax liability under the Code. (1989, c. 728, s. 1.4; 2011-145, s. 31A.1(d).)

§ 105-134.5. (Effective for taxable years beginning before January 1, 2012) North Carolina taxable income defined.

(a) Residents. - For residents of this State, the term "North Carolina taxable income" means the taxpayer's taxable income as determined under the Code, adjusted as provided in G.S. 105-134.6 and G.S. 105-134.7.

(b) Nonresidents. - For nonresident individuals, the term "North Carolina taxable income" means the taxpayer's taxable income as determined under the Code, adjusted as provided in G.S. 105-134.6 and G.S. 105-134.7, multiplied by a fraction the denominator of which is the taxpayer's gross income as determined under the Code, adjusted as provided in G.S. 105-134.6 and G.S. 105-134.7, and the numerator of which is the amount of that gross income, as adjusted, that is derived from North Carolina sources and is attributable to the ownership of any interest in real or tangible personal property in this State, is derived from a business, trade, profession, or occupation carried on in this State, or is derived from gambling activities in this State.

(c) Part-year Residents. - If an individual was a resident of this State for only part of the taxable year, having moved into or removed from the State during the year, the term "North Carolina taxable income" has the same meaning as in subsection (b) except that the numerator shall include gross income, adjusted as provided in G.S. 105-134.6 and G.S. 105-134.7, derived from all sources during the period the individual was a resident.

(d) S Corporations and Partnerships. - In order to calculate the numerator of the fraction provided in subsection (b), the amount of a shareholder's pro rata share of S Corporation income that is includable in the numerator shall be the shareholder's pro rata share of the S Corporation's income attributable to the State, as defined in G.S. 105-131(b)(4). In order to calculate the numerator of the fraction provided in subsection (b) for a member of a partnership or other unincorporated business with one or more nonresident members that operates in one or more other states, the amount of the member's distributive share of income of the business that is includable in the numerator shall be determined by multiplying the total net income of the business by the ratio ascertained under the provisions of G.S. 105-130.4. As used in this subsection, total net income means the entire gross income of the business less all expenses, taxes, interest, and other deductions allowable under the Code which were incurred in the operation of the business. (1989, c. 728, s. 1.4; 1995, c. 17, s. 4; 2005-276, s. 31.1(aa); 2005-344, s. 10.4.)

§ 105-134.5. (Effective for taxable years beginning on or after January 1, 2012 and recodified effective for taxable years beginning on or after January 1, 2014) North Carolina taxable income defined.

(a) Residents. - For an individual who is a resident of this State, the term "North Carolina taxable income" means the taxpayer's adjusted gross income as modified in G.S. 105-134.6 and G.S. 105-134.6A.

(b) Nonresidents. - For a nonresident individual, the term "North Carolina taxable income" means the taxpayer's adjusted gross income as modified in G.S. 105-134.6 and G.S. 105-134.6A multiplied by a fraction the denominator of which is the taxpayer's gross income as modified in G.S. 105-134.6 and G.S. 105-134.6A, and the numerator of which is the amount of that gross income, as modified, that is derived from North Carolina sources and is attributable to the ownership of any interest in real or tangible personal property in this State, is derived from a business, trade, profession, or occupation carried on in this State, or is derived from gambling activities in this State.

(c) Part-year Residents. - If an individual was a resident of this State for only part of the taxable year, having moved into or removed from the State during the year, the term "North Carolina taxable income" has the same meaning as in subsection (b) of this section except that the numerator includes gross income, as modified under G.S. 105-134.6 and G.S. 105-134.6A, derived from all sources during the period the individual was a resident.

(d) S Corporations and Partnerships. - In order to calculate the numerator of the fraction provided in subsection (b) of this section, the amount of a shareholder's pro rata share of S Corporation income that is includable in the numerator is the shareholder's pro rata share of the S Corporation's income attributable to the State, as defined in G.S. 105-131(b)(4). In order to calculate the numerator of the fraction provided in subsection (b) of this section for a member of a partnership or other unincorporated business that has one or more nonresident members and operates in one or more other states, the amount of the member's distributive share of income of the business that is includable in the numerator is determined by multiplying the total net income of the business by the ratio ascertained under the provisions of G.S. 105-130.4. As used in this subsection, total net income means the entire gross income of the business less all expenses, taxes, interest, and other deductions allowable under the Code that were incurred in the operation of the business.

(e) Tax Year. - A taxpayer must compute North Carolina taxable income on the basis of the taxable year used in computing the taxpayer's income tax liability under the Code. (1989, c. 728, s. 1.4; 1995, c. 17, s. 4; 2005-276, s. 31.1(aa); 2005-344, s. 10.4; 2011-145, s. 31A.1(b); 2012-79, s. 1.2; 2013-414, s. 55.)

§ 105-134.6. (Effective for taxable years beginning before January 1, 2012) Adjustments to taxable income.

(a) S Corporations. - Each shareholder's pro rata share of an S Corporation's income is subject to the adjustments provided in this section.

(b) Deductions. - The following deductions from taxable income shall be made in calculating North Carolina taxable income, to the extent each item is included in taxable income:

(1) Interest upon the obligations of any of the following:

a. The United States or its possessions.

b. This State, a political subdivision of this State, or a commission, an authority, or another agency of this State or of a political subdivision of this State.

c. A nonprofit educational institution organized or chartered under the laws of this State.

(2) Gain from the disposition of obligations issued before July 1, 1995, to the extent the gain is exempt from tax under the laws of this State.

(3) Benefits received under Title II of the Social Security Act and amounts received from retirement annuities or pensions paid under the provisions of the Railroad Retirement Act of 1937.

(4) Repealed by Session Laws 1989 (Reg. Sess., 1990), c. 1002, s. 2.

(5) Refunds of state, local, and foreign income taxes included in the taxpayer's gross income.

(5a) Reserved.

(5b) The amount received during the taxable year from one or more State, local, or federal government retirement plans to the extent the amount is exempt from tax under this Part pursuant to a court order in settlement of the following cases: Bailey v. State, 92 CVS 10221, 94 CVS 6904, 95 CVS 6625, 95 CVS 8230; Emory v. State, 98 CVS 0738; and Patton v. State, 95 CVS 04346. Amounts deducted under this subdivision may not also be deducted under subdivision (6) of this subsection.

(6) a. An amount, not to exceed four thousand dollars ($4,000), equal to the sum of the amount calculated in subparagraph b. plus the amount calculated in subparagraph c.

b. The amount calculated in this subparagraph is the amount received during the taxable year from one or more state, local, or federal government retirement plans.

c. The amount calculated in this subparagraph is the amount received during the taxable year from one or more retirement plans other than state, local, or federal government retirement plans, not to exceed a total of two thousand dollars ($2,000) in any taxable year.

d. In the case of a married couple filing a joint return where both spouses received retirement benefits during the taxable year, the maximum dollar amounts provided in this subdivision for various types of retirement benefits apply separately to each spouse's benefits.

(7) Recodified as G.S. 105-134.6(d)(1).

(8) Recodified as G.S. 105-134.6(d)(2).

(9) Income that is (i) earned or received by an enrolled member of a federally recognized Indian tribe and (ii) derived from activities on a federally recognized Indian reservation while the member resides on the reservation. Income from intangibles having a situs on the reservation and retirement income associated with activities on the reservation are considered income derived from activities on the reservation.

(10) The amount by which the basis of property under this Article exceeds the basis of the property under the Code, in the year the taxpayer disposes of the property.

(11) Severance wages received by a taxpayer from an employer as the result of the taxpayer's permanent, involuntary termination from employment through no fault of the employee. The amount of severance wages deducted as the result of the same termination may not exceed thirty-five thousand dollars ($35,000) for all taxable years in which the wages are received.

(12) Repealed by Session Laws 1998-171, s. 2, effective October 1, 1998.

(13) Repealed by Session Laws 2002-126, s. 30C.4, effective for taxable years beginning on or after January 1, 2002.

(14) The amount paid to the taxpayer by the State under G.S. 148-84 as compensation for pecuniary loss suffered by reason of erroneous conviction and imprisonment.

(15) Interest, investment earnings, and gains of a trust, the settlors of which are two or more manufacturers that signed a settlement agreement with this State to settle existing and potential claims of the State against the manufacturers for damages attributable to a product of the manufacturers, if the trust meets all of the following conditions:

a. The purpose of the trust is to address adverse economic consequences resulting from a decline in demand of the manufactured product potentially expected to occur because of market restrictions and other provisions in the settlement agreement.

b. A court of this State approves and retains jurisdiction over the trust.

c. Certain portions of the distributions from the trust are made in accordance with certifications that meet the criteria in the agreement creating the trust and are provided by a nonprofit entity, the governing board of which includes State officials.

(16) The amount paid to the taxpayer during the taxable year from the Hurricane Floyd Reserve Fund in the Office of State Budget and Management for hurricane relief or assistance, but not including payments for goods or services provided by the taxpayer.

(17) In each of the taxpayer's first five taxable years beginning on or after January 1, 2005, an amount equal to twenty percent (20%) of the amount added

to taxable income in a previous year as accelerated depreciation under subdivision (c)(8) of this section.

(17a) An amount equal to twenty percent (20%) of the amount added to federal taxable income as accelerated depreciation under subdivision (c)(8a) of this section. For a taxpayer who made the addition for accelerated depreciation in the 2008 taxable year, the deduction allowed by this subdivision applies to the first five taxable years beginning on or after January 1, 2009. For a taxpayer who made the addition for accelerated depreciation in the 2009 taxable year, the deduction allowed by this subdivision applies to the first five taxable years beginning on or after January 1, 2010.

(17b) An amount equal to twenty percent (20%) of the amount added to federal taxable income as accelerated depreciation under subdivision (c)(8b) of this section. For the amount added to taxable income in the 2010 taxable year, the deduction allowed by this subdivision applies to the first five taxable years beginning on or after January 1, 2011. For the amount added to taxable income in the 2011 taxable year, the deduction allowed by this subdivision applies to the first five taxable years beginning on or after January 1, 2012. For the amount added to taxable income in the 2012 taxable year, the deduction allowed by this subdivision applies to the first five taxable years beginning on or after January 1, 2013.

(18) The amount paid to the taxpayer during the taxable year from the Disaster Relief Reserve Fund in the Office of State Budget and Management for hurricane relief or assistance, but not including payments for goods or services provided by the taxpayer.

(19) (Expires for taxable years beginning on or after January 1, 2015) Five percent (5%) of the gross purchase price of a qualified sale of a manufactured home community. A qualified sale is a transfer of land comprising a manufactured home community in a single purchase to a group composed of a majority of the manufactured home community leaseholders or to a nonprofit organization that represents such a group. To be eligible for this deduction, a taxpayer must give notice of the sale to the North Carolina Housing Finance Agency under G.S. 42-14.3.

(20) The amount added to federal taxable income as deferred income under section 108(i)(1) of the Code. This deduction applies to taxable years beginning on or after January 1, 2014.

(21) An amount equal to twenty percent (20%) of the amount added to federal taxable income under subdivision (c)(15) of this section. For the amount added to taxable income in the 2010 taxable year, the deduction allowed by this subdivision applies to the first five taxable years beginning on or after January 1, 2011. For the amount added to taxable income in the 2011 taxable year, the deduction allowed by this subdivision applies to the first five taxable years beginning on or after January 1, 2012.

(c) Additions. - The following additions to taxable income shall be made in calculating North Carolina taxable income, to the extent each item is not included in taxable income:

(1) Interest upon the obligations of states other than this State, political subdivisions of those states, and agencies of those states and their political subdivisions.

(2) Any amount allowed as a deduction from gross income under the Code that is taxed under the Code by a separate tax other than the tax imposed in section 1 of the Code.

(3) Any amount deducted from gross income under section 164 of the Code as state, local, or foreign income tax or as state or local general sales tax to the extent that the taxpayer's total itemized deductions deducted under the Code for the taxable year exceed the standard deduction allowable to the taxpayer under the Code reduced by the amount the taxpayer is required to add to taxable income under subdivision (4) of this subsection.

(3a) The amount by which a shareholder's share of S Corporation income is reduced under section 1366(f)(2) of the Code for the taxable year by the amount of built-in gains tax imposed on the S Corporation under section 1374 of the Code.

(4) The amount by which the taxpayer's additional standard deduction for aged and blind has been increased for inflation under section 63(c)(4)(A) of the Code plus the amount by which the taxpayer's basic standard deduction, including adjustments for inflation, under the Code exceeds the appropriate amount in the following chart based on the taxpayer's filing status:

Filing Status	Standard Deduction
Married filing jointly/Surviving Spouse	$6,000

Head of Household	4,400
Single	3,000
Married filing separately	3,000

(4a) The amount by which each of the taxpayer's personal exemptions has been increased for inflation under section 151(d)(4)(A) of the Code. This amount is reduced by five hundred dollars ($500.00) for each personal exemption if the taxpayer's adjusted gross income (AGI), as calculated under the Code, is less than the following amounts:

Filing Status	AGI
Married, filing jointly	$100,000
Head of Household	80,000
Single	60,000
Married, filing separately	50,000.

For the purposes of this subdivision, if the taxpayer's personal exemptions have been reduced by the applicable percentage under section 151(d)(3) of the Code, the amount by which the personal exemptions have been increased for inflation is also reduced by the applicable percentage.

(5) The market price of the gleaned crop for which the taxpayer claims a credit for the taxable year under G.S. 105-151.14.

(5a) (Expires for taxable years beginning on or after January 1, 2013) The market price of the oyster shells for which the taxpayer claims a credit for the taxable year under G.S. 105-151.30.

(5b) The amount of a donation made to a nonprofit organization or a unit of State or local government for which a credit is claimed under G.S. 105-129.16H.

(6) The amount by which the basis of property under the Code exceeds the basis of the property under this Article, in the year the taxpayer disposes of the property.

(7) The amount of federal estate tax that is attributable to an item of income in respect of a decedent and is deducted from gross income under section 691(c) of the Code.

(8) For taxable years 2002-2005, the applicable percentage of the amount allowed as a special accelerated depreciation deduction under section 168(k) or section 1400L of the Code, as set out in the table below. In addition, a taxpayer who was allowed a special accelerated depreciation deduction under section 168(k) or section 1400L of the Code in a taxable year beginning before January 1, 2002, and whose North Carolina taxable income in that earlier year reflected that accelerated depreciation deduction must add to federal taxable income in the taxpayer's first taxable year beginning on or after January 1, 2002, an amount equal to the amount of the deduction allowed in the earlier taxable year. These adjustments do not result in a difference in basis of the affected assets for State and federal income tax purposes. The applicable percentage is as follows:

Taxable Year	Percentage
2002	100%
2003	70%
2004	70%
2005	0%

(8a) The applicable percentage of the amount allowed as a special accelerated depreciation deduction under section 168(k) or 168(n) of the Code for property placed in service after December 31, 2007, but before January 1, 2010. The applicable percentage under this subdivision is eighty-five percent (85%).

In addition, a taxpayer who was allowed a special accelerated depreciation deduction in taxable year 2007 or 2008 for property placed in service during that year, and whose North Carolina taxable income for that year reflected that accelerated depreciation deduction must make the adjustments set out below. These adjustments do not result in a difference in basis of the affected assets for State and federal income tax purposes.

a. A taxpayer must add to federal taxable income in the taxpayer's 2008 taxable year an amount equal to the applicable percentage of the accelerated depreciation deduction reflected in the taxpayer's 2007 North Carolina taxable income.

b. A taxpayer must add to federal taxable income in the taxpayer's 2009 taxable year an amount equal to the applicable percentage of the accelerated depreciation deduction reflected in the taxpayer's 2008 North Carolina taxable income.

(8b) For taxable years 2010 through 2012, eighty-five percent (85%) of the amount allowed as a special accelerated depreciation deduction under section 168(k) or 168(n) of the Code for property placed in service during the taxable year. In addition, for taxable year 2010, a taxpayer who placed property in service during the 2009 taxable year and whose North Carolina taxable income for the 2009 taxable year reflected a special accelerated depreciation deduction allowed for the property under section 168(k) of the Code must add eighty-five percent (85%) of the amount of the special accelerated depreciation deduction. These adjustments do not result in a difference in basis of the affected assets for State and federal income tax purposes.

(9) Repealed by Session Laws 2006-220, s. 3, effective for taxable years beginning on and after January 1, 2007.

(10) The amount excluded from gross income under section 199 of the Code.

(11) The amount of the taxpayer's real property tax deduction under section 63(c)(1)(C) of the Code.

(12) The amount of the taxpayer's deduction for motor vehicle sales taxes under section 164(a)(6) or section 63(c)(1)(E) of the Code.

(13) The amount of income deferred under section 108(i)(1) of the Code from the discharge of indebtedness in connection with a reacquisition of an applicable debt instrument.

(14) The amount allowed as a deduction under section 163(e)(5)(F) of the Code for an original issue discount on an applicable high yield discount obligation.

(15) For taxable years 2010 and 2011, eighty-five percent (85%) of the amount by which the taxpayer's expense deduction under section 179 of the Code for property placed in service in taxable year 2010 or 2011 exceeds the amount that would have been allowed for the respective taxable year under section 179 of the Code as of May 1, 2010. For purposes of this subdivision, the definition of section 179 property has the same meaning as under section 179 of the Code as of January 1, 2011. These adjustments do not result in a difference in basis of the affected assets for State and federal income tax purposes.

(d) Other Adjustments. – The following adjustments to taxable income shall be made in calculating North Carolina taxable income:

(1) The amount of inheritance or estate tax attributable to an item of income in respect of a decedent required to be included in gross income under the Code, adjusted as provided in G.S. 105-134.5, 105-134.6, and 105-134.7, may be deducted in the year the item of income is included. The amount of inheritance or estate tax attributable to an item of income in respect of a decedent is (i) the amount by which the inheritance or estate tax paid under Article 1 or 1A of this Chapter on property transferred to a beneficiary by a decedent exceeds the amount of the tax that would have been payable by the beneficiary if the item of income in respect of a decedent had not been included in the property transferred to the beneficiary by the decedent, (ii) multiplied by a fraction, the numerator of which is the amount required to be included in gross income for the taxable year under the Code, adjusted as provided in G.S. 105-134.5, 105-134.6, and 105-134.7, and the denominator of which is the total amount of income in respect of a decedent transferred to the beneficiary by the decedent. For an estate or trust, the deduction allowed by this subdivision shall be computed by excluding from the gross income of the estate or trust the portion, if any, of the items of income in respect of a decedent that are properly paid, credited, or to be distributed to the beneficiaries during the taxable year.

The Secretary may provide to a beneficiary of an item of income in respect of a decedent any information contained on an inheritance or estate tax return that the beneficiary needs to compute the deduction allowed by this subdivision.

(2) The taxpayer may deduct the amount by which the taxpayer's deductions allowed under the Code were reduced, and the amount of the taxpayer's deductions that were not allowed, because the taxpayer elected a federal tax credit in lieu of a deduction. This deduction is allowed only to the extent that a similar credit is not allowed by this Chapter for the amount.

(3) The taxpayer shall add to taxable income the amount of any recovery during the taxable year not included in taxable income, to the extent the taxpayer's deduction of the recovered amount in a prior taxable year reduced the taxpayer's tax imposed by this Part but, due to differences between the Code and this Part, did not reduce the amount of the taxpayer's tax imposed by the Code. The taxpayer may deduct from taxable income the amount of any recovery during the taxable year included in taxable income under section 111 of the Code, to the extent the taxpayer's deduction of the recovered amount in a prior taxable year reduced the taxpayer's tax imposed by the Code but, due to differences between the Code and this Part, did not reduce the amount of the taxpayer's tax imposed by this Part.

(4) A taxpayer may deduct from taxable income the amount, not to exceed two thousand five hundred dollars ($2,500), contributed to an account in the Parental Savings Trust Fund of the State Education Assistance Authority established pursuant to G.S. 116-209.25. In the case of a married couple filing a joint return, the maximum dollar amount of the deduction is five thousand dollars ($5,000).

(5) The taxpayer shall add to taxable income the amount deducted from taxable income in a prior taxable year under subdivision (4) of this subsection to the extent this amount was withdrawn from the Parental Savings Trust Fund of the State Education Assistance Authority established pursuant to G.S. 116-209.25 and not used to pay for the qualified higher education expenses of the designated beneficiary, unless the withdrawal was made without penalty under section 529 of the Code due to the death or permanent disability of the designated beneficiary.

(6) A taxpayer who is an eligible firefighter or an eligible rescue squad worker may deduct from taxable income the sum of two hundred fifty dollars ($250.00). In the case of a married couple filing a joint return, each spouse may qualify separately for the deduction allowed under this subdivision. In order to claim the deduction allowed under this subdivision, the taxpayer must submit with the tax return any documentation required by the Secretary. An individual may not claim a deduction as both an eligible firefighter and as an eligible rescue squad worker in a single taxable year. The following definitions apply in this subdivision:

a. Eligible firefighter. - An unpaid member of a volunteer fire department who attended at least 36 hours of fire department drills and meetings during the taxable year.

b. Eligible rescue squad worker. - An unpaid member of a volunteer rescue or emergency medical services squad who attended at least 36 hours of rescue squad training and meetings during the taxable year.

(7) The taxpayer shall add to taxable income the amounts listed in this subdivision. An addition is not required under this subdivision for a net operating loss deduction of an eligible small business as defined under section 172(b)(1)(H) of the Code. The amounts are:

a. For taxable years 2003, 2004, and 2005, the amount of any 2008 net operating loss deduction claimed on a federal return under section 172(b)(1)(H) or section 810(b)(4) of the Code.

b. For taxable years 2004, 2005, and 2006, the amount of any 2009 net operating loss deduction claimed on a federal return under section 172(b)(1)(H) or section 810(b)(4) of the Code.

(8) For taxable years 2011 through 2013, a taxpayer who made an addition under subdivision (7) of this subsection may deduct the following amounts:

a. For a taxpayer who made an addition under sub-subdivision (7)a. of this subsection, one-third of the taxpayer's net operating loss absorbed on the taxpayer's 2003, 2004, and 2005 federal returns under section 172(b)(1)(H) or section 810(b)(4) of the Code, with the exception of the portion of the net operating loss of an eligible small business absorbed on the taxpayer's 2003, 2004, and 2005 federal returns.

b. For a taxpayer who made an addition under sub-subdivision (7)b. of this subsection, one-third of the taxpayer's net operating loss absorbed on the taxpayer's 2004, 2005, and 2006 federal returns under section 172(b)(1)(H) or section 810(b)(4) of the Code, with the exception of the portion of the net operating loss of an eligible small business absorbed on the taxpayer's 2004, 2005, and 2006 federal returns. (1989, c. 718, s. 2; c. 728, s. 1.4; c. 770, ss. 41.2, 41.3; c. 792, s. 1.1; 1989 (Reg. Sess., 1990), c. 984, s. 4; c. 1002, s. 2; 1991, c. 45, s. 9; c. 453, s. 1; c. 689, ss. 253, 254; 1991 (Reg. Sess., 1992), c. 1007, s. 3; 1993, c. 12, s. 8; c. 443, s. 8; c. 485, s. 9; 1993 (Reg. Sess., 1994), c. 745, s. 7; 1995, c. 17, s. 5; c. 42, ss. 1, 2(a), (b); c. 46, s. 3; c. 370, s. 3; 1996, 2nd Ex. Sess., c. 13, s. 8.1; c. 14, s. 9; 1997-226, s. 3; 1997-328, s. 1; 1997-388, s. 4; 1997-525, s. 1; 1998-98, s. 69; 1998-171, ss. 2, 3; 1998-212, ss. 29A.2(c), 29A.13(a); 1999-333, s. 3; 1999-463, Ex Sess., s. 4.6 (a); 2000-140, ss. 65, 93.1(a); 2001-424, ss. 12.2(b), 34.19(a), (b); 2002-126, ss. 30B.1(a),

30B.1(b), 30C.2(b), 30C.2(d), 30C.4; 2003-284, s. 37A.2; 2005-1, s. 5.7(a); 2005-276, ss. 35.1(e), 39.1(f); 2005-435, s. 55; 2006-17, ss. 2, 3; 2006-66, ss. 24.12(a), 24.18(e); 2006-220, s. 3; 2006-221, s. 27(a); 2007-323, ss. 31.19(a)-(d), 31.24(a); 2007-397, s. 13(c); 2008-107, ss. 28.1(e), (f), (h), 28.25(c), 28.27(b), (c); 2008-134, s. 2(c); 2009-445, s. 43; 2009-451, s. 27A.6(e), (f); 2010-31, s. 31.1(b); 2011-5, ss. 2(c), (d), 3(c), (d); 2011-106, s. 1; 2011-330, ss. 11, 13, 36.)

§ 105-134.6. (Effective for taxable years beginning on or after January 1, 2012 and repealed effective for taxable years beginning on or after January 1, 2014 - see notes) Modifications to adjusted gross income.

(a) S Corporations. - Each shareholder's pro rata share of an S Corporation's income is subject to the adjustments provided in this section.

(a1) Personal Exemption. - In calculating North Carolina taxable income, a taxpayer may deduct an exemption amount equal to the amount listed in the table below based on the taxpayer's filing status and adjusted gross income. The taxpayer is allowed the same personal exemptions allowed under section 151 of the Code for the taxable year.

Filing Status	Adjusted Gross Income	Personal Exemption
Married, filing jointly	Up to $100,000	$2,500
	Over $100,000	$2,000
Head of Household	Up to $80,000	$2,500
	Over $80,000	$2,000
Single	Up to $60,000	$2,500

	Over $60,000	$2,000
Married, filing separately	Up to $50,000	$2,500
	Over $50,000	$2,000

(a2) Deduction Amount. - In calculating North Carolina taxable income, a taxpayer may deduct either the North Carolina standard deduction amount for that taxpayer's filing status or the itemized deductions amount claimed under the Code. The North Carolina standard deduction amount is the lesser of the amount shown in the table below or the amount allowed under the Code. In the case of a married couple filing separate returns, a taxpayer may not deduct the standard deduction amount if the taxpayer or the taxpayer's spouse claims itemized deductions for State purposes.

A taxpayer that deducts the standard deduction amount under this subsection and is entitled to an additional deduction amount under section 63(f) of the Code for the aged or blind may deduct an additional amount under this subsection. The additional amount the taxpayer may deduct is six hundred dollars ($600.00) in the case of an individual who is married and seven hundred fifty dollars ($750.00) in the case of an individual who is not married and is not a surviving spouse. The taxpayer is allowed the same number of additional amounts that the taxpayer claimed under the Code for the taxable year.

Filing Status	Standard Deduction
Married, filing jointly	$6,000
Head of Household	4,400
Single	3,000
Married, filing separately	3,000.

(b) Other Deductions. - In calculating North Carolina taxable income, a taxpayer may deduct any of the following items to the extent those items are included in the taxpayer's adjusted gross income.

(1) Interest upon the obligations of any of the following:

a. The United States or its possessions.

b. This State, a political subdivision of this State, or a commission, an authority, or another agency of this State or of a political subdivision of this State.

c. A nonprofit educational institution organized or chartered under the laws of this State.

(2) Gain from the disposition of obligations issued before July 1, 1995, to the extent the gain is exempt from tax under the laws of this State.

(3) Benefits received under Title II of the Social Security Act and amounts received from retirement annuities or pensions paid under the provisions of the Railroad Retirement Act of 1937.

(4) Repealed by Session Laws 1989 (Reg. Sess., 1990), c. 1002, s. 2.

(5) Refunds of state, local, and foreign income taxes included in the taxpayer's gross income.

(5a) Reserved.

(5b) The amount received during the taxable year from one or more State, local, or federal government retirement plans to the extent the amount is exempt from tax under this Part pursuant to a court order in settlement of the following cases: Bailey v. State, 92 CVS 10221, 94 CVS 6904, 95 CVS 6625, 95 CVS 8230; Emory v. State, 98 CVS 0738; and Patton v. State, 95 CVS 04346. Amounts deducted under this subdivision may not also be deducted under subdivision (6) of this subsection.

(6) a. An amount, not to exceed four thousand dollars ($4,000), equal to the sum of the amount calculated in subparagraph b. plus the amount calculated in subparagraph c.

b. The amount calculated in this subparagraph is the amount received during the taxable year from one or more state, local, or federal government retirement plans.

c. The amount calculated in this subparagraph is the amount received during the taxable year from one or more retirement plans other than state, local, or federal government retirement plans, not to exceed a total of two thousand dollars ($2,000) in any taxable year.

d. In the case of a married couple filing a joint return where both spouses received retirement benefits during the taxable year, the maximum dollar amounts provided in this subdivision for various types of retirement benefits apply separately to each spouse's benefits.

(7) Recodified as G.S. 105-134.6(d)(1).

(8) Recodified as G.S. 105-134.6(d)(2).

(9) Income that is (i) earned or received by an enrolled member of a federally recognized Indian tribe and (ii) derived from activities on a federally recognized Indian reservation while the member resides on the reservation. Income from intangibles having a situs on the reservation and retirement income associated with activities on the reservation are considered income derived from activities on the reservation.

(10) The amount by which the basis of property under this Article exceeds the basis of the property under the Code, in the year the taxpayer disposes of the property.

(11) Severance wages received by a taxpayer from an employer as the result of the taxpayer's permanent, involuntary termination from employment through no fault of the employee. The amount of severance wages deducted as the result of the same termination may not exceed thirty-five thousand dollars ($35,000) for all taxable years in which the wages are received.

(12) Repealed by Session Laws 1998-171, s. 2, effective October 1, 1998.

(13) Repealed by Session Laws 2002-126, s. 30C.4, effective for taxable years beginning on or after January 1, 2002.

(14) The amount paid to the taxpayer by the State under G.S. 148-84 as compensation for pecuniary loss suffered by reason of erroneous conviction and imprisonment.

(15) Interest, investment earnings, and gains of a trust, the settlors of which are two or more manufacturers that signed a settlement agreement with this State to settle existing and potential claims of the State against the

manufacturers for damages attributable to a product of the manufacturers, if the trust meets all of the following conditions:

a. The purpose of the trust is to address adverse economic consequences resulting from a decline in demand of the manufactured product potentially expected to occur because of market restrictions and other provisions in the settlement agreement.

b. A court of this State approves and retains jurisdiction over the trust.

c. Certain portions of the distributions from the trust are made in accordance with certifications that meet the criteria in the agreement creating the trust and are provided by a nonprofit entity, the governing board of which includes State officials.

(16) The amount paid to the taxpayer during the taxable year from the Hurricane Floyd Reserve Fund in the Office of State Budget and Management for hurricane relief or assistance, but not including payments for goods or services provided by the taxpayer.

(17) Repealed by Session Laws 2013-414, s. 34(c), effective August 23, 2013.

(17a), (17b) Repealed by Session Laws 2013-414, s. 34(c), effective August 23, 2013.

(18) The amount paid to the taxpayer during the taxable year from the Disaster Relief Reserve Fund in the Office of State Budget and Management for hurricane relief or assistance, but not including payments for goods or services provided by the taxpayer.

(19) (Expires for taxable years beginning on or after January 1, 2015) Five percent (5%) of the gross purchase price of a qualified sale of a manufactured home community. A qualified sale is a transfer of land comprising a manufactured home community in a single purchase to a group composed of a majority of the manufactured home community leaseholders or to a nonprofit organization that represents such a group. To be eligible for this deduction, a taxpayer must give notice of the sale to the North Carolina Housing Finance Agency under G.S. 42-14.3.

(20) The amount added to federal taxable income as deferred income under section 108(i)(1) of the Code. This deduction applies to taxable years beginning on or after January 1, 2014.

(21), (21a) Repealed by Session Laws 2013-414, s. 34(c), effective August 23, 2013.

(22) An amount not to exceed fifty thousand dollars ($50,000) of net business income the taxpayer receives during the taxable year. In the case of a married couple filing a joint return where both spouses receive or incur net business income, the maximum dollar amounts apply separately to each spouse's net business income, not to exceed a total of one hundred thousand dollars ($100,000). For purposes of this subdivision, the term "business income" does not include income that is considered passive income under the Code.

(23) The amount allowed as a deduction under G.S. 105-134.6A as a result of an add-back for federal accelerated depreciation and expensing.

(24) Amounts that were recognized as income under State law but not under federal law due to a taxpayer's use of a different installment method prior to January 1, 1989, shall be deducted from taxable income in the taxpayer's first taxable year beginning on or after January 1, 1989.

(c) Additions. - In calculating North Carolina taxable income, a taxpayer must add any of the following items to the extent those items are not included in the taxpayer's adjusted gross income. For a taxpayer who deducts the itemized deductions amount under subsection (a2) of this section, the taxpayer must add any of the following items to the extent those items are included in the itemized deductions amount.

(1) Interest upon the obligations of states other than this State, political subdivisions of those states, and agencies of those states and their political subdivisions.

(2) Any amount allowed as a deduction from gross income under the Code that is taxed under the Code by a separate tax other than the tax imposed in section 1 of the Code.

(3) Any amount deducted from gross income under section 164 of the Code as state, local, or foreign income tax, as state or local general sales tax, or as qualified motor vehicle tax to the extent that the taxpayer's total itemized

deductions deducted under the Code for the taxable year exceed the standard deduction allowable to the taxpayer under subsection (a2) of this section.

(3a) The amount by which a shareholder's share of S Corporation income is reduced under section 1366(f)(2) of the Code for the taxable year by the amount of built-in gains tax imposed on the S Corporation under section 1374 of the Code.

(4), (4a) Repealed by Session Laws 2011-145, s. 31A.1(c), effective for taxable years beginning on or after January 1, 2012.

(5) The market price of the gleaned crop for which the taxpayer claims a credit for the taxable year under G.S. 105-151.14.

(5a) (Expires for taxable years beginning on or after January 1, 2013) The market price of the oyster shells for which the taxpayer claims a credit for the taxable year under G.S. 105-151.30.

(5b) The amount of a donation made to a nonprofit organization or a unit of State or local government for which a credit is claimed under G.S. 105-129.16H.

(6) The amount by which the basis of property under the Code exceeds the basis of the property under this Article, in the year the taxpayer disposes of the property.

(7) The amount of federal estate tax that is attributable to an item of income in respect of a decedent and is deducted from gross income under section 691(c) of the Code.

(8) Repealed by Session Laws 2013-414, s. 34(c), effective August 23, 2013.

(8a), (8b) Repealed by Session Laws 2013-414, s. 34(c), effective August 23, 2013.

(9) Repealed by Session Laws 2006-220, s. 3, effective for taxable years beginning on and after January 1, 2007.

(10) The amount excluded from gross income under section 199 of the Code.

(11) Repealed by Session Laws 2011-145, s. 31A.1(c), effective for taxable years beginning on or after January 1, 2012.

(12) Repealed by Session Laws 2011-330, s. 12(e), effective for taxable years beginning on or after January 1, 2012.

(13) The amount of income deferred under section 108(i)(1) of the Code from the discharge of indebtedness in connection with a reacquisition of an applicable debt instrument.

(14) The amount allowed as a deduction under section 163(e)(5)(F) of the Code for an original issue discount on an applicable high yield discount obligation.

(15) For taxable years 2010 and 2011, eighty-five percent (85%) of the amount by which the taxpayer's expense deduction under section 179 of the Code for property placed in service in taxable year 2010 or 2011 exceeds the amount that would have been allowed for the respective taxable year under section 179 of the Code as of May 1, 2010. For purposes of this subdivision, the definition of section 179 property has the same meaning as under section 179 of the Code as of January 1, 2011. These adjustments do not result in a difference in basis of the affected assets for State and federal income tax purposes.

(15a) For taxable years 2012 and 2013, eighty-five percent (85%) of the amount by which the taxpayer's expense deduction under section 179 of the Code for property placed in service in taxable year 2012 or 2013 exceeds the amount that would have been allowed for the respective taxable year under section 179 of the Code as of May 1, 2010. For purposes of this subdivision, the definition of section 179 property has the same meaning as under section 179 of the Code as of January 2, 2013. These adjustments do not result in a difference in basis of the affected assets for State and federal income tax purposes.

(16) For taxable year 2013, the amount of the taxpayer's deduction for qualified tuition and related expenses under section 222 of the Code. The purpose of this subdivision is to decouple from the extension of the federal deduction under section 207 of the American Taxpayer Relief Act of 2012.

(17) For taxable year 2013, the amount excluded from the taxpayer's gross income for a qualified charitable distribution from an individual retirement plan by a person who has attained age 70 1/2 under section 408(d)(8) of the Code.

The purpose of this subdivision is to decouple from the extension of the income exclusion under section 208 of the American Taxpayer Relief Act of 2012.

(18) For taxable year 2013, the amount excluded from the taxpayer's gross income for the discharge of qualified principal residence indebtedness under section 108 of the Code. The purpose of this subdivision is to decouple from the extension of the income exclusion under section 202 of the American Taxpayer Relief Act of 2012.

(19) For taxable year 2013, the amount of the taxpayer's deduction for mortgage insurance premiums as qualified residence interest under section 163 of the Code. The purpose of this subdivision is to decouple from the extension of the income exclusion under section 204 of the American Taxpayer Relief Act of 2012.

(20) Amounts that were recognized as income under federal law but not under State law due to a taxpayer's use of the installment method set out in G.S. 105-142(f) prior to January 1, 1989, shall be added to taxable income in the taxpayer's first taxable year beginning on or after January 1, 1989.

(21) A loss or deduction that was incurred or paid and deducted from State taxable income in a taxable year beginning before January 1, 1989, and is carried forward and deducted in a taxable year beginning on or after January 1, 1989, under the Code.

(22) The amount required to be added under G.S. 105-134.6A when the State decouples from federal accelerated depreciation and expensing.

(d) Other Adjustments. - In calculating North Carolina taxable income, a taxpayer must make the following adjustments to adjusted gross income.

(1) The amount of inheritance or estate tax attributable to an item of income in respect of a decedent required to be included in gross income under the Code, adjusted as provided in G.S. 105-134.5, 105-134.6, and 105-134.6A, may be deducted in the year the item of income is included. The amount of inheritance or estate tax attributable to an item of income in respect of a decedent is (i) the amount by which the inheritance or estate tax paid under Article 1 or 1A of this Chapter on property transferred to a beneficiary by a decedent exceeds the amount of the tax that would have been payable by the beneficiary if the item of income in respect of a decedent had not been included in the property transferred to the beneficiary by the decedent, (ii) multiplied by a

fraction, the numerator of which is the amount required to be included in gross income for the taxable year under the Code, adjusted as provided in G.S. 105-134.5, 105-134.6, and 105-134.6A, and the denominator of which is the total amount of income in respect of a decedent transferred to the beneficiary by the decedent. For an estate or trust, the deduction allowed by this subdivision shall be computed by excluding from the gross income of the estate or trust the portion, if any, of the items of income in respect of a decedent that are properly paid, credited, or to be distributed to the beneficiaries during the taxable year.

The Secretary may provide to a beneficiary of an item of income in respect of a decedent any information contained on an inheritance or estate tax return that the beneficiary needs to compute the deduction allowed by this subdivision.

(2) The taxpayer may deduct the amount by which the taxpayer's deductions allowed under the Code were reduced, and the amount of the taxpayer's deductions that were not allowed, because the taxpayer elected a federal tax credit in lieu of a deduction. This deduction is not allowed in the following circumstances:

a. If a similar credit is allowed by this Chapter for the amount.

b. For taxable year 2013, if the taxpayer elected to claim the Hope scholarship credit, the Lifetime Learning credit, or the American Opportunity tax credit under section 25A of the Code in lieu of a deduction for qualified tuition and expenses under section 222 of the Code.

(3) The taxpayer shall add to adjusted gross income the amount of any recovery during the taxable year not included in adjusted gross income, to the extent the taxpayer's deduction of the recovered amount in a prior taxable year reduced the taxpayer's tax imposed by this Part but, due to differences between the Code and this Part, did not reduce the amount of the taxpayer's tax imposed by the Code. The taxpayer may deduct from adjusted gross income the amount of any recovery during the taxable year included in adjusted gross income under section 111 of the Code, to the extent the taxpayer's deduction of the recovered amount in a prior taxable year reduced the taxpayer's tax imposed by the Code but, due to differences between the Code and this Part, did not reduce the amount of the taxpayer's tax imposed by this Part.

(4) A taxpayer may deduct from adjusted gross income the amount, not to exceed two thousand five hundred dollars ($2,500), contributed to an account in the Parental Savings Trust Fund of the State Education Assistance Authority

established pursuant to G.S. 116-209.25. In the case of a married couple filing a joint return, the maximum dollar amount of the deduction is five thousand dollars ($5,000).

(5) The taxpayer shall add to adjusted gross income the amount deducted in a prior taxable year under subdivision (4) of this subsection to the extent this amount was withdrawn from the Parental Savings Trust Fund of the State Education Assistance Authority established pursuant to G.S. 116-209.25 and not used to pay for the qualified higher education expenses of the designated beneficiary, unless the withdrawal was made without penalty under section 529 of the Code due to the death or permanent disability of the designated beneficiary.

(6) A taxpayer who is an eligible firefighter or an eligible rescue squad worker may deduct from adjusted gross income the sum of two hundred fifty dollars ($250.00). In the case of a married couple filing a joint return, each spouse may qualify separately for the deduction allowed under this subdivision. In order to claim the deduction allowed under this subdivision, the taxpayer must submit with the tax return any documentation required by the Secretary. An individual may not claim a deduction as both an eligible firefighter and as an eligible rescue squad worker in a single taxable year. The following definitions apply in this subdivision:

a. Eligible firefighter. - An unpaid member of a volunteer fire department who attended at least 36 hours of fire department drills and meetings during the taxable year.

b. Eligible rescue squad worker. - An unpaid member of a volunteer rescue or emergency medical services squad who attended at least 36 hours of rescue squad training and meetings during the taxable year.

(7) The taxpayer shall add to taxable income the amounts listed in this subdivision. An addition is not required under this subdivision for a net operating loss deduction of an eligible small business as defined under section 172(b)(1)(H) of the Code. The amounts are:

a. For taxable years 2003, 2004, and 2005, the amount of any 2008 net operating loss deduction claimed on a federal return under section 172(b)(1)(H) or section 810(b)(4) of the Code.

b. For taxable years 2004, 2005, and 2006, the amount of any 2009 net operating loss deduction claimed on a federal return under section 172(b)(1)(H) or section 810(b)(4) of the Code.

(8) For taxable years 2011 through 2013, a taxpayer who made an addition under subdivision (7) of this subsection may deduct the following amounts:

a. For a taxpayer who made an addition under sub-subdivision (7)a. of this subsection, one-third of the taxpayer's net operating loss absorbed on the taxpayer's 2003, 2004, and 2005 federal returns under section 172(b)(1)(H) or section 810(b)(4) of the Code, with the exception of the portion of the net operating loss of an eligible small business absorbed on the taxpayer's 2003, 2004, and 2005 federal returns.

b. For a taxpayer who made an addition under sub-subdivision (7)b. of this subsection, one-third of the taxpayer's net operating loss absorbed on the taxpayer's 2004, 2005, and 2006 federal returns under section 172(b)(1)(H) or section 810(b)(4) of the Code, with the exception of the portion of the net operating loss of an eligible small business absorbed on the taxpayer's 2004, 2005, and 2006 federal returns.

(9) To the extent a deduction has not been claimed for educator expenses in determining federal adjusted gross income, an eligible educator may deduct an amount not to exceed two hundred fifty dollars ($250.00) paid or incurred in connection with items listed in this subdivision. This deduction is allowed only to the extent the expense has not been claimed under section 162 of the Code for the taxable year. For purposes of this subdivision, the term "eligible educator" has the same meaning as defined in section 62 of the Code, as it existed on December 31, 2011. In the case of a married couple filing a joint return where both spouses are eligible educators, the maximum dollar amount is five hundred dollars ($500.00).

a. Books.

b. Supplies, other than nonathletic supplies for courses of instruction in health or physical education.

c. Computer equipment, including related software and services.

d. Supplementary materials used by the eligible educator in the classroom.

(10) For taxable year 2013, the taxpayer who elects to itemize deductions under G.S. 105-134.6(a2) may deduct the amount that would have been allowed as a charitable deduction under section 170 of the Code had the taxpayer not elected to take the income exclusion under 408(d)(8) of the Code. However, this deduction is not subject to the charitable contribution limitation and carryover provisions under section 170 of the Code, but it is subject to the overall limitation on itemized deductions under section 68 of the Code.

(11) The transitional adjustments provided in Part 1A of this Article shall be made with respect to a shareholder's pro rata share of S Corporation income.

(12) The Secretary may by rule require other adjustments to be made to taxable income as necessary to assure that the transition to the tax changes effective January 1, 1989, will not result in double taxation of income, exemption of otherwise taxable income from taxation under this Division, or double allowance of deductions. (1989, c. 718, s. 2; c. 728, s. 1.4; c. 770, ss. 41.2, 41.3; c. 792, s. 1.1; 1989 (Reg. Sess., 1990), c. 984, s. 4; c. 1002, s. 2; 1991, c. 45, s. 9; c. 453, s. 1; c. 689, ss. 253, 254; 1991 (Reg. Sess., 1992), c. 1007, s. 3; 1993, c. 12, s. 8; c. 443, s. 8; c. 485, s. 9; 1993 (Reg. Sess., 1994), c. 745, s. 7; 1995, c. 17, s. 5; c. 42, ss. 1, 2(a), (b); c. 46, s. 3; c. 370, s. 3; 1996, 2nd Ex. Sess., c. 13, s. 8.1; c. 14, s. 9; 1997-226, s. 3; 1997-328, s. 1; 1997-388, s. 4; 1997-525, s. 1; 1998-98, s. 69; 1998-171, ss. 2, 3; 1998-212, ss. 29A.2(c), 29A.13(a); 1999-333, s. 3; 1999-463, Ex Sess., s. 4.6 (a); 2000-140, ss. 65, 93.1(a); 2001-424, ss. 12.2(b), 34.19(a), (b); 2002-126, ss. 30B.1(a), 30B.1(b), 30C.2(b), 30C.2(d), 30C.4; 2003-284, s. 37A.2; 2005-1, s. 5.7(a); 2005-276, ss. 35.1(e), 39.1(f); 2005-435, s. 55; 2006-17, ss. 2, 3; 2006-66, ss. 24.12(a), 24.18(e); 2006-220, s. 3; 2006-221, s. 27(a); 2007-323, ss. 31.19(a)-(d), 31.24(a); 2007-397, s. 13(c); 2008-107, ss. 28.1(e), (f), (h), 28.25(c), 28.27(b), (c); 2008-134, s. 2(c); 2009-445, s. 43; 2009-451, s. 27A.6(e), (f); 2010-31, s. 31.1(b); 2011-5, ss. 2(c), (d), 3(d), (c); 2011-106, s. 1; 2011-145, s. 31A.1(c); 2011-330, ss. 11, 12(b)-(e), 13, 36; 2012-74, s. 2(a); 2012-79, s. 1.3; 2013-10, ss. 2(c), (d), 3(c), (d), 5(a), (b), 6(a), (b), 7, 8; 2013-316, s. 1.1(b); 2013-414, ss. 5(a), 6(a)-(e), 34(c), 35(a).)

§ 105-134.6A. (Repealed effective January 1, 2014) Adjustments when State decouples from federal accelerated depreciation and expensing.

(a) Special Accelerated Depreciation. - A taxpayer who takes a special accelerated depreciation deduction for that property under section 168(k) or 168(n) of the Code must add to the taxpayer's federal taxable income or adjusted gross income, as appropriate, eighty-five percent (85%) of the amount taken for that year under those Code provisions. For taxable years before 2012, the taxpayer must add the amount to the taxpayer's federal taxable income. For taxable year 2012 and after, the taxpayer must add the amount to the taxpayer's adjusted gross income. A taxpayer is allowed to deduct twenty percent (20%) of the add-back in each of the first five taxable years following the year the taxpayer is required to include the add-back in income.

(b) 2009 Depreciation Exception. - A taxpayer who placed property in service during the 2009 taxable year and whose North Carolina taxable income for the 2009 taxable year reflected a special accelerated depreciation deduction allowed for the property under section 168(k) of the Code must add eighty-five percent (85%) of the amount of the special accelerated depreciation deduction to its federal taxable income for the 2010 taxable year. A taxpayer is allowed to deduct this add-back under subsection (a) of this section as if it were for property placed in service in 2010.

(c) Section 179 Expense. - For purposes of this subdivision, the definition of section 179 property has the same meaning as under section 179 of the Code as of January 2, 2013. A taxpayer who places section 179 property in service during a taxable year listed in the table below must add to the taxpayer's federal taxable income or adjusted gross income, as appropriate, eighty-five percent (85%) of the amount by which the taxpayer's expense deduction under section 179 of the Code exceeds the dollar and investment limitation listed in the table below for that taxable year. For taxable years before 2012, the taxpayer must add the amount to the taxpayer's federal taxable income. For taxable year 2012 and after, the taxpayer must add the amount to the taxpayer's adjusted gross income.

A taxpayer is allowed to deduct twenty percent (20%) of the add-back in each of the first five taxable years following the year the taxpayer is required to include the add-back in income.

Taxable Year of 85% Add-Back	Dollar Limitation	Investment Limitation
2010	$250,000	$800,000
2011	$250,000	$800,000

2012	$250,000	$800,000
2013	$25,000	$125,000

(d) Asset Basis. - The adjustments made in this section do not result in a difference in basis of the affected assets for State and federal income tax purposes, except as modified in subsection (e) of this section.

(e) Bonus Asset Basis. - In the event of an actual or deemed transfer of an asset occurring on or after January 1, 2013, wherein the tax basis of the asset carries over from the transferor to the transferee for federal income tax purposes, the transferee must add any remaining deductions allowed under subsection (a) of this section to the basis of the transferred asset and depreciate the adjusted basis over any remaining life of the asset. Notwithstanding the provisions of subsection (a) of this section, the transferor and any owner in a transferor are not allowed any remaining future bonus depreciation deductions associated with the transferred asset. This subsection applies only to the extent that each transferor or owner in a transferor that added bonus depreciation to its federal taxable income or adjusted gross income associated with the transferred asset certifies in writing to the transferee, that the transferor or owner in a transferor will not take any remaining future bonus depreciation deduction associated with the transferred asset.

(f) Prior Transactions. - For any transaction meeting the requirements of subsection (e) of this section prior to January 1, 2013, the transferor and transferee can make an election to make the basis adjustment allowed in that subsection on the transferee's 2013 tax return, to the extent that the transferor and any owner in a transferor has not taken the bonus depreciation deduction on a prior return and provided that the transferor is not allowed any remaining future bonus depreciation deductions associated with the transferred asset and each transferor or owner in a transferor certifies in writing to the transferee that the transferor or owner in a transferor will not take any remaining deductions allowed under subsection (a) of this section for tax years beginning on or after January 1, 2013, for depreciation associated with the transferred asset. The amount of the basis adjustment under this subsection is limited to the total remaining future bonus depreciation deductions forfeited by the transferor and any owner in the transferor at the time of the transfer.

(g) Tax Basis. - For transactions described in subsection (e) or (f) of this section, adjusted gross income must be increased or decreased to account for any difference in the amount of depreciation, amortization, or gains or losses applicable to property that has been depreciated or amortized by use of a different basis or rate for State income tax purposes than used for federal income tax purposes prior to the effective date of this section.

(h) Definitions. - For purposes of this section, a "transferor" is an individual, partnership, S Corporation, limited liability company, or an estate or trust that does not fully distribute income to its beneficiaries, and an "owner in a transferor" is a partner, shareholder, member, or beneficiary subject to tax under Part 2 or 3 of Article 4 of this Chapter, of a transferor. (S.L. 2013-414, ss. 34(d), 58(b)).

§ 105-134.7. Transitional adjustments.

(a) Repealed by Session Laws 2013-414, s. 6(f), effective for taxable years beginning on or after January 1, 2012.

(1), (2) Repealed by Session Laws 2013-414, s. 6(f), effective for taxable years beginning on or after January 1, 2012.

(3) Recodified as G.S. 105-134.6(b)(24) and (c)(20) by Session Laws 2013-414, s. 6(a) and (c), effective for taxable years beginning on or after January 1, 2012.

(4), (5) Repealed by Session Laws 2013-414, s. 6(f), effective for taxable years beginning on or after January 1, 2012.

(6) Recodified as G.S. 105-134.6(c)(21) by Session Laws 2013-414, s. 6(b), effective for taxable years beginning on or after January 1, 2012.

(7) Recodified as G.S. 105-134.6(b)(11) by Session Laws 2013-414, s. 6(d), effective for taxable years beginning on or after January 1, 2012.

(b) Recodified as G.S. 105-134.6(d)(12) by Session Laws 2013-414, s. 6(e), effective for taxable years beginning on or after January 1, 2012. (1989, c. 728, s. 1.4; 1993, c. 485, s. 10; 1998-98, s. 91;2013-316, s. 1.1(b); 2013-414, s. 6(a)-(f).)

§ 105-134.8. (Repealed effective for taxable years beginning on or after January 1, 2014 - see note) Inventory.

Whenever, in the opinion of the Secretary, it is necessary in order clearly to determine the income of any taxpayer, inventories shall be taken by the taxpayer as prescribed by the Secretary, conforming as nearly as possible to the best accounting practice in the trade or business and most clearly reflecting the income. (1989, c. 728, s. 1.4; 2013-316, s. 1.1(b).)

§§ 105-135 through 105-149: Repealed by Session Laws 1989, c. 728, s. 1.3.

§ 105-150. Repealed by Session Laws 1973, c. 1287, s. 5.

§ 105-151. (Recodified effective for taxable years beginning on or after January 1, 2014) Tax credits for income taxes paid to other states by individuals.

(a) An individual who is a resident of this State is allowed a credit against the taxes imposed by this Part for income taxes imposed by and paid to another state or country on income taxed under this Part, subject to the following conditions:

(1) The credit is allowed only for taxes paid to another state or country on income derived from sources within that state or country that is taxed under its laws irrespective of the residence or domicile of the recipient, except that whenever a taxpayer who is deemed to be a resident of this State under the provisions of this Part is deemed also to be a resident of another state or country under the laws of that state or country, the Secretary may allow a credit against the taxes imposed by this Part for taxes imposed by and paid to the other state or country on income taxed under this Part.

(2) The fraction of the gross income, as calculated under the Code and adjusted as provided in G.S. 105-134.6 and G.S. 105-134.6A, that is subject to income tax in another state or country shall be ascertained, and the North Carolina net income tax before credit under this section shall be multiplied by that fraction. The credit allowed is either the product thus calculated or the income tax actually paid the other state or country, whichever is smaller.

(3) Receipts showing the payment of income taxes to another state or country and a true copy of a return or returns upon the basis of which the taxes

are assessed shall be filed with the Secretary when the credit is claimed. If credit is claimed on account of a deficiency assessment, a true copy of the notice assessing or proposing to assess the deficiency, as well as a receipt showing the payment of the deficiency, shall be filed.

(b) If any taxes paid to another state or country for which a taxpayer has been allowed a credit under this section are at any time credited or refunded to the taxpayer, a tax equal to that portion of the credit allowed for the taxes so credited or refunded is due and payable from the taxpayer and is subject to the penalties and interest provided in Subchapter I of this Chapter. (1939, c. 158, s. 325; 1941, c. 50, s. 5; c. 204, s. 1; 1943, c. 400, s. 4; 1957, c. 1340, s. 4; 1963, c. 1169, s. 2; 1967, c. 1110, s. 3; 1973, c. 476, s. 193; 1989, c. 728, s. 1.5; 1989 (Reg. Sess., 1990), c. 814, s. 17; 1998-98, s. 92; 2013-316, s. 1.1(a); 2013-414, s. 5(b).)

§ 105-151.1. (Repealed effective for taxable years beginning on or after January 1, 2014 - see note) Credit for construction of dwelling units for handicapped persons.

An owner of multifamily rental units located in this State is allowed a credit against the tax imposed by this Part equal to five hundred fifty dollars ($550.00) for each dwelling unit constructed by the owner that conforms to Volume I-C of the North Carolina Building Code for the taxable year within which the construction of the dwelling unit is completed. The credit is allowed only for dwelling units completed during the taxable year that were required to be built in compliance with Volume I-C of the North Carolina Building Code. If the credit allowed by this section exceeds the tax imposed by this Part reduced by all other credits allowed, the excess may be carried forward for the next succeeding year. In order to claim the credit allowed by this section, the taxpayer must file with the income tax return a copy of the occupancy permit on the face of which is recorded by the building inspector the number of units completed during the taxable year that conform to Volume I-C of the North Carolina Building Code. After recording the number of these units on the face of the occupancy permit, the building inspector shall promptly forward a copy of the permit to the Building Accessibility Section of the Department of Insurance. (1973, c. 910, s. 2; 1979, c. 803, ss. 3, 4; 1981, c. 682, s. 17; 1989, c. 728, s. 1.6; 1997-6, s. 4; 1998-98, s. 69; 1998-100, s. 1; 2013-316, s. 1.1(b).)

§ 105-151.2. Repealed by Session Laws 1999-342, s. 1, effective for taxable years beginning on or after January 1, 2000.

§ 105-151.3. Repealed by Session Laws 1983 (Regular Session 1984), c. 1004, s. 2.

§ 105-151.4: Repealed by Session Laws 1989, c. 728, s. 1.8.

§ 105-151.5. Repealed by Session Laws 1999-342, s. 1, effective for taxable years beginning on or after January 1, 2000.

§ 105-151.6: Expired.

§ 105-151.6A: Repealed by Session Laws 1989, c. 728, s. 1.11.

§§ 105-151.7 through 105-151.10: Repealed by Session Laws 1999-342, s. 1, effective for taxable years beginning on or after January 1, 2000.

§ 105-151.11. (Repealed effective for taxable years beginning on or after January 1, 2014 - see note) Credit for child care and certain employment-related expenses.

(a) Credit. - A person who is allowed a credit against federal income tax for a percentage of employment-related expenses under section 21 of the Code shall be allowed as a credit against the tax imposed by this Part an amount equal to the applicable percentage of the employment-related expenses as defined in section 21(b)(2) of the Code. In order to claim the credit allowed by this section, the taxpayer must provide with the tax return the information required by the Secretary.

(a1) Applicable Percentage. - For employment-related expenses that are incurred only with respect to one or more dependents who are seven years old or older and are not physically or mentally incapable of caring for themselves, the applicable percentage is the appropriate percentage in the column labeled "Percentage A" in the table below, based on the taxpayer's adjusted gross income determined under the Code. For employment-related expenses with respect to any other qualifying individual, the applicable percentage is the appropriate percentage in the column labeled "Percentage B" in the table below, based on the taxpayer's adjusted gross income determined under the Code.

Filing Status	Adjusted Gross Income	Percentage A	Percentage B
Head of Household	Up to $20,000	9%	13%
	Over $20,000 up to $32,000	8%	11.5%
	Over $32,000	7%	10%
Surviving Spouse or Joint Return	Up to $25,000	9%	13%
	Over $25,000 up to $40,000	8%	11.5%
	Over $40,000	7%	10%

Filing Status	Income		
Single	Up to $15,000	9%	13%
	Over $15,000 up to $24,000	8%	11.5%
	Over $24,000	7%	10%
Married Filing Separately	Up to $12,500	9%	13%
	Over $12,500 up to $20,000	8%	11.5%
	Over $20,000	7%	10%

(b) Employment Related Expenses. - The amount of employment-related expenses for which a credit may be claimed may not exceed three thousand dollars ($3,000) if the taxpayer's household includes one qualifying individual, as defined in section 21(b)(1) of the Code, and may not exceed six thousand dollars ($6,000) if the taxpayer's household includes more than one qualifying individual. The amount of employment-related expenses for which a credit may be claimed is reduced by the amount of employer-provided dependent care assistance excluded from gross income.

(c) Limitations. - A nonresident or part-year resident who claims the credit allowed by this section shall reduce the amount of the credit by multiplying it by the fraction calculated under G.S. 105-134.5(b) or (c), as appropriate. No credit shall be allowed under this section for amounts deducted in calculating North Carolina taxable income. The credit allowed by this section may not exceed the amount of tax imposed by this Part for the taxable year reduced by the sum of all credits allowable, except for payments of tax made by or on behalf of the taxpayer. (1981, c. 899, s. 1; 1985, c. 656, ss. 8-11; 1989, c. 728, s. 1.16; 1993, c. 432, s. 1; 1998-98, ss. 69, 99; 1998-100, s. 2; 2006-18, s. 9; 2013-316, s. 1.1(b); 2013-414, s. 5(c).)

§ 105-151.12. (Repealed effective for taxable years beginning on or after January 1, 2014 - see note) Credit for certain real property donations.

(a) An individual or pass-through entity that makes a qualified donation of an interest in real property located in North Carolina during the taxable year that is useful for (i) public beach access or use, (ii) public access to public waters or trails, (iii) fish and wildlife conservation, (iv) forestland or farmland conservation, (v) watershed protection, (vi) conservation of natural areas as that term is defined in G.S. 113A-164.3(3), (vii) conservation of natural or scenic river areas as those terms are used in G.S. 113A-34, (viii) conservation of predominantly natural parkland, or (ix) historic landscape conservation is allowed a credit against the tax imposed by this Part equal to twenty-five percent (25%) of the fair market value of the donated property interest. To be eligible for this credit, the interest in property must be donated in perpetuity for one of the qualifying uses listed in this subsection and accepted in perpetuity for the qualifying use for which the property is donated. The person to whom the property is donated must be the State, a local government, or a body that is both organized to receive and administer lands for conservation purposes and qualified to receive charitable contributions under the Code. Lands required to be dedicated pursuant to local governmental regulation or ordinance and dedications made to increase building density levels permitted under a regulation or ordinance are not eligible for this credit.

To support the credit allowed by this section, the taxpayer must file with the income tax return for the taxable year in which the credit is claimed the following:

(1) A certification by the Department of Environment and Natural Resources that the property donated is suitable for one or more of the valid public benefits set forth in this subsection. The certification for a qualified donation made by a pass-through entity must be filed by the pass-through entity.

(2) A self-contained or summary appraisal report as defined in Standards Rule 2-2 in the latest edition of the Uniform Standards of Professional Appraisal Practice as promulgated by the Appraisal Foundation for the property. For fee simple absolute donations of real property, a taxpayer may submit documentation of the county's appraised value of the donated property, as adjusted by the sales assessment ratio, in lieu of an appraisal report.

(a1) Individuals. - The aggregate amount of credit allowed to an individual in a taxable year under this section for one or more qualified donations made during the taxable year, whether made directly or indirectly as owner of a pass-through entity, may not exceed two hundred fifty thousand dollars ($250,000). In the case of property owned by a married couple, if both spouses are required to file North Carolina income tax returns, the credit allowed by this section may be claimed only if the spouses file a joint return. The aggregate amount of credit allowed to a husband and wife filing a joint tax return may not exceed five hundred thousand dollars ($500,000). If only one spouse is required to file a North Carolina income tax return, that spouse may claim the credit allowed by this section on a separate return.

(a2) Pass-Through Entities. - The aggregate amount of credit allowed to a pass-through entity in a taxable year under this section for one or more qualified donations made during the taxable year, whether made directly or indirectly as owner of another pass-through entity, may not exceed five hundred thousand dollars ($500,000). Each individual who is an owner of a pass-through entity is allowed as a credit an amount equal to the owner's allocated share of the credit to which the pass-through entity is eligible under this subsection, not to exceed two hundred fifty thousand dollars ($250,000). Each corporation that is an owner of a pass-through entity is allowed as a credit an amount equal to the owner's allocated share of the credit to which the pass-through entity is eligible under this subsection, not to exceed five hundred thousand dollars ($500,000). If an owner's share of the pass-through entity's credit is limited due to the maximum allowable credit under this section for a taxable year, the pass-through entity and its owners may not reallocate the unused credit among the other owners.

(b) The credit allowed by this section may not exceed the amount of tax imposed by this Part for the taxable year reduced by the sum of all credits allowed, except payments of tax made by or on behalf of the taxpayer.

Any unused portion of this credit may be carried forward for the next succeeding five years.

(c) Repealed by Session Laws 1998-212, s. 29A.13(b).

(d) Repealed by Session Laws 2007-309, s. 2, effective for taxable years beginning on or after January 1, 2007.

(e) In the case of marshland for which a claim has been filed pursuant to G.S. 113-205, the offer of donation must be made before December 31, 2003 to qualify for the credit allowed by this section.

(f) Repealed by Session Laws 2007-309, s. 2, effective for taxable years beginning on or after January 1, 2007. (1983, c. 793, s. 3; 1985, c. 278, s. 2; 1989, c. 716, s. 2; c. 727, s. 218(43); c. 728, s. 1.17; 1989 (Reg. Sess., 1990), c. 869, s. 3; 1991, c. 45, s. 10; c. 453, ss. 2, 4; 1991 (Reg. Sess., 1992), c. 930, s. 21; 1993 (Reg. Sess., 1994), c. 717, s. 4; 1997-226, s. 2; 1997-443, s. 11A.119(a); 1998-98, s. 69; 1998-179, s. 2; 1998-212, s. 29A.13(b), (d); 2001-335, s. 2; 2002-72, s. 15(b); 2004-134, s. 1; 2006-66, s. 24.15(a); 2007-309, s. 2; 2009-445, s. 9(d); 2010-167, s. 5(b); 2013-316, s. 1.1(b).)

§ 105-151.13. (Repealed effective for taxable years beginning on or after January 1, 2014 - see note) Credit for conservation tillage equipment.

(a) A taxpayer who purchases conservation tillage equipment for use in a farming business, including tree farming, shall be allowed as a credit against the tax imposed by this Part an amount equal to twenty-five percent (25%) of the cost of the equipment paid during the taxable year. This credit may not exceed two thousand five hundred dollars ($2,500) for any taxable year. The credit may be claimed only by the first purchaser of the equipment and may not be claimed by a person who purchases the equipment for resale or for use outside this State. This credit may not exceed the amount of tax imposed by this Part for the taxable year reduced by the sum of all credits allowable, except tax payments made by or on behalf of the taxpayer. If the credit allowed by this section exceeds the tax imposed under this Part, the excess may be carried forward for the next succeeding five years. The basis in any equipment for which a credit is allowed under this section shall be reduced by the amount of the credit allowable.

(b)   As used in this section, "conservation tillage equipment" means:

(1)   A planter such as a planter commonly known as a "no-till" planter designed to minimize disturbance of the soil in planting crops or trees, including equipment that may be attached to equipment already owned by the taxpayer; or

(2)   Equipment designed to minimize disturbance of the soil in reforestation site preparation, including equipment that may be attached to equipment already owned by the taxpayer; provided, however, this shall include only those items of equipment generally known as a "KG-Blade", a "drum-chopper", or a "V-Blade".

(c)   In the case of conservation tillage equipment owned jointly by a husband and wife, if both spouses are required to file North Carolina income tax returns, the credit allowed by this section may be claimed only if the spouses file a joint return. If only one spouse is required to file a North Carolina income tax return, that spouse may claim the credit allowed by this section on a separate return. (1983 (Reg. Sess., 1984), c. 969, s. 2; 1989, c. 728, s. 1.18; 1991 (Reg. Sess., 1992), c. 930, s. 22; 1998-98, s. 100; 2013-316, s. 1.1(b).)

§ 105-151.14. (Repealed effective for taxable years beginning on or after January 1, 2014 - see note) Credit for gleaned crop.

(a)   A taxpayer who grows a crop and permits the gleaning of the crop during the taxable year shall be allowed as a credit against the tax imposed by this Part an amount equal to ten percent (10%) of the market price of the quantity of the gleaned crop. This credit may not exceed the amount of tax imposed by this Part for the taxable year reduced by the sum of all credits allowable, except tax payments made by or on behalf of the taxpayer. In order to claim the credit allowed under this section, the taxpayer must add the market price of the gleaned crop to taxable income as provided in G.S. 105-134.6(c). Any unused portion of the credit may be carried forward for the next succeeding five years.

(b) The following definitions apply to this section:

(1) "Gleaning" means the harvesting of a crop that has been donated by the grower to a nonprofit organization which will distribute the crop to individuals or other nonprofit organizations it considers appropriate recipients of the food.

(2) "Market price" means the season average price of the crop as determined by the North Carolina Crop and Livestock Reporting Service in the Department of Agriculture and Consumer Services, or the average price of the crop in the nearest local market for the month in which the crop is gleaned if the Crop and Livestock Reporting Service does not determine the season average price for that crop; and

(3) "Nonprofit organization" means an organization to which charitable contributions are deductible from gross income under the Code. (1983 (Reg. Sess., 1984), c. 1018, s. 2; 1989, c. 728, s. 1.19; 1991, c. 453, s. 3; 1997-261, s. 13; 1998-98, s. 101; 2013-316, s. 1.1(b).)

§ 105-151.15: Repealed by Session Laws 1996, 2nd Extra Session, c. 14, s. 1.

§ 105-151.16: Repealed by Session Laws 1989, c. 728, s. 1.21.

§ 105-151.17: Recodified as § 105-129.8 by Session Laws 1996, 2nd Extra Session, c. 13, s. 3.4.

§ 105-151.18. (Repealed effective for taxable years beginning on or after January 1, 2014 - see note) Credit for the disabled.

(a) Disabled Taxpayer. - A taxpayer who (i) is retired on disability, (ii) at the time of retirement, was permanently and totally disabled, and (iii) claims a federal income tax credit under section 22 of the Code for the taxable year, is allowed as a credit against the tax imposed by this Part an amount equal to one-third of the amount of the federal income tax credit for which the taxpayer is eligible under section 22 of the Code.

(b) Disabled Dependent. - If a dependent or spouse for whom a taxpayer is allowed an exemption under the Code is permanently and totally disabled, the taxpayer is allowed a credit against the tax imposed by this Part. In order to claim the credit allowed by this subsection, the taxpayer must attach to the tax return on which the credit is claimed a statement from a physician or local health department certifying that the dependent or spouse for whom the credit is claimed is permanently and totally disabled, as defined in this section. The amount of the credit allowed is determined as follows: For a taxpayer whose North Carolina adjusted gross income does not exceed the appropriate income amount provided in the table below, based on the taxpayer's filing status, the credit allowed is the appropriate initial credit provided in the table below. For a taxpayer whose North Carolina adjusted gross income does exceed the appropriate income amount, the credit allowed is the appropriate initial credit reduced by four dollars ($4.00) for every one thousand dollars ($1,000) by which the taxpayer's North Carolina adjusted gross income exceeds the appropriate income amount.

Filing Status	Income Amount	Initial Credit
Head of Household	$16,000	$64.00
Surviving Spouse or Joint Return	$20,000	$80.00
Single	$12,000	$48.00
Married Filing Separately	$10,000	$40.00

(c)　　Definitions. - The following definitions apply in this section:

(1)　　North Carolina adjusted gross income. - Adjusted gross income, as determined under the Code, adjusted as provided in G.S. 105-134.6 and G.S. 105-134.6A.

(2)　　Permanently and totally disabled. - Unable to engage in any substantial gainful activity by reason of any medically determinable physical or mental impairment that can be expected to result in death or that has lasted or can be expected to last for a continuous period of not less than 12 months. For the purpose of this section, a minor is permanently and totally disabled if the impact of the impairment on the minor's ability to function is equivalent in severity to that which would make an adult unable to engage in any substantial gainful activity.

(d)   Limitations. - A nonresident or part-year resident who claims the credit allowed by this section shall reduce the amount of the credit by multiplying it by the fraction calculated under G.S. 105-134.5(b) or (c), as appropriate. The credit allowed under this section may not exceed the amount of tax imposed by this Part for the taxable year reduced by the sum of all credits allowable, except payments of tax made by or on behalf of the taxpayer. (1989, c. 728, s. 1.22; 1989 (Reg. Sess., 1990), c. 984, s. 5; 1998-98, ss. 69, 102; 2013-316, s. 1.1(b); 2013-414, s. 7.)

§ 105-151.19: Repealed by Session Laws 1996, 2nd Extra Session, c. 14, s. 2.

§ 105-151.20. (Repealed effective for taxable years beginning on or after January 1, 2014 - see note) Credit or partial refund for tax paid on certain federal retirement benefits.

(a)   Purpose; Definitions. - The purpose of this section is to benefit certain retired federal government workers on account of their public service. The following definitions apply in this section:

(1)   Federal retirement benefits. - Retirement benefits received from one or more federal government retirement plans.

(2)   Net pension tax. - The amount of tax a taxpayer paid under this Part for the 1985, 1986, 1987, and 1988 tax years on federal retirement benefits, without interest, less any part of the tax for which the taxpayer received a credit under this section before 1997 and any part of the tax refunded to the taxpayer before 1997.

(3)   Tax year. - The taxpayer's taxable year beginning on a day in the applicable calendar year.

(b)   Credit. - A taxpayer who received federal retirement benefits during the 1985, 1986, 1987, or 1988 tax year may claim a credit against the tax imposed by this Part equal to the net pension tax on those benefits. The credit allowed under this section shall be taken in equal installments over the taxpayer's first three taxable years beginning on or after January 1, 1996. The credit allowed under this section may not exceed the amount of tax imposed by this Part reduced by the sum of all credits allowed against the tax, except payments of tax made by or on behalf of the taxpayer; any unused portion of a credit installment may be carried forward to the 1999 and 2000 tax years.

(c)   Partial Refund Alternative. - If the amount of tax imposed by this Part on the taxpayer for the taxpayer's 1996 tax year, reduced by the sum of all credits allowed against the tax except payments of tax made by or on behalf of the taxpayer, is less than five percent (5%) of the taxpayer's net pension tax for which credit is allowed, the taxpayer is eligible to elect a partial refund under this subsection in lieu of claiming the credit. The partial refund allowed under this subsection is equal to the lesser of eighty-five percent (85%) of the taxpayer's net pension tax or the reduced amount determined by the Secretary as provided in this subsection. To elect the partial refund, an eligible taxpayer must file with the Secretary on or before April 15, 1997, a written request for a partial refund of the taxpayer's net pension. The Secretary shall calculate from these requests eighty-five percent (85%) of the total amount of net pension tax for which partial refunds have been claimed and, if this sum exceeds the amount in the Federal Retiree Refund Account created in this section, shall allocate the amount in the Account among the eligible taxpayers claiming partial refunds by reducing each taxpayer's claimed refund in proportion to the size of the claimed refund. The Secretary shall remit these partial refunds before January 1, 1998.

(d)   Substantiation; Deceased Taxpayers. - In order to claim a refund or credit under this section, a taxpayer must provide any information required by the Secretary to establish the taxpayer's eligibility for tax benefit and the amount of the tax benefit. In the case of a taxpayer who is deceased, the representative of the taxpayer's estate may claim the refund in the name of the deceased taxpayer and, if the taxpayer does not qualify for a refund, the surviving spouse may claim the deceased taxpayer's credit. If there is no surviving spouse, the representative of the taxpayer's estate may claim the credit in the name of the taxpayer but may not carry forward any unused portion of the credit to the 1999 or 2000 tax year.

(e)   Federal Retiree Accounts. - There are created in the Department of Revenue two special accounts to be known as the Federal Retiree Refund Account and the Federal Retiree Administration Account. Funds in the Federal Retiree Refund Account shall be spent only for partial refunds pursuant to subsection (c) of this section. The Department of Revenue may use funds in the Federal Retiree Administration Account only for the costs of administering this section. Funds in the Federal Retiree Refund Account and the Federal Retiree

Administration Account shall not revert to the General Fund until the Director of the Budget certifies that the Department of Revenue has completed all duties necessary to implement this section, including processing the escheat of refund checks that have not been cashed. (1989 (Reg. Sess., 1990), c. 984, s. 6; 1991, c. 45, s. 11; 1996, 2nd Ex. Sess., c. 19, s. 1; 1997-499, ss. 1, 2; 1998-98, s. 69; 2013-316, s. 1.1(b).)

§ 105-151.21. (Repealed effective for taxable years beginning on or after January 1, 2014 - see note) Credit for property taxes paid on farm machinery.

(a) Credit. - An individual engaged in the business of farming is allowed a credit against the tax imposed by this Part equal to the amount of property taxes the individual paid at par during the taxable year on farm machinery and on attachments and repair parts for farm machinery. In addition, an individual shareholder of an S Corporation engaged in the business of farming is allowed a credit against the tax imposed by this Part equal to the shareholder's pro rata share of the amount of property taxes the S Corporation paid at par during the taxable year on farm machinery and on attachments and repair parts for farm machinery. The total credit allowed under this section may not exceed one thousand dollars ($1,000) for the taxable year and may not exceed the amount of tax imposed by this Part for the taxable year reduced by the sum of all credits allowable, except payments of tax made by or on behalf of the taxpayer. To claim the credit, the taxpayer shall attach to the retur

n a copy of the tax receipt for the property taxes for which credit is claimed. The receipt must indicate that the taxes have been paid and the amount and date of the payment.

(b) Definitions. - The following definitions apply in this section:

(1) Farm machinery. - Machinery exempt from State sales tax under G.S. 105-164.13(1)b.

(2) Property taxes. - The principal amount of taxes levied and assessed by a taxing unit under Subchapter II of this Chapter. The term does not include costs, penalties, interest, or other charges that may be added to the principal amount.

(3) Taxing unit. - Defined in G.S. 105-273.

(c) Adjustment. If a taxing unit gives a taxpayer a credit or refund for any of the property taxes for which the taxpayer claimed a credit under this section, the taxpayer shall notify the Secretary within 90 days. The Secretary shall then recompute the credit allowed under this section and make any resulting adjustment of income tax for the taxable year for which the credit was claimed. (1985, c. 656, s. 13(3); 1987, c. 804, s. 6; 1991, c. 45, s. 14(a); 1998-98, s. 103; 2001-414, s. 11; 2005-276, s. 33.25; 2013-316, s. 1.1(b).)

§ 105-151.22. (Repealed effective for taxable years beginning after January 1, 2014) Credit for North Carolina State Ports Authority wharfage, handling, and throughput charges.

(a) Credit. - A taxpayer whose waterborne cargo is loaded onto or unloaded from an ocean carrier calling at the State-owned port terminal at Wilmington or Morehead City, without consideration of the terms under which the cargo is moved, is allowed a credit against the tax imposed by this Part. The amount of credit allowed is equal to the excess of the wharfage, handling (in or out), and throughput charges assessed on the cargo for the current taxable year over an amount equal to the average of the charges for the current taxable year and the two preceding taxable years. The credit applies to forest products, break-bulk cargo and container cargo, including less-than-container-load cargo, that is loaded onto or unloaded from an ocean carrier calling at either the Wilmington or Morehead City port terminal and to bulk cargo that is loaded onto or unloaded from an ocean carrier calling at the Morehead City port terminal. To obtain the credit, taxpayers must provide to the Secretary a statement from the State Ports Authority certifying the amount of charges for which a credit is claimed and any other information required by the Secretary.

(b) Limitations. - This credit may not exceed fifty percent (50%) of the amount of tax imposed by this Part for the taxable year reduced by the sum of all credits allowable, except tax payments made by or on behalf of the taxpayer. Any unused portion of the credit may be carried forward for the succeeding five years. The maximum cumulative credit that may be claimed by a taxpayer under this section is two million dollars ($2,000,000).

(c) Definitions. - For purposes of this section, the terms "handling" (in or out) and "wharfage" have the meanings provided in the State Ports Tariff Publications, "Wilmington Tariff, Terminal Tariff #6," and "Morehead City Tariff, Terminal Tariff #1." For purposes of this section, the term "throughput" has the same meaning as "wharfage" but applies only to bulk products, both dry and liquid.

(c1) Report. - The Department must include in the economic incentives report required by G.S. 105-256 the following information itemized by taxpayer:

(1)   The number of taxpayers taking a credit allowed in this section.

(2)   The total amount of charges assessed for the taxable year.

(2a)   The amount of the charges attributable to imports.

(2b)   The amount of the charges attributable to exports.

(3)   The total cost to the General Fund of the credits taken.

(d) Sunset. - This section is repealed effective for taxable years beginning on or after January 1, 2014. (1991 (Reg. Sess., 1992), c. 977, s. 2; 1993 (Reg. Sess., 1994), c. 681, s. 2; 1995, c. 17, s. 17; c. 495, ss. 2-4; 1996, 2nd Ex. Sess., c. 18, s. 15.3(b); 1997-443, s. 29.1 (a), (b), (d); 1998-98, s. 69; 2001-517, ss. 1, 2; 2002-99, s. 6(d); 2003-414, s. 8; 2005-429, s. 2.11; 2007-527, s. 26(b); 2008-107, s. 28.5(c), (d); 2010-166, s. 1.15.)

§ 105-151.23: Recodified as §§ 105-129.35 through 105-129.37 by Session Laws 1999-389, s. 6, effective for taxable years beginning on or after January 1, 1999.

§ 105-151.24. (Recodified effective for taxable years beginning on or after January 1, 2014 - see editor's note) Credit for children.

(a) Credit. - An individual who is allowed a federal child tax credit under section 24 of the Code for the taxable year and whose adjusted gross income (AGI), as calculated under the Code, is less than the amount listed below is allowed a credit against the tax imposed by this Part in an amount equal to one hundred dollars ($100.00) for each dependent child for whom the individual is allowed the federal credit for the taxable year:

Filing Status	AGI
Married, filing jointly	$100,000
Head of Household	80,000
Single	60,000
Married, filing separately	50,000.

(b) Limitations. - A nonresident or part-year resident who claims the credit allowed by this section shall reduce the amount of the credit by multiplying it by the fraction calculated under G.S. 105-134.5(b) or (c), as appropriate. The credit allowed under this section may not exceed the amount of tax imposed by this Part for the taxable year reduced by the sum of all credits allowed, except payments of tax made by or on behalf of the taxpayer. (1995, c. 42, s. 3; 1998-98, s. 69; 2001-424, s. 34.20(a); 2002-126, s. 30B.2(a), (b); 2003-284, s. 39B.2; 2013-316, s. 1.1(a).)

§ 105-151.25. (Repealed effective for taxable years beginning on or after January 1, 2014 - see note) Credit for construction of a poultry composting facility.

(a) Credit. - A taxpayer who constructs in this State a poultry composting facility as defined in G.S. 106-549.51 for the composting of whole, unprocessed poultry carcasses from commercial operations in which poultry is raised or produced is allowed as a credit against the tax imposed by this Division an amount equal to twenty-five percent (25%) of the installation, materials, and equipment costs of construction paid during the taxable year. This credit may not exceed one thousand dollars ($1,000) for any single installation. The credit allowed by this section may not exceed the amount of tax imposed by this Division for the taxable year reduced by the sum of all credits allowable, except payments of tax by or on behalf of the taxpayer. The credit allowed by this section does not apply to costs paid with funds provided the taxpayer by a State or federal agency.

(b) Property Owned by the Entirety. - In the case of property owned by the entirety, if both spouses are required to file North Carolina income tax returns, the credit allowed by this section may be claimed only if the spouses file a joint return. If only one spouse is required to file a North Carolina income tax return, that spouse may claim the credit allowed by this section on a separate return. (1995, c. 543, s. 1; 1998-134, ss. 2, 3; 2013-316, s. 1.1(b).)

§ 105-151.26. (Effective for taxable years beginning before January 1, 2012) Credit for charitable contributions by nonitemizers.

A taxpayer who elects the standard deduction under section 63 of the Code for federal tax purposes is allowed as a credit against the tax imposed by this Part an amount equal to seven percent (7%) of the taxpayer's excess charitable contributions. The taxpayer's excess charitable contributions are the amount by which the taxpayer's charitable contributions for the taxable year that would have been deductible under section 170 of the Code if the taxpayer had not elected the standard deduction exceed two percent (2%) of the taxpayer's adjusted gross income as calculated under the Code.

No credit shall be allowed under this section for amounts deducted from gross income in calculating taxable income under the Code or for contributions for which a credit was claimed under G.S. 105-151.12 or G.S. 105-151.14. A nonresident or part-year resident who claims the credit allowed by this section shall reduce the amount of the credit by multiplying it by the fraction calculated under G.S. 105-134.5(b) or (c), as appropriate. The credit allowed under this section may not exceed the amount of tax imposed by this Part for the taxable year reduced by the sum of all credits allowed, except payments of tax made by or on behalf of the taxpayer. (1996, 2nd Ex. Sess., c. 13, s. 7.1; 1998-98, s. 69; 1998-183, s. 1; 2006-66, s. 24.18(d).)

§ 105-151.26. (Effective for taxable years beginning on or after January 1, 2012 and before January 1, 2013) Credit for charitable contributions by nonitemizers.

A taxpayer who elects the standard deduction under G.S. 105-134.6(a2) is allowed as a credit against the tax imposed by this Part an amount equal to seven percent (7%) of the taxpayer's excess charitable contributions. The taxpayer's excess charitable contributions are the amount by which the taxpayer's charitable contributions for the taxable year that would have been deductible under section 170 of the Code if the taxpayer had not elected the standard deduction exceed two percent (2%) of the taxpayer's adjusted gross income.

No credit shall be allowed under this section for contributions for which a credit was claimed under G.S. 105-151.12, 105-151.14, or 151.30 [105-151.30]. A nonresident or part-year resident who claims the credit allowed by this section shall reduce the amount of the credit by multiplying it by the fraction calculated under G.S. 105-134.5(b) or (c), as appropriate. The credit allowed under this section may not exceed the amount of tax imposed by this Part for the taxable year reduced by the sum of all credits allowed, except payments of tax made by or on behalf of the taxpayer. (1996, 2nd Ex. Sess., c. 13, s. 7.1; 1998-98, s. 69; 1998-183, s. 1; 2006-66, s. 24.18(d); 2011-145, s. 31A.1(e); 2011-330, s. 36.)

§ 105-151.26. (Effective for taxable years beginning on or after January 1, 2013, and repealed effective for taxable years beginning on or after January 1, 2014 - see notes) Credit for charitable contributions by nonitemizers.

A taxpayer who elects the standard deduction under G.S. 105-134.6(a2) is allowed as a credit against the tax imposed by this Part an amount equal to seven percent (7%) of the taxpayer's excess charitable contributions. The taxpayer's excess charitable contributions are the amount by which the taxpayer's charitable contributions for the taxable year that would have been deductible under section 170 of the Code if the taxpayer had not elected the standard deduction exceed two percent (2%) of the taxpayer's adjusted gross income. For tax year 2013, the taxpayer's excess charitable contributions also include the amount by which the taxpayer's charitable contributions for the taxable year would have been deductible under section 170 of the Code had the taxpayer not elected to take the income exclusion under section 408(d)(8) of the Code that exceed two percent (2%) of the taxpayer's adjusted gross income. For purposes of computing this tax credit, charitable contributions are not subject to the charitable contribution limitation and carryover provisions under section 170 of the Code.

No credit shall be allowed under this section for contributions for which a credit was claimed under G.S. 105-151.12 or G.S. 105-151.14. A nonresident or part-year resident who claims the credit allowed by this section shall reduce the amount of the credit by multiplying it by the fraction calculated under G.S. 105-134.5(b) or (c), as appropriate. The credit allowed under this section may not exceed the amount of tax imposed by this Part for the taxable year reduced by the sum of all credits allowed, except payments of tax made by or on behalf of the taxpayer. (1996, 2nd Ex. Sess., c. 13, s. 7.1; 1998-98, s. 69; 1998-183, s. 1; 2006-66, s. 24.18(d); 2011-145, s. 31A.1(e); 2011-330, s. 36; 2013-316, s. 1.1(b); 2013-414, s. 37(a).)

§ 105-151.27: Repealed by Session Laws 2001-424, s. 34.21(a), effective for taxable years beginning on or after January 1, 2001.

§ 105-151.28. (Repealed for taxable years beginning on or after January 1, 2014) Credit for premiums paid on long-term care insurance.

(a) Credit. - A taxpayer whose adjusted gross income (AGI), as calculated under the Code, is less than the amount listed in this section is allowed, as a credit against the tax imposed by this Part, an amount equal to fifteen percent (15%) of the premium costs the taxpayer paid during the taxable year on a qualified long-term care insurance contract that offers coverage to either the taxpayer, the taxpayer's spouse, or a dependent for whom the taxpayer was allowed to deduct a personal exemption under section 151(c) of the Code for the taxable year. The credit allowed by this section may not exceed three hundred fifty dollars ($350.00) for each qualified long-term care insurance contract for which a credit is claimed. The credit allowed under this section may not exceed the amount of tax imposed by this Part for the taxable year reduced by the sum of all credits allowed, except payments of tax made by or on behalf of the taxpayer. A nonresident or part-year resident who claims the credit allowed by this subsection shall reduce the amount of the credit by multiplying it by the fraction calculated under G.S. 105-134.5(b) or (c), as appropriate.

Filing Status	AGI
Married, filing jointly	$100,000
Head of Household	80,000
Single	60,000
Married, filing separately	50,000

(b) No Double Benefit. - No credit is allowed for payments that are deducted from, or not included in, the taxpayer's gross income for the taxable year. If the taxpayer claimed a deduction for health insurance costs of self-employed individuals under section 162(l) of the Code for the taxable year, the amount of credit otherwise allowed the taxpayer under this section is reduced by the applicable percentage provided in section 162(l) of the Code. If the taxpayer claimed a deduction for medical care expenses under section 213 of the Code for the taxable year, the taxpayer is not allowed a credit under this section. A taxpayer who claims the credit allowed by this section must provide any information required by the Secretary to demonstrate that the amount paid for premiums for which the credit is claimed was not excluded from the taxpayer's gross income for the taxable year.

(c) Definition. - For purposes of this section, the term "qualified long-term care insurance contract" has the same meaning as defined in section 7702B of the Code.

(d) Sunset. - This section is repealed for taxable years beginning on or after January 1, 2014. (1998-212, s. 29A.6(a); 2007-323, s. 31.5(a); 2012-36, s. 7.)

§ 105-151.29. (Repealed for qualifying expenses occurring on or after January 1, 2015) Credit for qualifying expenses of a production company.

(a) Definitions. - The following definitions apply in this section:

(1) Highly compensated individual. - An individual who directly or indirectly receives compensation in excess of one million dollars ($1,000,000) for personal services with respect to a single production. An individual receives compensation indirectly when a production company pays a personal service company or an employee leasing company that pays the individual.

(2) Live sporting event. - A scheduled sporting competition, game, or race that is not originated by a production company, but originated solely by an amateur, collegiate, or professional organization, institution, or association for live or tape-delayed television or satellite broadcast. A live sporting event does not include commercial advertising, an episodic television series, a television pilot, a music video, a motion picture, or a documentary production in which sporting events are presented through archived historical footage or similar footage taken at least 30 days before it is used.

(3) Production company. - Defined in G.S. 105-164.3.

(4) Qualifying expenses. - The sum of the following amounts spent in this State by a production company in connection with a production, less the amount paid in excess of one million dollars ($1,000,000) to a highly compensated individual:

a. Goods and services leased or purchased. For goods with a purchase price of twenty-five thousand dollars ($25,000) or more, the amount included in qualifying expenses is the purchase price less the fair market value of the good at the time the production is completed.

b. Compensation and wages on which withholding payments are remitted to the Department of Revenue under Article 4A of this Chapter.

c. The cost of production-related insurance coverage obtained on the production. Expenses for insurance coverage purchased from a related member are not qualifying expenses.

d. Employee fringe contributions, including health, pension, and welfare contributions.

e. Per diems, stipends, and living allowances paid for work being performed in this State.

(5) Related member. - Defined in G.S. 105-130.7A.

(b) Credit. - A taxpayer that is a production company and has qualifying expenses of at least two hundred fifty thousand dollars ($250,000) with respect to a production is allowed a credit against the taxes imposed by this Part equal to twenty-five percent (25%) of the production company's qualifying expenses. For the purposes of this section, in the case of an episodic television series, an entire season of episodes is one production. The credit is computed based on all of the taxpayer's qualifying expenses incurred with respect to the production, not just the qualifying expenses incurred during the taxable year.

(b1) Repealed by Session Laws 2009-529, s. 2, effective January 1, 2011.

(c) Pass-Through Entity. - Notwithstanding the provisions of G.S. 105-131.8 and G.S. 105-269.15, a pass-through entity that qualifies for a credit provided in this section does not distribute the credit among any of its owners. The pass-through entity is considered the taxpayer for purposes of claiming a credit allowed by this section. If a return filed by a pass-through entity indicates that the entity is paying tax on behalf of the owners of the entity, a credit allowed under this section does not affect the entity's payment of tax on behalf of its owners.

(d) Return. - A taxpayer may claim a credit allowed by this section on a return filed for the taxable year in which the production activities are completed. The return must state the name of the production, a description of the production, and a detailed accounting of the qualifying expenses with respect to which a credit is claimed. The qualifying expenses are subject to audit by the Secretary before the credit is allowed.

(e) Credit Refundable. - If a credit allowed by this section exceeds the amount of tax imposed by this Part for the taxable year reduced by the sum of all credits allowable, the Secretary must refund the excess to the taxpayer. The refundable excess is governed by the provisions governing a refund of an overpayment by the taxpayer of the tax imposed in this Part. In computing the amount of tax against which multiple credits are allowed, nonrefundable credits are subtracted before refundable credits.

(f) Limitations. - The amount of credit allowed under this section with respect to a production that is a feature film may not exceed twenty million dollars ($20,000,000). No credit is allowed under this section for any production that satisfies one of the following conditions:

(1) It is political advertising.

(2) It is a television production of a news program or live sporting event.

(3) It contains material that is obscene, as defined in G.S. 14-190.1.

(4) It is a radio production.

(g) Substantiation. - A taxpayer allowed a credit under this section must maintain and make available for inspection any information or records required by the Secretary of Revenue. The taxpayer has the burden of proving eligibility for a credit and the amount of the credit. The Secretary may consult with the North Carolina Film Office of the Department of Commerce and the regional film commissions in order to determine the amount of qualifying expenses.

(h) Report. - The Department must include in the economic incentives report required by G.S. 105-256 the following information itemized by taxpayer:

(1)   The location of sites used in a production for which a credit was taken.

(2)   The qualifying expenses for which a credit was taken, classified by whether the expenses were for goods, services, or compensation paid by the production company.

(3)   The number of people employed in the State with respect to credits taken.

(4)   The total cost to the General Fund of the credits taken.

(i)   Repealed by Session Laws 2006-220, s. 4, effective for taxable years beginning on and after January 1, 2007.

(j)   NC Film Office. - To claim a credit under this section, a taxpayer must notify the Division of Tourism, Film, and Sports Development in the Department of Commerce of the taxpayer's intent to claim the production tax credit. The notification must include the title of the production, the name of the production company, a financial contact for the production company, the proposed dates on which the production company plans to begin filming the production, and any other information required by the Division. For productions that have production credits, a taxpayer claiming a credit under this section must acknowledge in the production credits both the North Carolina Film Office and the regional film office responsible for the geographic area in which the filming of the production occurred.

(k)   Sunset. - This section is repealed for qualifying expenses occurring on or after January 1, 2015. (2005-276, s. 39.1(b); 2005-345, ss. 47(c), 47(d); 2006-162, s. 4(b); 2006-220, s. 4; 2007-527, s. 24; 2008-107, s. 28.24(b); 2009-445, s. 8(b); 2009-529, s. 2; 2010-147, s. 2.2; 2010-166, s. 1.16; 2012-194, s. 79.10(b).)

§ 105-151.30. (Repealed for taxable years beginning on or after January 1, 2014) Credit for recycling oyster shells.

(a)   Credit. - A taxpayer who donates oyster shells to the Division of Marine Fisheries of the Department of Environment and Natural Resources is eligible for a credit against the tax imposed by this Part. The amount of the credit is equal to one dollar ($1.00) per bushel of oyster shells donated.

(b) Limitation. - The credit allowed under this section may not exceed the amount of tax imposed by this Part for the taxable year reduced by the sum of all credits allowable, except tax payment made by or on behalf of the taxpayer.

(c) Carryforward. - Any unused portion of a credit allowed in this section may be carried forward for the succeeding five years.

(d) Documentation of Credit. - Upon request, to support the credit allowed by this section, the taxpayer must file with its income tax return, for the taxable year in which the credit is claimed, a certification by the Department of Environment and Natural Resources stating the number of bushels of oyster shells donated by the taxpayer.

(e) No Double Benefit. - A taxpayer who claims a credit under this section must add back to adjusted gross income any amount deducted under G.S. 105-134.6(a2) for the donation of the oyster shells.

(f) Sunset. - This section is repealed effective for taxable years beginning on or after January 1, 2014. (2006-66, s. 24.18(c); 2007-527, s. 9(b); 2010-147, s. 4.2; 2011-330, s. 36; 2012-36, s. 6(b); 2013-414, s. 5(d).)

§ 105-151.31. (Repealed for taxable years beginning on or after January 1, 2014) Earned income tax credit.

(a) Credit. - An individual who claims for the taxable year an earned income tax credit under section 32 of the Code is allowed a credit against the tax imposed by this Part equal to a percentage of the amount of credit the individual qualified for under section 32 of the Code. A nonresident or part-year resident who claims the credit allowed by this section must reduce the amount of the credit by multiplying it by the fraction calculated under G.S. 105-134.5(b) or (c), as appropriate. The percentage is as follows:

(1) For taxable year 2013, four and one-half percent (4.5%).

(2) For all other taxable years, five percent (5%).

(b) Credit Refundable. - If the credit allowed by this section exceeds the amount of tax imposed by this Part for the taxable year reduced by the sum of all credits allowable, the Secretary must refund the excess to the taxpayer. The refundable excess is governed by the provisions governing a refund of an overpayment by the taxpayer of the tax imposed in this Part. Section 3507 of the Code, Advance Payment of Earned Income Credit, does not apply to the credit allowed by this section. In computing the amount of tax against which multiple credits are allowed, nonrefundable credits are subtracted before refundable credits.

(c) Sunset. - This section is repealed effective for taxable years beginning on or after January 1, 2014. (2007-323, s. 31.4(a); 2008-107, s. 28.9(a); 2012-36, s. 8; 2013-10, s. 9.)

§ 105-151.32. (Repealed for taxable years beginning on or after January 1, 2014) Credit for adoption expenses.

(a) Credit. - An individual who is allowed a federal adoption tax credit under section 36C of the Code for the taxable year is allowed a credit against the tax imposed by this Part. The credit is equal to a percentage of the amount of credit allowed under section 36C of the Code. The percentage is as follows:

(1) For taxable year 2013, thirty percent (30%).

(2) For all other taxable years, fifty percent (50%).

(b) Limitations. - A nonresident or part-year resident who claims the credit allowed by this section shall reduce the amount of the credit by multiplying it by the fraction calculated under G.S. 105-134.5(b) or (c), as appropriate. The credit allowed under this section may not exceed the amount of tax imposed by this Part for the taxable year reduced by the sum of all credits allowed, except payments of tax made by or on behalf of the taxpayer. Any unused portion of this credit may be carried forward for the next succeeding five years.

(c) Sunset. - This section is repealed effective for taxable years beginning on or after January 1, 2014. (2007-323, s. 31.6(a); 2012-36, s. 9; 2013-10, s. 10.)

§ 105-151.33. (Repealed effective for taxable years beginning on or after January 1, 2014 - see note) Education expenses credit.

(a) Credit. - A taxpayer is allowed a credit against the tax imposed by this Part for each of the taxpayer's eligible dependent children who is a resident of this State and who for one or two semesters during the taxable year is enrolled in grades kindergarten through 12 in a nonpublic school or in a public school at which tuition is charged in accordance with G.S. 115C-366.1. As used in this section, the term "eligible dependent child" means a child who meets all of the following criteria:

(1) Is a child with a disability as defined by G.S. 115C-106.3(1).

(2) Was determined to require an individualized education program as defined by G.S. 115C-106.3(8).

(3) Receives special education or related services on a daily basis.

(4) Is a child for whom the taxpayer is entitled to deduct a personal exemption under section 151(c) of the Code for the taxable year.

For the initial eligibility for the tax credit, for at least the preceding two semesters, the eligible dependent child shall have been either (i) enrolled in a public school or (ii) receiving special education or related services through the public schools as a preschool child with a disability as defined by G.S. 115C-106.3(17). An eligible dependent child shall be reevaluated every three years by the local educational agency in order to verify that the child continues to be a child with a disability as defined by G.S. 115C-106.3(1).

(b) Amount. - The credit is equal to the amount the taxpayer paid for tuition and special education and related services expenses, not to exceed three thousand dollars ($3,000) per semester. For home schools, as defined in G.S. 115C-563(a), the credit is equal to the amount the taxpayer paid for special education and related services expenses, not to exceed three thousand dollars ($3,000) per semester.

(c) Semesters. - For the purposes of this section, there are two semesters during each taxable year. The spring semester is the first six months of the taxable year, and the fall semester is the second six months of the taxable year. An eligible dependent child is enrolled in a school for a semester if the eligible dependent child is enrolled in that school for more than 70 days during that semester.

(d) Disqualification. - A taxpayer may not qualify for a credit for any semester during which the taxpayer's eligible dependent child for whom the credit would otherwise be claimed met any of the following conditions:

(1) Was placed in a nonpublic school or facility by a public agency at public expense.

(2) Spent any time enrolled as a full-time student taking at least 12 hours of academic credit in a postsecondary educational institution.

(3) Was 22 years or older during the entire semester.

(4) Graduated from high school prior to the end of the semester.

(e) Reduction of Credit. - The amount of the credit is reduced for any semester in which the eligible dependent child spent any time enrolled in a public school. The amount of the reduction is a percentage equal to the percentage of the semester that the eligible dependent child spent enrolled in a public school.

(f) Information. - In order to claim the credit allowed by this section, the taxpayer shall provide, when requested, the following to the Secretary:

(1) The name, address, and social security number of each eligible dependent child for whom the credit is claimed and the name and address of the school or schools in which the eligible dependent child was enrolled for more than 70 days each semester.

(2) The taxpayer's certification that the eligible dependent child did not meet any of the disqualifying conditions set out in this section.

(3) The name of the local school administrative unit in which the eligible dependent child resides.

(4) The amount of tuition paid to a public school at which tuition is charged in accordance with G.S. 115C-366.1 for each semester the eligible dependent child for whom the credit is claimed was enrolled in the school.

(5) The eligibility determination that the eligible dependent child is a child with a disability who requires special education and related services.

(6) A listing of the tuition and special education and related services expenses on which the amount of the credit is based.

(7) For home schools as defined in G.S. 115C-563(a), a listing of the special education and related services expenses on which the amount of the credit is based.

(g) Carryforward. - The credit allowed under this section may not exceed the amount of tax imposed by this Part reduced by the sum of all credits allowed against the tax, except payments of tax made by or on behalf of the taxpayer. Any unused portion of the credit may be carried forward for the succeeding three years.

(h) Transfer. - At the end of each fiscal year, the Secretary shall transfer to the Fund for Special Education and Related Services established under G.S. 115C-472.15 from the net individual income tax collections under G.S. 105-134.2 an amount equal to two thousand dollars ($2,000) multiplied by the number of credits taken under this section during the fiscal year.

(i) Definitions. - The following definitions apply in this section:

(1) "Related services" is as defined in The Individuals with Disabilities Education Improvement Act, 20 U.S.C. § 1400, et seq., (2004), as amended, and federal regulations adopted under this act.

(2) "Special education" means specially designed instruction to meet the unique needs of a child with a disability. The term includes instruction in physical education and instruction conducted in a classroom, the home, a hospital, or institution, and other settings. (2011-395, ss. 1, 2; 2013-316, s. 1.1(b); 2013-364, s. 2.)

§ 105-152. (Recodified for taxable years beginning on or after January 1, 2014 - see editor's note) Income tax returns.

(a) Who Must File. - The following individuals shall file with the Secretary an income tax return under affirmation:

(1) Every resident required to file an income tax return for the taxable year under the Code and every nonresident who (i) derived gross income from North

Carolina sources during the taxable year attributable to the ownership of any interest in real or tangible personal property in this State or derived from a business, trade, profession, or occupation carried on in this State and (ii) is required to file an income tax return for the taxable year under the Code.

(2) Repealed by Session Laws 1991 (Reg. Sess., 1992), c. 930, s. 1.

(3) Any individual whom the Secretary believes to be liable for a tax under this Part, when so notified by the Secretary and requested to file a return.

(b) Taxpayer Deceased or Unable to Make Return. - If the taxpayer is unable to file the income tax return, the return shall be filed by a duly authorized agent or by a guardian or other person charged with the care of the person or property of the taxpayer. If an individual who was required to file an income tax return for the taxable year while living has died before making the return, the administrator or executor of the estate shall file the return in the decedent's name and behalf, and the tax shall be levied upon and collected from the estate.

(c) Information Required With Return. - The income tax return shall show the adjusted gross income and adjustments required by this Part and any other information the Secretary requires. The Secretary may require some or all individuals required to file an income tax return to attach to the return a copy of their federal income tax return for the taxable year. The Secretary may require a taxpayer to provide the Department with copies of any other return the taxpayer has filed with the Internal Revenue Service and to verify any information in the return.

(d) Secretary May Require Additional Information. - When the Secretary has reason to believe that any taxpayer conducts a trade or business in a way that directly or indirectly distorts the taxpayer's adjusted gross income or North Carolina taxable income, the Secretary may require any additional information for the proper computation of the taxpayer's adjusted gross income and North Carolina taxable income. In computing the taxpayer's adjusted gross income and North Carolina taxable income, the Secretary shall consider the fair profit that would normally arise from the conduct of the trade or business.

(e) Joint Returns. - A husband and wife whose federal taxable income is determined on a joint federal return shall file a single income tax return jointly if each spouse either is a resident of this State or has North Carolina taxable income and may file a single income tax return jointly if one spouse is not a resident and has no North Carolina taxable income. Except as otherwise provided in this Part, a wife and husband filing jointly are treated as one taxpayer for the purpose of determining the tax imposed by this Part. A husband and wife filing jointly are jointly and severally liable for the tax imposed by this Part reduced by the sum of all credits allowable including tax payments made by or on behalf of the husband and wife. However, if a spouse qualifies for relief of liability for federal tax attributable to a substantial understatement by the other spouse pursuant to section 6015 of the Code, that spouse is not liable for the corresponding tax imposed by this Part attributable to the same substantial understatement by the other spouse. A wife and husband filing jointly have expressly agreed that if the amount of the payments made by them with respect to the taxes for which they are liable, including withheld and estimated taxes, exceeds the total of the taxes due, refund of the excess may be made payable to both spouses jointly or, if either is deceased, to the survivor alone.

(f)   Repealed by Session Laws 1991 (Reg. Sess., 1992), c. 930, s. 1. (1939, c. 158, s. 326; 1941, c. 50, s. 5; 1943, c. 400, s. 4; 1945, c. 708, s. 4; 1951, c. 643, s. 4; 1957, c. 1340, s. 4; 1967, c. 1110, s. 3; 1973, c. 476, s. 193; c. 903, s. 1; c. 1287, s. 5; 1977, c. 315; 1989, c. 728, s. 1.23; 1991 (Reg. Sess., 1992), c. 930, s. 1; 1998-98, ss. 69, 104; 1999-337, s. 25; 2006-66, s. 24.11(a); 2012-79, s. 2.5; 2013-316, s. 1.1(a); 2013-414, s. 5(e).)

§ 105-152.1: Repealed by Session Laws 1991 (Regular Session, 1992), c. 930, s. 12.

§ 105-153. Repealed by Session Laws 1967, c. 1110, s. 3.

§ 105-153.1. (Effective for taxable years beginning on or after January 1, 2014) Short title.

This Part of the income tax Article shall be known as the Individual Income Tax Act. (1967, c. 1110, s. 3; 1989, c. 728, s. 1.1; 1998-98, ss. 44, 68; 2013-316, s. 1.1(a).)

§ 105-153.2. (Effective for taxable years beginning on or before January 1, 2014) Purpose.

The general purpose of this Part is to impose a tax for the use of the State government upon the taxable income collectible annually:

(1) Of every resident of this State.

(2) Of every nonresident individual deriving income from North Carolina sources attributable to the ownership of any interest in real or tangible personal property in this State, deriving income from a business, trade, profession, or occupation carried on in this State, or deriving income from gambling activities in this State. (1939, c. 158, s. 301; 1967, c. 1110, s. 3; 1989, c. 728, s. 1.2; 1998-98, s. 69; 2005-276, s. 31.1(dd), (jj); 2005-344, s. 10.3; 2006-259, s. 8(j); 2006-264, s. 91(a); 2013-316, s. 1.1(a).)

§ 105-153.3. (Effective for taxable years beginning on or after January 1, 2014) Definitions.

The following definitions apply in this Part:

(1) Adjusted gross income. - Defined in section 62 of the Code.

(2) Code. - Defined in G.S. 105-228.90.

(3) Department. - The Department of Revenue.

(4) Educational institution. - An educational institution that normally maintains a regular faculty and curriculum and normally has a regularly organized body of students in attendance at the place where its educational activities are carried on.

(5) Fiscal year. - Defined in section 441(e) of the Code.

(6) Gross income. - Defined in section 61 of the Code.

(7) Head of household. - Defined in section 2(b) of the Code.

(8) Individual. - A human being.

(9) Limited liability company. - Either a domestic limited liability company organized under Chapter 57D of the General Statutes or a foreign limited liability company authorized by that Chapter to transact business in this State that is classified for federal income tax purposes as a partnership. As applied to a

limited liability company that is a partnership under this Part, the term "partner" means a member of the limited liability company.

(10) Married individual. - An individual who is married and is considered married as provided in section 7703 of the Code.

(11) Nonresident individual. - An individual who is not a resident of this State.

(12) North Carolina taxable income. - Defined in G.S. 105-153.4.

(13) Partnership. - A domestic partnership, a foreign partnership, or a limited liability company.

(14) Person. - Defined in G.S. 105-228.90.

(15) Resident. - An individual who is domiciled in this State at any time during the taxable year or who resides in this State during the taxable year for other than a temporary or transitory purpose. In the absence of convincing proof to the contrary, an individual who is present within the State for more than 183 days during the taxable year is presumed to be a resident, but the absence of an individual from the state for more than 183 days raises no presumption that the individual is not a resident. A resident who removes from the State during a taxable year is considered a resident until he has both established a definite domicile elsewhere and abandoned any domicile in this State. The fact of marriage does not raise any presumption as to domicile or residence.

(16) S Corporation. - Defined in G.S. 105-131(b).

(17) Secretary. - The Secretary of Revenue.

(18) Taxable year. - Defined in section 441(b) of the Code.

(19) Taxpayer. - An individual subject to the tax imposed by this Part.

(20) This State. - The State of North Carolina. (1989, c. 728, s. 1.4; c. 792, s. 1.2; 1989 (Reg. Sess., 1990), c. 814, s. 15; c. 981, s. 5; 1991, c. 689, s. 252; 1991 (Reg. Sess., 1992), c. 922, s. 6; 1993, c. 12, s. 7; c. 354, s. 13; 1996, 2nd Ex. Sess., c. 13, s. 8.2; 1998-98, ss. 9, 69; 2011-145, s. 31A.1(a); 2011-330, s. 12(a); 2013-157, s. 28; 2013-316, s. 1.1(a), (c); 2013-414, s. 58(c).)

§ 105-153.4. North Carolina taxable income defined.

(a) Residents. - For an individual who is a resident of this State, the term "North Carolina taxable income" means the taxpayer's adjusted gross income as modified in G.S. 105-153.5 and G.S. 105-153.6 and G.S. 105-134.6A.

(b) Nonresidents. - For a nonresident individual, the term "North Carolina taxable income" means the taxpayer's adjusted gross income as modified in G.S. 105-153.5 and G.S. 105-153.6 and G.S. 105-134.6A, multiplied by a fraction the denominator of which is the taxpayer's gross income as modified in G.S. 105-153.5 and G.S. 105-153.6 and G.S. 105-134.6A, and the numerator of which is the amount of that gross income, as modified, that is derived from North Carolina sources and is attributable to the ownership of any interest in real or tangible personal property in this State, is derived from a business, trade, profession, or occupation carried on in this State, or is derived from gambling activities in this State.

(c) Part-year Residents. - If an individual was a resident of this State for only part of the taxable year, having moved into or removed from the State during the year, the term "North Carolina taxable income" has the same meaning as in subsection (b) of this section except that the numerator includes gross income, as modified under G.S. 105-153.5 and G.S. 105-153.6 and G.S. 105-134.6A, derived from all sources during the period the individual was a resident.

(d) S Corporations and Partnerships. - In order to calculate the numerator of the fraction provided in subsection (b) of this section, the amount of a shareholder's pro rata share of S Corporation income that is includable in the numerator is the shareholder's pro rata share of the S Corporation's income attributable to the State, as defined in G.S. 105-131(b)(4). In order to calculate the numerator of the fraction provided in subsection (b) of this section for a member of a partnership or other unincorporated business that has one or more nonresident members and operates in one or more other states, the amount of the member's distributive share of income of the business that is includable in the numerator is determined by multiplying the total net income of the business by the ratio ascertained under the provisions of G.S. 105-130.4. As used in this subsection, total net income means the entire gross income of the business less all expenses, taxes, interest, and other deductions allowable under the Code that were incurred in the operation of the business.

(e) Tax Year. - A taxpayer must compute North Carolina taxable income on the basis of the taxable year used in computing the taxpayer's income tax liability under the Code. (1989, c. 728, s. 1.4; 1995, c. 17, s. 4; 2005-276, s. 31.1(aa); 2005-344, s. 10.4; 2011-145, s. 31A.1(b); 2012-79, s. 1.2; 2013-316, ss. 1.1(a), 1.3(c); 2013-414, s. 55.)

§ 105-153.5. (Effective for taxable years beginning on or after January 1, 2014) Modifications to adjusted gross income.

(a) Deduction Amount. - In calculating North Carolina taxable income, a taxpayer may deduct from adjusted gross income either the standard deduction amount provided in subdivision (1) of this subsection or the itemized deduction amount provided in subdivision (2) of this subsection that the taxpayer claimed under the Code. In the case of a married couple filing separate returns, a taxpayer may not deduct the standard deduction amount if the taxpayer or the taxpayer's spouse claims the itemized deductions amount:

(1) Standard deduction amount. - An amount equal to the amount listed in the table below based on the taxpayer's filing status:

Filing Status	Standard Deduction
Married, filing jointly	$15,000
Head of Household	12,000
Single	7,500
Married, filing separately	7,500.

(2) Itemized deduction amount. - An amount equal to the sum of the items listed in this subdivision. The amounts allowed under this subdivision are not subject to the overall limitation on itemized deductions under section 68 of the Code:

a. The amount allowed as a deduction for charitable contributions under section 170 of the Code for that taxable year.

b. The amount allowed as a deduction for interest paid or accrued during the taxable year under section 163(h) of the Code with respect to any qualified residence plus the amount claimed by the taxpayer as a deduction for property taxes paid or accrued on real estate under section 164 of the Code for that taxable year. The amount allowed under this sub-subdivision may not exceed twenty thousand dollars ($20,000).

(b) Other Deductions. - In calculating North Carolina taxable income, a taxpayer may deduct from the taxpayer's adjusted gross income any of the following items that are included in the taxpayer's adjusted gross income:

(1) Interest upon the obligations of any of the following:

a. The United States or its possessions.

b. This State, a political subdivision of this State, or a commission, an authority, or another agency of this State or of a political subdivision of this State.

c. A nonprofit educational institution organized or chartered under the laws of this State.

(2) Gain from the disposition of obligations issued before July 1, 1995, to the extent the gain is exempt from tax under the laws of this State.

(3) Benefits received under Title II of the Social Security Act and amounts received from retirement annuities or pensions paid under the provisions of the Railroad Retirement Act of 1937.

(4) Refunds of State, local, and foreign income taxes included in the taxpayer's gross income.

(5) The amount received during the taxable year from one or more State, local, or federal government retirement plans to the extent the amount is exempt from tax under this Part pursuant to a court order in settlement of any of the following cases:

a. Bailey v. State, 92 CVS 10221, 94 CVS 6904, 95 CVS 6625, 95 CVS 8230.

b. Emory v. State, 98 CVS 0738.

c. Patton v. State, 95 CVS 04346.

(6) Income that meets both of the following requirements:

a. Is earned or received by an enrolled member of a federally recognized Indian tribe.

b. Is derived from activities on a federally recognized Indian reservation while the member resides on the reservation. Income from intangibles having a situs on the reservation and retirement income associated with activities on the reservation are considered income derived from activities on the reservation.

(7) The amount by which the basis of property under this Article exceeds the basis of the property under the Code, in the year the taxpayer disposes of the property.

(8) The amount allowed as a deduction under G.S. 105-153.6 as a result of an add-back for federal accelerated depreciation and expensing.

(9) (Effective for taxable years beginning on or after January 1, 2015) The amount paid to the taxpayer during the taxable year from the Eugenics Sterilization Compensation Fund as compensation to a qualified recipient under the Eugenics Asexualization and Sterilization Compensation Program under Part 30 of Article 9 of Chapter 143B of the General Statutes. This subdivision expires for taxable years beginning on or after January 1, 2016.

(c) Additions. - In calculating North Carolina taxable income, a taxpayer must add to the taxpayer's adjusted gross income any of the following items that are not included in the taxpayer's adjusted gross income:

(1) Interest upon the obligations of states other than this State, political subdivisions of those states, and agencies of those states and their political subdivisions.

(2) The amount by which a shareholder's share of S Corporation income is reduced under section 1366(f)(2) of the Code for the taxable year by the amount of built-in gains tax imposed on the S Corporation under section 1374 of the Code.

(3) The amount by which the basis of property under the Code exceeds the basis of the property under this Article, in the year the taxpayer disposes of the property.

(4) The amount excluded from gross income under section 199 of the Code.

(5) The amount required to be added under G.S. 105-153.6 when the State decouples from federal accelerated depreciation and expensing.

(d) S Corporations. - Each shareholder's pro rata share of an S Corporation's income is subject to the adjustments provided in this section and in G.S. 105-153.6. (2013-316, s. 1.1(d); 2013-360, s. 6.18(b).)

§ 105-153.6. (Effective for taxable years beginning on or after January 1, 2014) Adjustments when State decouples from federal accelerated depreciation and expensing.

(a) Special Accelerated Depreciation. - A taxpayer who takes a special accelerated depreciation deduction for that property under section 168(k) or 168(n) of the Code must add to the taxpayer's federal taxable income or adjusted gross income, as appropriate, eighty-five percent (85%) of the amount taken for that year under those Code provisions. For taxable years before 2012, the taxpayer must add the amount to the taxpayer's federal taxable income. For taxable year 2012 and after, the taxpayer must add the amount to the taxpayer's adjusted gross income. A taxpayer is allowed to deduct twenty percent (20%) of the add-back in each of the first five taxable years following the year the taxpayer is required to include the add-back in income.

(b) 2009 Depreciation Exception. - A taxpayer who placed property in service during the 2009 taxable year and whose North Carolina taxable income for the 2009 taxable year reflected a special accelerated depreciation deduction allowed for the property under section 168(k) of the Code must add eighty-five percent (85%) of the amount of the special accelerated depreciation deduction to its federal taxable income for the 2010 taxable year. A taxpayer is allowed to deduct this add-back under subsection (a) of this section as if it were for property placed in service in 2010.

(c) Section 179 Expense. - For purposes of this subdivision, the definition of section 179 property has the same meaning as under section 179 of the Code as of January 2, 2013. A taxpayer who places section 179 property in service during a taxable year listed in the table below must add to the taxpayer's federal taxable income or adjusted gross income, as appropriate, eighty-five percent (85%) of the amount by which the taxpayer's expense deduction under section 179 of the Code exceeds the dollar and investment limitation listed in the table below for that taxable year. For taxable years before 2012, the taxpayer must add the amount to the taxpayer's federal taxable income. For taxable year 2012 and after, the taxpayer must add the amount to the taxpayer's adjusted gross income.

A taxpayer is allowed to deduct twenty percent (20%) of the add-back in each of the first five taxable years following the year the taxpayer is required to include the add-back in income.

Taxable Year of 85% Add-Back	Dollar Limitation	Investment Limitation
2010	$250,000	$800,000
2011	$250,000	$800,000
2012	$250,000	$800,000
2013	$25,000	$125,000

(d)   Asset Basis. - The adjustments made in this section do not result in a difference in basis of the affected assets for State and federal income tax purposes, except as modified in subsection (e) of this section.

(e)   Bonus Asset Basis. - In the event of an actual or deemed transfer of an asset occurring on or after January 1, 2013, wherein the tax basis of the asset carries over from the transferor to the transferee for federal income tax purposes, the transferee must add any remaining deductions allowed under subsection (a) of this section to the basis of the transferred asset and depreciate the adjusted basis over any remaining life of the asset. Notwithstanding the provisions of subsection (a) of this section, the transferor and any owner in a transferor are not allowed any remaining future bonus depreciation deductions associated with the transferred asset. This subsection applies only to the extent that each transferor or owner in a transferor that added bonus depreciation to its federal taxable income or adjusted gross income associated with the transferred asset certifies in writing to the transferee, that the transferor or owner in a transferor will not take any remaining future bonus depreciation deduction associated with the transferred asset.

(f) Prior Transactions. - For any transaction meeting the requirements of subsection (e) of this section prior to January 1, 2013, the transferor and transferee can make an election to make the basis adjustment allowed in that subsection on the transferee's 2013 tax return, to the extent that the transferor and any owner in a transferor has not taken the bonus depreciation deduction on a prior return and provided that the transferor is not allowed any remaining future bonus depreciation deductions associated with the transferred asset and each transferor or owner in a transferor certifies in writing to the transferee that the transferor or owner in a transferor will not take any remaining deductions allowed under subsection (a) of this section for tax years beginning on or after January 1, 2013, for depreciation associated with the transferred asset. The amount of the basis adjustment under this subsection is limited to the total remaining future bonus depreciation deductions forfeited by the transferor and any owner in the transferor at the time of the transfer.

(g) Tax Basis. - For transactions described in subsection (e) or (f) of this section, adjusted gross income must be increased or decreased to account for any difference in the amount of depreciation, amortization, or gains or losses applicable to property that has been depreciated or amortized by use of a different basis or rate for State income tax purposes than used for federal income tax purposes prior to the effective date of this section.

(h) Definitions. - For purposes of this section, a "transferor" is an individual, partnership, S Corporation, limited liability company, or an estate or trust that does not fully distribute income to its beneficiaries, and an "owner in a transferor" is a partner, shareholder, member, or beneficiary subject to tax under Part 2 or 3 of Article 4 of this Chapter of a transferor. (2013-316, s. 1.1(d); 2013-414, s. 58(a).)

§ 105-153.7. (Effective for taxable years beginning on or after January 1, 2014) Individual income tax imposed.

(a) (Effective for taxable years beginning on or after January 1, 2014 and before January 1, 2015) Tax. - A tax is imposed for each taxable year on the North Carolina taxable income of every individual. The tax shall be levied, collected, and paid annually. The tax is five and eight-tenths percent (5.8%) of the taxpayer's North Carolina taxable income.

(a) (Effective for taxable years beginning on or after January 1, 2015) Tax. - A tax is imposed for each taxable year on the North Carolina taxable income of every individual. The tax shall be levied, collected, and paid annually. The tax is five and seventy-five hundredths percent (5.75%) of the taxpayer's North Carolina taxable income.

(b) Withholding Tables. - The Secretary may provide tables that compute the amount of tax due for a taxable year under this Part. The tables do not apply to an individual who files a return under section 443(a)(1) of the Code for a period of less than 12 months due to a change in the individual's annual accounting period or to an estate or trust. (2013-316, s. 1.1(d), 1.2(a).)

§ 105-153.8. (Effective for taxable years beginning on or after January 1, 2014) Income tax returns.

(a) Who Must File. - The following individuals must file with the Secretary an income tax return under affirmation:

(1) Every resident required to file an income tax return for the taxable year under the Code.

(2) Every nonresident individual who meets all of the following requirements:

a. Receives during the taxable year gross income that is derived from North Carolina sources and is attributable to the ownership of any interest in real or tangible personal property in this State, is derived from a business, trade, profession, or occupation carried on in this State, or is derived from gambling activities in this State.

b. Is required to file an income tax return for the taxable year under the Code.

(3) Any individual whom the Secretary believes to be liable for a tax under this Part, when so notified by the Secretary and requested to file a return.

(b) Taxpayer Deceased or Unable to Make Return. - If a taxpayer is unable to file an income tax return, a duly authorized agent of the taxpayer or a guardian or other person charged with the care of the person or property of the taxpayer must file the return. If an individual who was required to file an income tax return for the taxable year while living has died before making the return, the administrator or executor of the estate must file the return in the decedent's name and behalf, and the tax is payable by the estate.

(c) Information Required With Return. - The income tax return must show the adjusted gross income and modifications required by this Part, and any other information the Secretary requires. The Secretary may require some or all individuals required to file an income tax return to attach to the return a copy of their federal income tax return for the taxable year. The Secretary may require a taxpayer to provide the Department with copies of any other return the taxpayer has filed with the Internal Revenue Service and to verify any information in the return.

(d) Secretary May Require Additional Information. - When the Secretary has reason to believe that any taxpayer conducts a trade or business in a way that directly or indirectly distorts the taxpayer's adjusted gross income or North Carolina taxable income, the Secretary may require any additional information for the proper computation of the taxpayer's adjusted gross income and North Carolina taxable income. In computing the taxpayer's adjusted gross income and North Carolina taxable income, the Secretary must consider the fair profit that would normally arise from the conduct of the trade or business.

(e) Joint Returns. - A husband and wife whose adjusted gross income is determined on a joint federal return must file a single income tax return jointly if each spouse either is a resident of this State or has North Carolina taxable income and may file a single income tax return jointly if one spouse is not a resident and has no North Carolina taxable income. Except as otherwise provided in this Part, a wife and husband filing jointly are treated as one taxpayer for the purpose of determining the tax imposed by this Part. A husband and wife filing jointly are jointly and severally liable for the tax imposed by this Part reduced by the sum of all credits allowable including tax payments made by or on behalf of the husband and wife. However, if a spouse qualifies for relief of liability for federal tax attributable to a substantial understatement by the other spouse pursuant to section 6015 of the Code, that spouse is not liable for the corresponding tax imposed by this Part attributable to the same substantial understatement by the other spouse. A wife and husband filing jointly have expressly agreed that if the amount of the payments made by them with respect to the taxes for which they are liable, including withheld and estimated taxes, exceeds the total of the taxes due, refund of the excess may be made payable to both spouses jointly or, if either is deceased, to the survivor alone. (1939, c. 158, s. 326; 1941, c. 50, s. 5; 1943, c. 400, s. 4; 1945, c. 708, s. 4; 1951, c. 643, s. 4; 1957, c. 1340, s. 4; 1967, c. 1110, s. 3; 1973, c. 476, s. 193; c. 903, s. 1; c. 1287, s. 5; 1977, c. 315; 1989, c. 728, s. 1.23; 1991 (Reg. Sess., 1992), c. 930, s. 1; 1998-98, ss. 69, 104; 1999-337, s. 25; 2006-66, s. 24.11(a); 2012-79, s. 2.5; 2013-316, ss. 1.1(a), 1.3(d).)

§ 105-153.9. (Effective for taxable years beginning on or after January 1, 2014) Tax credits for income taxes paid to other states by individuals.

(a) An individual who is a resident of this State is allowed a credit against the taxes imposed by this Part for income taxes imposed by and paid to another state or country on income taxed under this Part, subject to the following conditions:

(1) The credit is allowed only for taxes paid to another state or country on income that is derived from sources within that state or country and is taxed under its laws irrespective of the residence or domicile of the recipient, except that whenever a taxpayer who is considered a resident of this State under this Part is considered a resident of another state or country under the laws of that state or country, the Secretary may allow a credit against the taxes imposed by this Part for taxes imposed by and paid to the other state or country on income taxed under this Part.

(2) The fraction of the gross income, as modified as provided in G.S. 105-134.6A, G.S. 105-153.5, and G.S. 105-153.6, that is subject to income tax in another state or country shall be ascertained, and the North Carolina net income tax before credit under this section shall be multiplied by that fraction. The credit allowed is either the product thus calculated or the income tax actually paid the other state or country, whichever is smaller.

(3) Receipts showing the payment of income taxes to another state or country and a true copy of a return or returns upon the basis of which the taxes are assessed shall be filed with the Secretary when the credit is claimed. If credit is claimed on account of a deficiency assessment, a true copy of the notice assessing or proposing to assess the deficiency, as well as a receipt showing the payment of the deficiency, shall be filed.

(b) If any taxes paid to another state or country for which a taxpayer has been allowed a credit under this section are at any time credited or refunded to the taxpayer, a tax equal to that portion of the credit allowed for the taxes so credited or refunded is due and payable from the taxpayer and is subject to the penalties and interest provided in Subchapter I of this Chapter. (1939, c. 158, s. 325; 1941, c. 50, s. 5; c. 204, s. 1; 1943, c. 400, s. 4; 1957, c. 1340, s. 4; 1963, c. 1169, s. 2; 1967, c. 1110, s. 3; 1973, c. 476, s. 193; 1989, c. 728, s. 1.5; 1989 (Reg. Sess., 1990), c. 814, s. 17; 1998-98, s. 92; 2013-316, ss. 1.1(a), 1.3(d); 2013-414, s. 5(b).)

§ 105-153.10. (Effective for taxable years beginning on or after January 1, 2014) Credit for children.

(a) Credit. - A taxpayer who is allowed a federal child tax credit under section 24 of the Code for the taxable year is allowed a credit against the tax imposed by this Part for each dependent child for whom the taxpayer is allowed the federal credit. The amount of credit allowed under this section for the taxable year is equal to the amount listed in the table below based on the taxpayer's adjusted gross income, as calculated under the Code:

Filing Status	AGI	Credit Amount
Married, filing jointly	Up to $40,000	$125.00
	Over $40,000	
	Up to $100,000	$100.00
	Over $100,000	0
Head of Household	Up to $32,000	$125.00
	Over $32,000	
	Up to $80,000	$100.00
	Over $80,000	0

Single	Up to $20,000	$125.00
	Over $20,000	
	Up to $50,000	$100.00
	Over $50,000	0
Married, filing separately	Up to $20,000	$125.00
	Over $20,000	
	Up to $50,000	$100.00
	Over $50,000	0.

(b) Limitations. - A nonresident or part-year resident who claims the credit allowed by this section shall reduce the amount of the credit by multiplying it by the fraction calculated under G.S. 105-134.5(b) or (c), as appropriate. The credit allowed under this section may not exceed the amount of tax imposed by this Part for the taxable year reduced by the sum of all credits allowed, except payments of tax made by or on behalf of the taxpayer. (1995, c. 42, s. 3; 1998-98, s. 69; 2001-424, s. 34.20(a); 2002-126, s. 30B.2(a), (b); 2003-284, s. 39B.2; 2013-316, s. 1.1(a), (e).)

§ 105-154. Information at the source returns.

(a) Repealed by Session Laws 1993, c. 354, s. 14.

(b) Information Returns of Payers. - A person who is a resident of this State, has a place of business in this State, or has an employee, an agent, or another representative in any capacity in this State shall file an information return as required by the Secretary if the person directly or indirectly pays or controls the payment of any income to any taxpayer. The return shall contain all information required by the Secretary. The filing of any return in compliance with this section by a foreign corporation is not evidence that the corporation is doing business in this State.

(c) Information Returns of Partnerships. - A partnership doing business in this State and required to file a return under the Code shall file an information return with the Secretary. A partnership that the Secretary believes to be doing business in this State and to be required to file a return under the Code shall file an information return when requested to do so by the Secretary. The information return shall contain all information required by the Secretary. It shall state specifically the items of the partnership's gross income, the deductions allowed under the Code, and the adjustments required by this Part. The information return shall also include the name and address of each person who would be entitled to share in the partnership's net income, if distributable, and the amount each person's distributive share would be. The information return shall specify the part of each person's distributive share of the net income that represents corporation dividends. The information return shall be signed by one of the partners under affirmation in the form required by the Secretary.

A partnership that files an information return under this subsection shall furnish to each person who would be entitled to share in the partnership's net income, if distributable, any information necessary for that person to properly file a State income tax return. The information shall be in the form prescribed by the Secretary and must be furnished on or before the due date of the information return.

(d) (Effective for taxable years beginning before January 1, 2014) Payment of Tax on Behalf of Nonresident Owner or Partner. - If a business conducted in this State is owned by a nonresident individual or by a partnership having one or more nonresident members, the manager of the business shall report the earnings of the business in this State, the distributive share of the income of each nonresident owner or partner, and any other information required by the Secretary. The manager of the business shall pay with the return the tax on each nonresident owner or partner's share of the income computed at the rate levied on individuals under G.S. 105-134.2(a)(3). The business may deduct the payment for each nonresident owner or partner from the owner or partner's distributive share of the profits of the business in this State. If the nonresident partner is not an individual and the partner has executed an affirmation that the partner will pay the tax with its corporate, partnership, trust, or estate income tax return, the manager of the business is not required to pay the tax on the partner's share. In this case, the manager shall include a copy of the affirmation with the report required by this subsection.

(d) (Effective for taxable years beginning on or after January 1, 2014) Payment of Tax on Behalf of Nonresident Owner or Partner. - If a business conducted in this State is owned by a nonresident individual or by a partnership having one or more nonresident members, the manager of the business shall report the earnings of the business in this State, the distributive share of the income of each nonresident owner or partner, and any other information required by the Secretary. The manager of the business shall pay with the return the tax on each nonresident owner or partner's share of the income computed at the rate levied on individuals under G.S. 105-153.7. The business may deduct the payment for each nonresident owner or partner from the owner or partner's distributive share of the profits of the business in this State. If the nonresident partner is not an individual and the partner has executed an affirmation that the partner will pay the tax with its corporate, partnership, trust, or estate income tax return, the manager of the business is not required to pay the tax on the partner's share. In this case, the manager shall include a copy of the affirmation with the report required by this subsection.

(e) Publicly Traded Partnership. - The information return and payment requirements under this section are modified as follows for a publicly traded partnership that is described in section 7704(c) of the Code:

(1) The information return required under subsection (c) of this section is limited to partners whose distributive share of the partnership's net income during the tax year was more than five hundred dollars ($500.00).

(2) The payment requirements under subsection (d) of this section do not apply. (1939, c. 158, s. 328; 1945, c. 708, s. 4; 1957, c. 1340, s. 4; 1967, c. 1110, s. 3; 1973, c. 476, s. 193; c. 1287, s. 5; 1989, c. 728, s. 1.25; 1989 (Reg. Sess., 1990), c. 814, s. 19; 1991 (Reg. Sess., 1992), c. 930, s. 2; 1993, c. 314, s. 1; c. 354, s. 14; 1998-98, s. 69; 1999-337, s. 26; 2008-107, s. 28.8(a); 2013-316, s. 1.3(e).)

§ 105-155. Time and place of filing returns; extensions; affirmation.

(a) Return. - An income tax return shall be filed at the place and in the form prescribed by the Secretary. The income tax return of every taxpayer reporting on a calendar year basis is due on or before the fifteenth day of April in each year. The income tax return of every taxpayer reporting on a fiscal year basis is due on or before the fifteenth day of the fourth month following the close of the fiscal year. These dates do not apply to a nonresident alien whose federal income tax return is due at a later date under section 6072(c) of the Code. The return of a nonresident alien affected by that Code section is due on or before the fifteenth day of the sixth month following the close of the taxable year. An information return shall be filed at the times prescribed by the Secretary. A taxpayer may ask the Secretary for an extension of time to file a return under G.S. 105-263.

(b)   Repealed by 1991 (Regular Session, 1992), c. 930, s. 3.

(c)   Repealed by Session Laws 1998-217, s. 44, effective October 31, 1998.

(d)   Forms. - Returns and affirmations shall be in the form prescribed by the Secretary. (1939, c. 158, s. 329; 1943, c. 400, s. 4; 1951, c. 643, s. 4; 1953, c. 1302, s. 4; 1955, c. 17, s. 1; 1957, c. 1340, s. 4; 1963, c. 1169, s. 2; 1967, c. 1110, s. 3; 1973, c. 476, s. 193; 1989, c. 728, s. 1.26; 1989 (Reg. Sess., 1990), c. 984, s. 10; 1991, c. 45, s. 12; 1991 (Reg. Sess., 1992), c. 930, s. 3; 1998-217, s. 44; 2006-18, s. 8.)

§ 105-156: Repealed by Session Laws 2009-445, s. 7, effective August 7, 2009.

§ 105-156.1: Repealed by Session Laws 1989, c. 728, s. 1.28.

§ 105-157. When tax must be paid.

(a)   Except as otherwise provided in this section and in Article 4A of this Chapter, the full amount of the tax payable as shown on the return must be paid to the Secretary within the time allowed for filing the return. If the amount shown to be due is less than one dollar ($1.00), no payment need be made.

(b)   Repealed by Session Laws 1993, c. 450, s. 4. (1939, c. 158, s. 332; 1943, c. 400, s. 4; 1947, c. 501, s. 4; 1951, c. 643, s. 4; 1955, c. 17, s. 2; 1959, c. 1259, s. 2; 1963, c. 1169, s. 2; 1967, c. 702, s. 1; c. 1110, s. 3; 1973, c. 476, s. 193; c. 903, s. 2; c. 1287, s. 5; 1989, c. 728, s. 1.29; 1989 (Reg. Sess., 1990), c. 984, s. 11; 1991 (Reg. Sess., 1992), c. 930, s. 4; 1993, c. 450, s. 4.)

§ 105-158. Taxation of certain Armed Forces personnel and other individuals upon death.

An individual is not subject to the tax imposed by this Part for a taxable year if, under section 692 of the Code, the individual is not subject to federal income tax for that same taxable year. (1969, c. 1116; 1979, c. 179, s. 2; 1989, c. 728, s. 1.30; 1991, c. 439, s. 2; 1998-98, s. 69; 2011-183, s. 72.)

§ 105-159. Federal corrections.

If a taxpayer's adjusted gross income or federal tax credit that affects the amount of State tax payable is corrected or otherwise determined by the federal government, the taxpayer must, within six months after being notified of the correction or final determination by the federal government, file an income tax return with the Secretary reflecting the corrected or determined adjusted gross income or federal tax credit that affects the amount of State tax payable. The Secretary must propose an assessment for any additional tax due from the taxpayer as provided in Article 9 of this Chapter. The Secretary must refund any overpayment of tax as provided in Article 9 of this Chapter. A taxpayer who fails to comply with this section is subject to the penalties in G.S. 105-236 and forfeits the right to any refund due by reason of the determination. (1939, c. 158, s. 334; 1947, c. 501, s. 4; 1949, c. 392, s. 3; 1957, c. 1340, s. 14; 1963, c. 1169, s. 2; 1967, c. 1110, s. 3; 1973, c. 476, s. 193; 1989, c. 728, s. 1.31; 1993 (Reg. Sess., 1994), c. 582, s. 1; 2006-18, s. 5; 2007-491, s. 16; 2013-414, s. 38.)

§ 105-159.1. (Repealed effective July 1, 2013) Designation of tax by individual to political party.

(a) Every individual whose income tax liability for the taxable year is three dollars ($3.00) or more may designate on his or her income tax return that three dollars ($3.00) of the tax shall be credited to the North Carolina Political Parties Financing Fund for the use of the political party designated by the taxpayer. In the case of a married couple filing a joint return whose income tax liability for the taxable year is six dollars ($6.00) or more, each spouse may designate on the income tax return that three dollars ($3.00) of the tax shall be credited to the North Carolina Political Parties Financing Fund for the use of the political party designated by the taxpayer. Amounts credited to the Fund shall be allocated among the political parties according to the designation of the taxpayer. Where any taxpayer elects to designate but does not specify a particular political party, those funds shall be distributed among the political parties on a pro rata basis according to their respective party voter registrations as determined by the most recent certification of the State Board of Elections. As used in this section, the term "political party" has the same meaning as defined in G.S. 163-96.

(b)   Amounts designated under subsection (a) shall be credited to the North Carolina Political Parties Financing Fund on a quarterly basis. Interest earned by the Fund shall be credited to the Fund and shall be allocated among the political parties on the same basis as the principal of the Fund. The State Board of Elections, which administers the Fund, shall make a quarterly report to each State party chairman stating the amount of funds allocated to each party for that quarter, the cumulative total of funds allocated to each party to date for the year, and an estimate of the probable total amount to be collected and allocated to each party for that calendar year.

(c)   Repealed by Session Laws 1983, c. 481.

(d)   Return. - The first page of the income tax return must give an individual the opportunity to make the political contribution authorized in this section. The return or its accompanying explanatory instructions must readily indicate that a contribution neither increases nor decreases an individual's tax liability.

(e)   An income tax return preparer may not designate on a return that the taxpayer does or does not desire to make the political contribution authorized in this section unless the taxpayer or the taxpayer's spouse has consented to the designation. (1977, 2nd Sess., c. 1298, s. 1; 1979, c. 801, s. 69; 1981, c. 963, s. 1; 1983, cc. 139, 480, 481; 1989, c. 37, s. 4; c. 713; c. 728, s. 1.32; c. 770, s. 41.1; 1991, c. 45, s. 13; c. 347, s. 3; c. 690, ss. 8, 9; 1997-515, s. 10(a); 1999-438, s. 3; 2002-106, s. 3; 2005-345, s. 46; 2010-95, s. 3; 2013-381, s. 38.1(e).)

§ 105-159.2. (See Editor's note for repeal) Designation of tax to North Carolina Public Campaign Fund.

(a)   Allocation to the North Carolina Public Campaign Fund. - To ensure the financial viability of the North Carolina Public Campaign Fund established in Article 22D of Chapter 163 of the General Statutes, the Department must allocate to that Fund three dollars ($3.00) from the income taxes paid each year by each individual with an income tax liability of at least that amount, if the individual agrees. A taxpayer must be given the opportunity to indicate an agreement or objection to that allocation in the manner described in subsection (b) of this section. In the case of a married couple filing a joint return, each individual must have the option of agreeing or objecting to the allocation. The amounts allocated under this subsection to the Fund must be credited to it on a monthly basis.

(b)   Returns. - Individual income tax returns must give an individual an opportunity to agree to the allocation of three dollars ($3.00) of the individual's tax liability to the North Carolina Public Campaign Fund. The Department must make it clear to the taxpayer that the dollars will support a nonpartisan court system, that the dollars will go to the Fund if the taxpayer marks an agreement, and that allocation of the dollars neither increases nor decreases the individual's tax liability. The following statement must be used to meet this requirement: "Mark 'Yes' if you want to designate $3 of taxes to this special Fund for voter education materials and for candidates who accept spending limits. Marking 'Yes' does not change your tax or refund." The Department must consult with the State Board of Elections to ensure that the information given to taxpayers complies with the intent of this section.

The Department must inform the entities it approves to reproduce the return that they must comply with the requirements of this section and that a return may not reflect an agreement or objection unless the individual completing the return decided to agree or object after being presented with the statement required by subsection (b) of this section and, as available background information or instructions, the information required by subsection (c) of this section. No software package used in preparing North Carolina income tax returns may default to an agreement or objection. A paid preparer of tax returns may not mark an agreement or objection for a taxpayer without the taxpayer's consent.

(c)   Instructions. - The instruction for individual income tax returns must include the following explanatory statement: "The N.C. Public Campaign Fund provides an alternative source of campaign money to qualified candidates who accept strict campaign spending and fund-raising limits. The Fund also helps finance a Voter Guide with educational materials about voter registration, the role of the appellate courts, and the candidates seeking election as appellate judges in North Carolina. Three dollars from the taxes you pay will go to the Fund if you mark an agreement. Regardless of what choice you make, your tax will not increase, nor will any refund be reduced." (2002-158, s. 4; 2005-276, s. 23A.1(d); 2006-192, s. 18; 2013-360, s. 21.1(c); 2013-381, s. 38.1(f).)

Part 3. Income Tax - Estates, Trusts, and Beneficiaries.

§ 105-160. Short title.

This Part shall be known as the Income Tax Act for Estates, Trusts, and Beneficiaries. (1967, c. 1110, s. 3; 1989, c. 728, s. 1.36; 1998-98, ss. 45, 68.)

§ 105-160.1. Definitions.

The definitions provided in Part 2 of this Article shall apply in this Part except where the context clearly indicates a different meaning. In addition, as used in this Part, "taxable income" is defined in sections 641 through 692 of the Code. (1989, c. 728, s. 1.38; 1998-98, ss. 69, 71; 2013-414, s. 5(f).)

§ 105-160.2. Imposition of tax.

The tax imposed by this Part applies to the taxable income of estates and trusts as determined under the provisions of the Code except as otherwise provided in this Part. The taxable income of an estate or trust is the same as taxable income for such an estate or trust under the provisions of the Code, adjusted as provided in G.S. 105-134.6 and G.S. 105-134.6A, except that the adjustments provided in G.S. 105-134.6 and G.S. 105-134.6A are apportioned between the estate or trust and the beneficiaries based on the distributions made during the taxable year. The tax is computed on the amount of the taxable income of the estate or trust that is for the benefit of a resident of this State, or for the benefit of a nonresident to the extent that the income (i) is derived from North Carolina sources and is attributable to the ownership of any interest in real or tangible personal property in this State or (ii) is derived from a business, trade, profession, or occupation carried on in this State. For purposes of the preceding sentence, taxable income and gross income is computed subject to the adjustments provided in G.S. 105-134.6 and G.S. 105-134.6A. The tax on the amount computed above is at the rates levied in G.S. 105-134.2(a)(3). The fiduciary responsible for administering the estate or trust shall pay the tax computed under the provisions of this Part. (1989, c. 728, s. 1.38; 1989 (Reg. Sess., 1990), c. 814, s. 21; 1991, c. 689, s. 302; 1998-98, s. 69; 2013-414, s. 5(g).)

§ 105-160.3. Tax credits.

(a) Except as otherwise provided in this section, the credits allowed to an individual against the tax imposed by Part 2 of this Article shall be allowed to the same extent to an estate or a trust against the tax imposed by this Part. Any credit computed as a percentage of income received shall be apportioned between the estate or trust and the beneficiaries based on the distributions made during the taxable year. No credit may exceed the amount of the tax imposed by this Part for the taxable year reduced by the sum of all credits allowable, except for payments of tax made by or on behalf of the estate or trust.

(b) (Effective for taxable years beginning before January 1, 2014) The following credits are not allowed to an estate or trust:

(1) G.S. 105-151. Tax credits for income taxes paid to other states by individuals.

(2) G.S. 105-151.11. Credit for child care and certain employment-related expenses.

(3) G.S. 105-151.18. Credit for the disabled.

(4) G.S. 105-151.24. Credit for children.

(5) G.S. 105-151.26. Credit for charitable contributions by nonitemizers.

(6) Repealed by Session Laws 2004-170, s. 17, effective August 2, 2004.

(7) G.S. 105-151.28. Credit for long-term care insurance.

(8) (Expires for taxable years beginning on or after January 1, 2013) G.S. 105-151.30. Credit for recycling oyster shells.

(9) G.S. 105-151.31. Earned income tax credit.

(10) G.S. 105-151.32. Credit for adoption expenses.

(11) G.S. 105-151.33. Education expenses credit.

(b) (Effective for taxable years beginning on or after January 1, 2014) The tax credits allowed under G.S. 105-153.9 and G.S. 105-153.10 may not be claimed by an estate or trust. (1989, c. 728, s. 1.38; 1998-1, s. 5(b); 1998-98, ss. 10, 105; 1998-212, s. 29A.6(b); 2004-170, s. 17; 2006-66, s. 24.18(f); 2007-323, ss. 31.4(b), 31.5(b), 31.6(b); 2011-330, s. 36; 2012-79, s. 2.6; 2013-316, s. 1.3(f); 2013-364, s. 3.)

§ 105-160.4. Tax credits for income taxes paid to other states by estates and trusts.

(a) If a fiduciary is required to pay income tax to this State for an estate or a trust, the fiduciary shall be allowed a credit against the tax imposed by this Part for income taxes imposed by and paid to another state or country on income derived from sources within that other state or country in accordance with the formula contained in subsection (b) and the requirements of subsection (c).

(b) The fraction of the gross income for North Carolina income tax purposes that is derived from sources within and subject to income tax in another state or country shall be ascertained and the North Carolina income tax before credit under this section shall be multiplied by that fraction. The credit allowed shall be either the product thus calculated or the income tax actually paid the other state or country, whichever is smaller.

(c) Receipts showing the payment of income taxes to another state or country and a true copy of the return upon the basis of which the taxes are assessed shall be filed with the Secretary at or before the time credit is claimed. If credit is claimed on account of a deficiency assessment, a true copy of the notice assessing or proposing to assess the deficiency, as well as a receipt showing the payment of the deficiency, shall be filed with the Secretary.

(d) If any taxes paid to another state or country for which a fiduciary has been allowed a credit under this section are at any time credited or refunded to the fiduciary, a tax equal to that portion of the credit allowed for the taxes so credited or refunded shall be due and payable from the fiduciary and shall be subject to the penalties and interest on delinquent payments provided in G.S. 105-236 and G.S. 105-241.21.

(e) A resident beneficiary of an estate or trust who is taxed under the provisions of Part 2 of this Article on income from an estate or trust determined to be includable in the resident's gross income is allowed a credit against the tax imposed for income taxes paid by the fiduciary to another state or country on the income in accordance with the formula contained in subsection (b) of this section and the requirements of subsection (c) of this section; provided, that if any taxes paid to another state or country for which a beneficiary has been allowed credit under this section are at any time credited or refunded to the beneficiary, a tax equal to that portion of the credit allowed for the taxes so credited or refunded shall be due and payable from the beneficiary and shall be subject to the penalties and interest on delinquent payments provided in G.S. 105-236 and G.S. 105-241.21. (1989, c. 728, s. 1.38; 1998-98, ss. 69, 71; 2007-491, s. 44(1)b.)

§ 105-160.5. Returns.

The fiduciary of an estate or trust described below shall file an income tax return under affirmation, showing specifically the taxable income and the adjustments required by this Part and such other facts as the Secretary may require for the purpose of making any computation required by this Part:

(1) Every estate or trust which has taxable income under this Part during the taxable year and is required to file an income tax return for the taxable year under the Code.

(2) Every estate or trust which the Secretary believes to be liable for a tax under this Part, when so notified by the Secretary and requested to file a return. (1989, c. 728, s. 1.38; 1998-98, s. 69.)

§ 105-160.6. Time and place of filing returns.

An income tax return of an estate or a trust shall be filed as prescribed by the Secretary at the place prescribed by the Secretary. The return of every fiduciary reporting on a calendar year basis shall be filed on or before the 15th day of April in each year, and the return of every fiduciary reporting on a fiscal year basis shall be filed on or before the 15th day of the fourth month following the close of the fiscal year. A fiduciary may ask the Secretary for an extension of time to file a return under G.S. 105-263. (1989, c. 728, s. 1.38; 1989 (Reg. Sess., 1990), c. 984, s. 12; 1991 (Reg. Sess., 1992), c. 930, s. 7.)

§ 105-160.7. When tax must be paid.

(a) The full amount of the tax payable as shown on the return must be paid to the Secretary within the time allowed for filing the return. However, if the amount shown to be due after all credits is less than one dollar ($1.00), no payment need be made.

(b) Repealed by Session Laws 1993, c. 450, s. 5. (1989, c. 728, s. 1.38; 1989 (Reg. Sess., 1990), c. 984, s. 13; 1991 (Reg. Sess., 1992), c. 930, s. 8; 1993, c. 450, s. 5.)

§ 105-160.8. Federal corrections.

For purposes of this Part, the provisions of G.S. 105-159 requiring an individual to report the correction or determination of taxable income by the federal government apply to fiduciaries required to file returns for estates and trusts. (1989, c. 728, s. 1.38; 1993 (Reg. Sess., 1994), c. 582, s. 3; 1998-98, s. 69.)

§§ 105-161 through 105-163: Repealed by Session Laws 1989, c. 728, s. 1.37.

§§ 105-163.01 through 105-163.06: Repealed by Session Laws 1991, c. 45, s. 14(b).

§ 105-163.07: Recodified as § 105-151.21 by Session Laws 1991, c. 45, s. 14.

§§ 105-163.08 through 105-163.09: Repealed by Session Laws 1991, c. 45, s. 14(b).

Part 5. Tax Credits for Qualified Business Investments.

§ 105-163.010. (Repealed effective for investments made on or after January 1, 2014) Definitions.

The following definitions apply in this Part:

(1) Affiliate. - An individual or business that controls, is controlled by, or is under common control with another individual or business.

(2) Business. - A corporation, partnership, limited liability company, association, or sole proprietorship operated for profit.

(3) Control. - A person controls an entity if the person owns, directly or indirectly, more than ten percent (10%) of the voting securities of that entity. As used in this subdivision, the term "voting security" means a security that (i) confers upon the holder the right to vote for the election of members of the board of directors or similar governing body of the business or (ii) is convertible into, or entitles the holder to receive upon its exercise, a security that confers such a right to vote. A general partnership interest is a voting security.

(4) Equity security. - Common stock, preferred stock, or an interest in a partnership, or subordinated debt that is convertible into, or entitles the holder to receive upon its exercise, common stock, preferred stock, or an interest in a partnership.

(5) Financial institution. - A business that is (i) a bank holding company, as defined in the Bank Holding Company Act of 1956, 12 U.S.C. §§ 1841, et seq., or its wholly owned subsidiary, (ii) registered as a broker-dealer under the Securities Exchange Act of 1934, 15 U.S.C. §§ 78a, et seq., or its wholly owned subsidiary, (iii) an investment company as defined in the Investment Company Act of 1940, 15 U.S.C. §§ 80a-1, et seq., whether or not it is required to register under that act, (iv) a small business investment company as defined in the Small Business Investment Act of 1958, 15 U.S.C. §§ 661, et seq., (v) a pension or profit-sharing fund or trust, or (vi) a bank, savings institution, trust company, financial services company, or insurance company. The term does not include, however, a business, other than a small business investment company, whose net worth, when added to the net worth of all of its affiliates, is less than ten million dollars ($10,000,000). The term also does not include a business that does not generally market its services to the public and is controlled by a business that is not a financial institution.

(5a) Granting entity. - Any of the following:

a. A domestic or foreign corporation that (i) is tax-exempt pursuant to section 501(c)(3) of the Code, (ii) has as its principal purpose the stimulation of the development of the biotechnology industry, and (iii) in furtherance of that purpose has received, or is a successor in interest to an organization that has received, direct appropriations from the State in at least three fiscal years.

b. A domestic or foreign corporation that meets the following three conditions:

1. It is tax-exempt pursuant to section 501(c)(3) of the Code, is a private foundation pursuant to section 509 of the Code, or is an affiliate of either of the foregoing.

2. It has as its principal purpose one of the following: conducting research and development in, or stimulating the development of, electronic, photonic, information, or other technologies, which may include investing in companies that provide research, development, products, or services in these technologies.

3. It meets one of the following conditions:

I. It received direct appropriations in furtherance of one of these purposes from the State in at least three fiscal years.

II. It was organized to perform one of these purposes for an organization that meets condition I of this sub-subdivision.

III. It is an affiliate of an entity that meets condition II of this sub-subdivision.

c. An institute that (i) is administratively located within a constituent institution of The University of North Carolina, (ii) is financed in part by a domestic or foreign corporation that is tax-exempt pursuant to section 501(c)(3) of the Code, (iii) has as a principal purpose the stimulation of economic development based on the advancement of science, engineering, and technology, and (iv) funds, either directly or in collaboration with other entities, small businesses engaging in developing technology.

(6) North Carolina Enterprise Corporation. - A corporation established in accordance with Article 3 of Chapter 53A of the General Statutes or a limited partnership in which a North Carolina Enterprise Corporation is the only general partner.

(7) Pass-through entity. - Defined in G.S. 105-228.90.

(7b) Qualified business. - A qualified business venture, a qualified grantee business, or a qualified licensee business.

(8) Qualified business venture. - A business that (i) engages primarily in manufacturing, processing, warehousing, wholesaling, research and development, or a service-related industry, and (ii) is registered with the Secretary of State under G.S. 105-163.013.

(9) Qualified grantee business. - A business that (i) is registered with the Secretary of State under G.S. 105-163.013, and (ii) has received during the current year or any of the preceding three years a grant, an investment, or other funding from a federal agency under the Small Business Innovation Research Program administered by the United States Small Business Administration or from a granting entity as defined in this section.

(9a) Qualified licensee business. - A business that meets all of the following conditions:

a. It is registered with the Secretary of State under G.S. 105-163.013.

b. During its most recent fiscal year before filing an application for registration under G.S. 105-163.013, it had gross revenues, as determined in accordance with generally accepted accounting principles, of one million dollars ($1,000,000) or less on a consolidated basis.

c. It has been certified by a constituent institution of The University of North Carolina or a research university as currently performing under a licensing agreement with the institution or university for the purpose of commercializing technology developed at the institution or university. For the purpose of this section, a research university is an institution of higher education classified as a Doctoral/Research University, Extensive or Intensive, in the most recent edition of "A Classification of Institutions of Higher Education", the official report of The Carnegie Foundation for the Advancement of Teaching.

(10) Real estate-related business. - A business that is involved in or related to the brokerage, selling, purchasing, leasing, operating, or managing of hotels, motels, nursing homes or other lodging facilities, golf courses, sports or social clubs, restaurants, storage facilities, or commercial or residential lots or buildings is a real estate-related business, except that a real estate-related business does not include (i) a business that purchases or leases real estate from others for the purpose of providing itself with facilities from which to conduct a business that is not itself a real estate-related business or (ii) a business that is not otherwise a real estate-related business but that leases, subleases, or otherwise provides to one or more other persons a number of

square feet of space which in the aggregate does not exceed fifty percent (50%) of the number of square feet of space occupied by the business for its other activities.

(10a) Related person. - A person described in one of the relationships set forth in section 267(b) or 707(b) of the Code.

(11) Security. - A security as defined in Section 2(1) of the Securities Act of 1933, 15 U.S.C. § 77b(1).

(12) Selling or leasing at retail. - A business is selling or leasing at retail if the business either (i) sells or leases any product or service of any nature from a store or other location open to the public generally or (ii) sells or leases products or services of any nature by means other than to or through one or more other businesses.

(13) Service-related industry. - A business is engaged in a service-related industry, whether or not it also sells a product, if it provides services to customers or clients and does not as a substantial part of its business engage in a business described in G.S. 105-163.013(b)(4). A business is engaged as a substantial part of its business in an activity described in G.S. 105-163.013(b)(4) if (i) its gross revenues derived from all activities described in that subdivision exceed twenty-five percent (25%) of its gross revenues in any fiscal year or (ii) it is established as one of its primary purposes to engage in any activities described in that subdivision, whether or not its purposes were stated in its articles of incorporation or similar organization documents.

(14) Subordinated debt. - Indebtedness that is not secured and is subordinated to all other indebtedness of the issuer issued or to be issued to a financial institution other than a financial institution described in subdivisions (5)(ii) through (5)(v) of this section. Except as provided in G.S. 105-163.014(d1), any portion of indebtedness that matures earlier than five years after its issuance is not subordinated debt. (1987, c. 852, s. 1; 1987 (Reg. Sess., 1988), c. 882, s. 2; 1989 (Reg. Sess., 1990), c. 848, s. 2; 1991, c. 637, s. 1; 1993, c. 443, s. 1; 1996, 2nd Ex. Sess., c. 14, s. 7; 1997-6, s. 5; 1998-98, ss. 46, 69; 1998-212, ss. 29A.15(a), 29A.16(c), (d); 1999-369, s. 5.6; 2002-99, s. 3; 2003-414, s. 2; 2003-416, s. 4(a).)

§ 105-163.011. (Repealed effective for investments made on or after January 1, 2014) Tax credits allowed.

(a) No Credit for Brokered Investments. - No credit is allowed under this section for a purchase of equity securities or subordinated debt if a broker's fee or commission or other similar remuneration is paid or given directly or indirectly for soliciting the purchase.

(b) Individuals. - Subject to the limitations contained in G.S. 105-163.012, an individual who purchases the equity securities or subordinated debt of a qualified business directly from that business is allowed as a credit against the tax imposed by Part 2 of this Article for the taxable year an amount equal to twenty-five percent (25%) of the amount invested. The aggregate amount of credit allowed an individual for one or more investments made in a single taxable year under this Part, whether directly or indirectly as owner of a pass-through entity, may not exceed fifty thousand dollars ($50,000). The credit may not be taken for the year in which the investment is made but may be taken for the taxable year beginning during the calendar year in which the application for the credit becomes effective as provided in subsection (c) of this section.

(b1) Pass-Through Entities. - This subsection does not apply to a pass-through entity that has committed capital under management in excess of five million dollars ($5,000,000) or to a pass-through entity that is a qualified business or a North Carolina Enterprise Corporation. Subject to the limitations provided in G.S. 105-163.012, a pass-through entity that purchases the equity securities or subordinated debt of a qualified business directly from the business is eligible for a tax credit equal to twenty-five percent (25%) of the amount invested. The aggregate amount of credit allowed a pass-through entity for one or more investments made in a single taxable year under this Part, whether directly or indirectly as owner of another pass-through entity, may not exceed seven hundred fifty thousand dollars ($750,000). The pass-through entity is not eligible for the credit for the year in which the investment by the pass-through entity is made but is eligible for the credit for the taxable year beginning during the calendar year in which the application for the credit becomes effective as provided in subsection (c) of this section.

Each individual who is an owner of a pass-through entity is allowed as a credit against the tax imposed by Part 2 of this Article for the taxable year an amount equal to the owner's allocated share of the credits for which the pass-through entity is eligible under this subsection. The aggregate amount of credit allowed an individual for one or more investments made in a single taxable year under this Part, whether directly or indirectly as owner of a pass-through entity, may not exceed fifty thousand dollars ($50,000).

If an owner's share of the pass-through entity's credit is limited due to the maximum allowable credit under this section for a taxable year, the pass-through entity and its owners may not reallocate the unused credit among the other owners.

(c) Application. - To be eligible for the tax credit provided in this section, the taxpayer must file an application for the credit with the Secretary. The application should be filed on or before April 15 of the year following the calendar year in which the investment was made. The Secretary may not accept an application filed after October 15 of the year following the calendar year in which the investment was made. An application is effective for the year in which it is timely filed. The application must be on a form prescribed by the Secretary and must include any supporting documentation that the Secretary may require. If an investment for which a credit is applied for was paid for other than in money, the taxpayer must include with the application a certified appraisal of the value of the property used to pay for the investment. The application for a credit for an investment made by a pass-through entity must be filed by the pass-through entity.

(d) Penalties. - The penalties provided in G.S. 105-236 apply in this Part. (1987, c. 852, s. 1; 1987 (Reg. Sess., 1988), c. 882, ss. 3, 3.1; 1989 (Reg. Sess., 1990), c. 848, s. 3; 1991, c. 637, s. 2; 1993, c. 443, s. 2; 1995, c. 491, s. 1; 1996, 2nd Ex. Sess., c. 14, s. 7; 1998-98, s. 71; 1998-212, s. 29A.15(a); 1999-337, s. 27; 2003-414, s. 3; 2007-422, s. 2; 2009-445, s. 9(a).)

§ 105-163.012. (Repealed effective for investments made on or after January 1, 2014) Limit; carry-over; ceiling; reduction in basis.

(a) The credit allowed a taxpayer under G.S. 105-163.011 may not exceed the amount of income tax imposed by Part 2 of this Article for the taxable year reduced by the sum of all other credits allowable except tax payments made by or on behalf of the taxpayer. The amount of unused credit allowed under G.S. 105-163.011 may be carried forward for the next five succeeding years.

(b) The total amount of all tax credits allowed to taxpayers under G.S. 105-163.011 for investments made in a calendar year may not exceed seven million five hundred thousand dollars ($7,500,000). The Secretary of Revenue shall calculate the total amount of tax credits claimed from the applications filed pursuant to G.S. 105-163.011(c). If the total amount of tax credits claimed for investments made in a calendar year exceeds this maximum amount, the Secretary shall allow a portion of the credits claimed by allocating the maximum amount in tax credits in proportion to the size of the credit claimed by each taxpayer.

(c) If a credit claimed under G.S. 105-163.011 is reduced as provided in this section, the Secretary shall notify the taxpayer of the amount of the reduction of the credit on or before December 31 of the year following the calendar year in which the investment was made. The Secretary's allocations based on applications filed pursuant to G.S. 105-163.011(c) are final and shall not be adjusted to account for credits applied for but not claimed.

(d) The taxpayer's basis in the equity securities or subordinated debt acquired as a result of an investment in a qualified business shall be reduced for the purposes of this Article by the amount of allowable credit. "Allowable credit" means the amount of credit allowed under G.S. 105-163.011 reduced as provided in subsection (c) of this section. (1987, c. 852, s. 1; 1987 (Reg. Sess., 1988), c. 882, ss. 4, 4.1; 1989 (Reg. Sess., 1990), c. 848, s. 4; 1991, c. 637, s. 3; 1993, c. 443, s. 3; 1993 (Reg. Sess., 1994), c. 745, s. 8; 1996, 2nd Ex. Sess., c. 14, ss. 6, 7; 1998-98, s. 71; 1998-212, s. 29A.15(a); 2003-414, s. 4; 2004-124, s. 32C.1; 2008-107, s. 28.26(a); 2009-445, s. 9(b).)

§ 105-163.013. (Repealed for investments made on or after January 1, 2014) Registration.

(a) Repealed by Session Laws 1993, c. 443, s. 4.

(b) Qualified Business Ventures. - In order to qualify as a qualified business venture under this Part, a business must be registered with the Securities Division of the Department of the Secretary of State. To register, the business must file with the Secretary of State an application and any supporting documents the Secretary of State may require from time to time to determine that the business meets the requirements for registration as a qualified business venture. A business meets the requirements for registration as a qualified business venture if all of the following are true as of the date the business files the required application:

(1) Repealed by Session Laws 1996, Second Extra Session, c. 14, s. 7.

(1a) Reserved for future codification purposes.

(1b) Either (i) it was organized after January 1 of the calendar year in which its application is filed or (ii) during its most recent fiscal year before filing the application, it had gross revenues, as determined in accordance with generally accepted accounting principles, of five million dollars ($5,000,000) or less on a consolidated basis.

(2) Repealed by Session Laws 1996, Second Extra Session, c. 14, s. 7.

(3) It is organized to engage primarily in manufacturing, processing, warehousing, wholesaling, research and development, or a service-related industry.

(4) It does not engage as a substantial part of its business in any of the following:

a. Providing a professional service as defined in Chapter 55B of the General Statutes.

b. Construction or contracting.

c. Selling or leasing at retail.

d. The purchase, sale, or development, or purchasing, selling, or holding for investment of commercial paper, notes, other indebtedness, financial instruments, securities, or real property, or otherwise make investments.

e. Providing personal grooming or cosmetics services.

f. Offering any form of entertainment, amusement, recreation, or athletic or fitness activity for which an admission or a membership is charged.

(5) It was not formed for the primary purpose of acquiring all or part of the stock or assets of one or more existing businesses.

(6) It is not a real estate-related business.

The effective date of registration for a qualified business venture whose application is accepted for registration is 60 days before the date its application is filed. No credit is allowed under this Part for an investment made before the effective date of the registration or after the registration is revoked. For the purpose of this Article, if a taxpayer's investment is placed initially in escrow conditioned upon other investors' commitment of additional funds, the date of the investment is the date escrowed funds are transferred to the qualified business venture free of the condition.

To remain qualified as a qualified business venture, the business must renew its registration annually as prescribed by rule by filing a financial statement for the most recent fiscal year showing gross revenues, as determined in accordance with generally accepted accounting principles, of five million dollars ($5,000,000) or less on a consolidated basis and an application for renewal in which the business certifies the facts required in the original application.

Failure of a qualified business venture to renew its registration by the applicable deadline shall result in revocation of its registration effective as of the next day after the renewal deadline, but shall not result in forfeiture of tax credits previously allowed to taxpayers who invested in the business except as provided in G.S. 105-163.014. The Secretary of State shall send the qualified business venture notice of revocation within 60 days after the renewal deadline. A qualified business venture may apply to have its registration reinstated by the Secretary of State by filing an application for reinstatement, accompanied by the reinstatement application fee and a late filing penalty of one thousand dollars ($1,000), within 30 days after receipt of the revocation notice from the Secretary of State. A business that seeks approval of a new application for registration after its registration has been revoked must also pay a penalty of one thousand dollars ($1,000). A registration that has been reinstated is treated as if it had not been revoked.

If the gross revenues of a qualified business venture exceed five million dollars ($5,000,000) in a fiscal year, the business must notify the Secretary of State in writing of this fact by filing a financial statement showing the revenues of the business for that year.

(b1) Qualified Licensee Businesses. - In order to qualify as a qualified licensee business under this Part, a business must be registered with the Securities Division of the Department of the Secretary of State. To register, the business must file with the Secretary of State an application and any supporting documents the Secretary of State may require from time to time to determine that the business meets the requirements for registration as a qualified licensee business. The requirements for registration as a qualified licensee business are set out in G.S. 105-163.010.

The effective date of registration for a qualified licensee business whose application is accepted for registration is the filing date of its application. No credit is allowed under this Part for an investment made before the effective date of the registration or after the registration is revoked.

To remain qualified as a qualified licensee business, the business must renew its registration annually as prescribed by rule by filing a financial statement for the most recent fiscal year showing gross revenues, as determined in accordance with generally accepted accounting principles, of one million dollars ($1,000,000) or less on a consolidated basis and an application for renewal in which the business certifies the facts required in the original application.

Failure of a qualified licensee venture to renew its registration by the applicable deadline results in revocation of its registration effective as of the next day after the renewal deadline, but does not result in forfeiture of tax credits previously allowed to taxpayers who invested in the business except as provided in G.S. 105-163.014. The Secretary of State shall send the qualified licensee business notice of revocation within 60 days after the renewal deadline. A qualified licensee business may apply to have its registration reinstated by the Secretary of State by filing an application for reinstatement, accompanied by the reinstatement application fee and a late filing penalty of one thousand dollars ($1,000), within 30 days after receipt of the revocation notice from the Secretary of State. A business that seeks approval of a new application for registration after its registration has been revoked must also pay a penalty of one thousand dollars ($1,000). A registration that has been reinstated is treated as if it had not been revoked.

If the gross revenues of a qualified business venture exceed one million dollars ($1,000,000) in a fiscal year, the business must notify the Secretary of State in writing of this fact by filing a financial statement showing the revenues of the business for that year.

(c) Qualified Grantee Businesses. - In order to qualify as a qualified grantee business under this Part, a business must be registered with the Securities Division of the Department of the Secretary of State. To register, the business must file with the Secretary of State an application and any supporting documents the Secretary of State may require from time to time to determine that the business meets the requirements for registration as a qualified grantee business. The requirements for registration as a qualified grantee business are set out in G.S. 105-163.010.

The effective date of registration for a qualified grantee business whose application is accepted for registration is the filing date of its application. No credit is allowed under this Part for an investment made before the effective date of the registration or after the registration is revoked.

To remain qualified as a qualified grantee business, the business must renew its registration annually as prescribed by rule by filing an application for renewal in which the business certifies the facts demonstrating that it continues to meet the applicable requirements for qualification.

(d)   Application Forms; Rules; Fees. - Applications for registration, renewal of registration, and reinstatement of registration under this section shall be in the form required by the Secretary of State. The Secretary of State may, by rule, require applicants to furnish supporting information in addition to the information required by subsections (b), (b1), and (c) of this section. The Secretary of State may adopt rules in accordance with Chapter 150B of the General Statutes that are needed to carry out the Secretary's responsibilities under this Part. The Secretary of State shall prepare blank forms for the applications and shall distribute them throughout the State and furnish them on request. Each application shall be signed by the owners of the business or, in the case of a corporation, by its president, vice-president, treasurer, or secretary. There shall be annexed to the application the affirmation of the person making the application in the following form: "Under penalties prescribed by law, I certify and affirm that to the best of my knowledge and belief this application is true and complete." A person who submits a false application is guilty of a Class 1 misdemeanor.

The fee for filing an application for registration under this section is one hundred dollars ($100.00). The fee for filing an application for renewal of registration under this section is fifty dollars ($50.00). The fee for filing an application for reinstatement of registration under this section is fifty dollars ($50.00).

An application for renewal of registration under this section must indicate whether the applicant is a minority business, as defined in G.S. 143-128, and include a report of the number of jobs the business created during the preceding year that are attributable to investments that qualify under this section for a tax credit and the average wages paid by each job. An application that does not contain this information is incomplete and the applicant's registration may not be renewed until the information is provided.

(e)   Revocation of Registration. - If the Securities Division of the Department of the Secretary of State finds that any of the information contained in an application of a business registered under this section is false, it shall revoke the registration of the business. The Secretary of State shall not revoke the registration of a business solely because it ceases business operations for an indefinite period of time, as long as the business renews its registration each year as required under this section.

(f)   Transfer of Registration. - A registration as a qualified business may not be sold or otherwise transferred, except that if a qualified business enters into a merger, conversion, consolidation, or other similar transaction with another business and the surviving company would otherwise meet the criteria for being a qualified business, the surviving company retains the registration without further application to the Secretary of State. In such a case, the qualified business must provide the Secretary of State with written notice of the merger, conversion, consolidation, or similar transaction and the name, address, and jurisdiction of incorporation or organization of the surviving company.

(g)   Report by Secretary of State. - The Secretary of State shall report to the Revenue Laws Study Committee by October 1 of each year all of the businesses that have registered with the Secretary of State as qualified business ventures, qualified licensee businesses, and qualified grantee businesses. The report shall include the name and address of each business, the location of its headquarters and principal place of business, a detailed description of the types of business in which it engages, whether the business is a minority business as defined in G.S. 143-128, the number of jobs created by the business during the period covered by the report, and the average wages paid by these jobs. (1987, c. 852, s. 1; 1991, c. 637, s. 4; 1993, c. 443, ss. 4, 9; c. 485, s. 12; c. 553, s. 80.1; 1994, Ex. Sess., c. 14, s. 50; 1993 (Reg. Sess., 1994), c. 745, ss. 9, 10; 1996, 2nd Ex. Sess., c. 14, s. 7; 1998-98, s. 69; 1998-212, ss. 29A.15(a), 29A.16(e); 1999-369, s. 5.7; 2001-414, s. 12; 2002-99, s. 4; 2003-414, s. 5.)

§ 105-163.014. (Repealed for investments made on or after January 1, 2014) Forfeiture of credit.

(a) Participation in Business. - A taxpayer who has received a credit under this Part for an investment in a qualified business forfeits the credit if, within three years after the investment was made, the taxpayer participates in the operation of the qualified business. For the purpose of this section, a taxpayer participates in the operation of a qualified business if the taxpayer, the taxpayer's spouse, parent, sibling, or child, or an employee of any of these individuals or of a business controlled by any of these individuals, provides services of any nature to the qualified business for compensation, whether as an employee, a contractor, or otherwise. However, a person who provides services to a qualified business, whether as an officer, a member of the board of directors, or otherwise does not participate in its operation if the person receives as compensation only reasonable reimbursement of expenses incurred in providing the services, participation in a stock option or stock bonus plan, or both.

(b) False Application. - A taxpayer who has received a credit under this Part for an investment in a qualified business forfeits the credit if the registration of the qualified business is revoked because information in the registration application was false at the time the application was filed with the Secretary of State.

(c) Repealed by Session Laws 1996, Second Extra Session, c. 14, s. 7.

(d) Transfer or Redemption of Investment. - A taxpayer who has received a credit under this Part for an investment in a qualified business forfeits the credit in the following cases:

(1) Within one year after the investment was made, the taxpayer transfers any of the securities received in the investment that qualified for the tax credit to another person or entity, other than in a transfer resulting from one of the following:

a. The death of the taxpayer.

b. A final distribution in liquidation to the owners of a taxpayer that is a corporation or other entity.

c. A merger, conversion, consolidation, or similar transaction requiring approval by the owners of the qualified business under applicable State law, to the extent the taxpayer does not receive cash or tangible property in the merger, conversion, consolidation, or other similar transaction.

(2) Except as provided in subsection (d1) of this section, within five years after the investment was made, the qualified business in which the investment was made makes a redemption with respect to the securities received in the investment.

In the event the taxpayer transfers fewer than all the securities in a manner that would result in a forfeiture, the amount of the credit that is forfeited is the product obtained by multiplying the aggregate credit attributable to the investment by a fraction whose numerator equals the number of securities transferred and whose denominator equals the number of securities received on account of the investment to which the credit was attributable. In addition, if the redemption amount is less than the amount invested by the taxpayer in the securities to which the redemption is attributable, the amount of the credit that is forfeited is further reduced by multiplying it by a fraction whose numerator equals the redemption amount and whose denominator equals the aggregate amount invested by the taxpayer in the securities involved in the redemption. The term "redemption amount" means all amounts paid that are treated as a distribution in part or full payment in exchange for securities under section 302(a) of the Code.

(d1) Certain Redemptions Allowed. - Forfeiture of a credit does not occur under this section if a qualified business venture that engages primarily in motion picture film production makes a redemption with respect to securities received in an investment and the following conditions are met:

(1) The redemption occurred because the qualified business venture completed production of a film, sold the film, and was liquidated.

(2) Neither the qualified business venture nor a related person continues to engage in business with respect to the film produced by the qualified business venture.

(e) Effect of Forfeiture. - A taxpayer who forfeits a credit under this section is liable for all past taxes avoided as a result of the credit plus interest at the rate established under G.S. 105-241.21, computed from the date the taxes would have been due if the credit had not been allowed. The past taxes and interest are due 30 days after the date the credit is forfeited; a taxpayer who fails to pay the past taxes and interest by the due date is subject to the penalties provided in G.S. 105-236. (1987, c. 852, s. 1; 1991, c. 637, s. 5; 1993, c. 443, s. 5; 1996, 2nd Ex. Sess., c. 14, s. 7; 1998-98, s. 69; 1998-212, ss. 29A.15(a), 29A.16(a), (b); 1999-369, s. 5.8; 2003-414, s. 6; 2007-491, s. 44(1)a.)

§ 105-163.015. Sunset.

This Part is repealed effective for investments made on or after January 1, 2014. (2002-99, s. 5; 2003-414, s. 1; 2004-124, s. 32C.2; 2007-422, s. 1; 2010-31, s. 31.5(b); 2012-36, s. 10.)

Article 4A.

Withholding; Estimated Income Tax for Individuals.

§ 105-163.1. Definitions.

The following definitions apply in this Article:

(1) Compensation. - Consideration a payer pays to any of the following:

a. A nonresident individual or nonresident entity for personal services performed in this State.

b. An ITIN holder who is a contractor and not an employee for services performed in this State.

(2) Repealed by Session Laws 2009-476, s. 1, effective for taxable years beginning on or after January 1, 2010.

(3) Dependent. - An individual with respect to whom an income tax exemption is allowed under the Code.

(4) Employee. - An individual, whether a resident or a nonresident of this State, who performs services in this State for wages or an individual who is a resident of this State and performs services outside this State for wages. The term includes an ordained or licensed member of the clergy who elects to be considered an employee under G.S. 105-163.1A, an officer of a corporation, and an elected public official.

(5) Employer. - A person for whom an individual performs services for wages. In applying the requirements to withhold income taxes from wages and pay the withheld taxes, the term includes a person who:

a. Controls the payment of wages to an individual for services performed for another.

b. Pays wages on behalf of a person who is not engaged in trade or business in this State.

c. Pays wages on behalf of a unit of government that is not located in this State.

d. Pays wages for any other reason.

(6) Individual. - Defined in G.S. 105-134.1.

(6a) ITIN contractor. - An ITIN holder who performs services in this State for compensation other than wages.

(6b) ITIN holder. - A person whose taxpayer identification number is an Individual Taxpayer Identification Number (ITIN).

(7) Miscellaneous payroll period. - A payroll period other than a daily, weekly, biweekly, semimonthly, monthly, quarterly, semiannual, or annual payroll period.

(8) Nonresident entity. - Any of the following:

a. A foreign limited liability company, defined using the same definition for the term "foreign LLC" in G.S. 57D-1-03, that has not obtained a certificate of authority from the Secretary of State pursuant to Article 7 of Chapter 57D of the General Statutes.

b. A foreign limited partnership as defined in G.S. 59-102 or a general partnership formed under the laws of any jurisdiction other than this State, unless the partnership maintains a permanent place of business in this State.

c. A foreign corporation, as defined in G.S. 55-1-40, that has not obtained a certificate of authority from the Secretary of State pursuant to Article 15 of Chapter 55 of the General Statutes.

(9) Pass-through entity. - Defined in G.S. 105-228.90.

(10) Payer. - A person who, in the course of a trade or business, pays compensation to any of the following:

a. A nonresident individual or a nonresident entity compensation for personal services performed in this State.

b. An ITIN holder who is a contractor and not an employee for services performed in this State.

(11) Payroll period. - A period for which an employer ordinarily pays wages to an employee of the employer.

(11a) Pension payer. - A payor or a plan administrator with respect to a pension payment under section 3405 of the Code.

(11b) Pension payment. - A periodic payment or a nonperiodic distribution as those terms are defined in section 3405 of the Code.

(12) Taxable year. - Defined in section 441(b) of the Code.

(13) Wages. - The term has the same meaning as in section 3401 of the Code except it does not include either of the following:

a. The amount of severance wages paid to an employee during the taxable year that is exempt from State income tax for that taxable year under G.S. 105-134.6(b)(11).

b. The amount an employer pays an employee as reimbursement for ordinary and necessary expenses incurred by the employee on behalf of the employer and in the furtherance of the business of the employer.

(14) Withholding agent. - An employer, a pension payer, or a payer. (1959, c. 1259, s. 1; 1967, c. 716, s. 3; 1973, c. 476, s. 193; 1977, c. 657, s. 5; 1979, c. 801, s. 70; 1983, c. 713, ss. 79, 82; 1985, c. 394, s. 1; c. 656, s. 7; 1985 (Reg. Sess., 1986), c. 853, s. 1; 1987, c. 778, s. 1; 1987 (Reg. Sess., 1988), c. 1015, s. 5; 1989, c. 36, s. 5; c. 728, s. 1.40; 1989 (Reg. Sess., 1990), c. 945, s. 5; c. 981, s. 6; 1991, c. 689, s. 255; 1991 (Reg. Sess., 1992), c. 922, s. 7; 1993, c. 12, s. 9; c. 354, s. 15; 1997-6, s. 6; 1997-109, ss. 1, 2, 4; 1998-162, ss. 1, 2; 1999-414, ss. 1, 2; 2000-126, s. 2; 2003-416, s. 4(b); 2009-476, s. 1; 2013-157, s. 29.)

§ 105-163.1A. Ordained or licensed clergyman may elect to be considered an employee.

An ordained or licensed clergyman who performs services for a church of any religious denomination may file an election with the Secretary and the church he serves to be considered an employee of the church instead of self-employed. Until a clergyman files an election, amounts paid by a church to a clergyman are not subject to withholding. A church shall withhold taxes from a clergyman's wages after the clergyman files an election with it under this section. (1985, c. 394, s. 2; 1985 (Reg. Sess., 1986), c. 826, s. 9; 1989 (Reg. Sess., 1990), c. 945, s. 6.)

§ 105-163.2. Employers must withhold taxes.

(a) Withholding Required. - An employer shall deduct and withhold from the wages of each employee the State income taxes payable by the employee on the wages. For each payroll period, the employer shall withhold from the employee's wages an amount that would approximate the employee's income tax liability under Article 4 of this Chapter if the employer withheld the same amount from the employee's wages for each similar payroll period in a calendar year. In calculating an employee's anticipated income tax liability, the employer shall allow for the exemptions, deductions, and credits to which the employee is entitled under Article 4 of this Chapter. The amount of State income taxes withheld by an employer is held in trust for the Secretary.

(b) Withholding Tables. - The manner of withholding and the amount to be withheld shall be determined in accordance with tables and rules adopted by the Secretary. The withholding exemption allowed by these tables and rules shall, as nearly as possible, approximate the exemptions, deductions, and credits to which an employee would be entitled under Article 4 of this Chapter. The Secretary shall promulgate tables for computing amounts to be withheld with respect to different rates of wages for different payroll periods applicable to the various combinations of exemptions to which an employee may be entitled and taking into account the appropriate standard deduction. The tables may provide for the same amount to be withheld within reasonable salary brackets or ranges so designed as to result in the withholding during a year of approximately the amount of an employee's indicated income tax liability for that year. The withholding of wages pursuant to and in accordance with these tables shall be deemed as a matter of law to constitute compliance with the provisions of subsection (a) of this section, notwithstanding any other provisions of this Article.

(c) Withholding if No Payroll Period. - If wages are paid with respect to a period that is not a payroll period, the amount to be deducted and withheld shall be that applicable in the case of a miscellaneous payroll period containing a number of days, excluding Sundays and holidays, equal to the number of days in the period with respect to which such wages are paid. In any case in which wages are paid by an employer without regard to any payroll period or other period, the amount to be deducted and withheld shall be that applicable in the case of a miscellaneous payroll period containing a number of days equal to the number of days, excluding Sundays and holidays, which have elapsed since the date of the last payment of such wages by such employer during the calendar year, or the date of commencement of employment with such employer during such year, or January 1 of such year, whichever is the later.

(d) Estimated Withholding. - The Secretary may, by rule, authorize employers to estimate the wages to be paid to an employee during a calendar quarter, calculate the amount to be withheld for each period based on the estimated wages, and, upon payment of wages to the employee, adjust the withholding so that the amount actually withheld is the amount that would be required to be withheld if the employee's payroll period were quarterly.

(e) Alternatives to Tables. - If the Secretary determines that use of the withholding tables would be impractical, would impose an unreasonable burden on an employer, or would produce substantially incorrect results, the Secretary may authorize or require an employer to use some other method of determining the amounts to be withheld under this Article. The alternative method authorized by the Secretary must reasonably approximate the predicted income tax liability of the affected employees. In addition, with the agreement of the employer and employee, the Secretary may authorize an employer to use an alternative method that results in withholding of a greater amount than otherwise required under this section.

The Secretary's authorization of an alternative method is discretionary and may be cancelled at any time without advance notice if the Secretary finds that the method is being abused or is not resulting in the withholding of an amount reasonably approximating the predicted income tax liability of the affected employees. The Secretary shall give an employer written notice of any cancellation and the findings upon which the cancellation is based. The cancellation becomes effective upon the employer's receipt of this notice or on the third day after the notice was mailed to the employer, whichever occurs first. If the employer requests a hearing on the cancellation within 30 days after the cancellation, the Secretary shall grant a hearing. After a hearing, the Secretary's findings are conclusive. (1959, c. 1259, s. 1; 1973, c. 476, s. 193; 1981, c. 13; 1989, c. 728, s. 1.41; 1989 (Reg. Sess., 1990), c. 945, s. 7; 1997-109, s. 2.)

§ 105-163.2A. Pension payers must withhold taxes.

(a) Definitions. - The definitions provided in section 3405 of the Code apply in this section.

(b) Withholding Required. - A pension payer required to withhold federal taxes under section 3405 of the Code on a pension payment to a resident of this State must deduct and withhold from the payment the State income taxes payable on the payment. Liability for withholding and paying taxes under this section on a pension payment falls on the person who would be liable under section 3405 of the Code for withholding federal taxes on the payment.

Except as otherwise provided in this section, the provisions of this Article apply to a pension payer's pension payment to a resident of this State as if it were an employer's payment of wages to an employee. If a pension payer has more than one arrangement under which it may make pension payments to a resident of this State, each arrangement must be treated separately under this section.

(c) Amount. - In the case of a periodic payment, the pension payer must withhold the amount that would be required to be withheld under this Article if the payment were a payment of wages by an employer to an employee for the appropriate payroll period. If the recipient of periodic payments fails to file an exemption certificate under G.S. 105-163.5, the pension payer must compute the amount to be withheld as if the recipient were a married individual claiming three withholding exemptions.

In the case of a nonperiodic distribution, the pension payer must withhold taxes equal to four percent (4%) of the nonperiodic distribution.

(d) Election of No Withholding. - The recipient may elect not to have taxes withheld under this section to the extent permitted by section 3405 of the Code. The election must be in the form required by the Secretary. In the case of periodic payments, the election remains in effect until revoked by the recipient.

In the case of a nonperiodic distribution, the election applies on a distribution-by-distribution basis unless it meets conditions prescribed by the Secretary for it to apply to subsequent nonperiodic distributions by the pension payer.

A pension payer must notify each recipient of the right to elect not to have taxes withheld under this section. The notice must comply with the requirements of section 3405 of the Code and any additional requirements prescribed by the Secretary.

A recipient's election not to have taxes withheld under this section is void if the recipient fails to furnish the recipient's tax identification number to the pension payer, or the Secretary has notified the pension payer that the tax identification number furnished by the recipient is incorrect.

(e) Exemptions. - This section does not apply to the following pension payments:

(1) A pension payment that is wages under this Article.

(2) Any portion of a pension payment that meets both of the following conditions:

a. It is not a distribution or payment from an individual retirement plan as defined in section 7701 of the Code.

b. The pension payer reasonably believes it is not taxable to the recipient under Article 4 of this Chapter.

(3) A distribution described in section 404(k)(2) of the Code, relating to dividends on corporate securities.

(4) A pension payment that consists only of securities of the recipient's employer corporation plus cash not in excess of two hundred dollars ($200.00) in lieu of securities of the employer corporation. (1999-414, s. 3; 2000-126, s. 3.)

§ 105-163.2B. (Effective for taxable years beginning before January 1, 2014) North Carolina State Lottery Commission must withhold taxes.

The North Carolina State Lottery Commission, established by Chapter 18C of the General Statutes, must deduct and withhold State income taxes from the payment of winnings in an amount of six hundred dollars ($600.00) or more. The amount of taxes to be withheld is seven percent (7%) of the winnings. The Commission must file a return, pay the withheld taxes, and report the amount withheld in the time and manner required under G.S. 105-163.6 as if the winnings were wages. The taxes the Commission withholds are held in trust for the Secretary. (2005-276, s. 31.1(bb); 2005-344, s. 10.2(a); 2006-259, s. 8(f); 2006-264, s. 91(b).)

§ 105-163.2B. (Effective for taxable years beginning on or after January 1, 2014) North Carolina State Lottery Commission must withhold taxes.

The North Carolina State Lottery Commission, established by Chapter 18C of the General Statutes, must deduct and withhold State income taxes from the payment of winnings in an amount of six hundred dollars ($600.00) or more. The amount of taxes to be withheld is a percentage of the winnings. The percentage is the individual income tax rate in G.S. 105-153.7. The Commission must file a return, pay the withheld taxes, and report the amount withheld in the time and manner required under G.S. 105-163.6 as if the winnings were wages. The taxes the Commission withholds are held in trust for the Secretary. (2005-276, s. 31.1(bb); 2005-344, s. 10.2(a); 2006-259, s. 8(f); 2006-264, s. 91(b); 2013-316, s. 1.3(g).)

§ 105-163.3. Certain payers must withhold taxes.

(a) Requirement. - Every payer who pays more than one thousand five hundred dollars ($1,500) during a calendar year to either a nonresident contractor or an ITIN contractor must deduct and withhold from compensation paid to the contractor the State income taxes payable by the contractor on the compensation as provided in this section. The amount of taxes to be withheld is four percent (4%) of the compensation paid to the contractor. The taxes a payer withholds are held in trust for the Secretary.

(b) Exemptions. - The withholding requirement does not apply to the following:

(1) Compensation that is subject to the withholding requirement of G.S. 105-163.2.

(2) Compensation paid to an ordained or licensed member of the clergy.

(3) Compensation paid to an entity exempt from tax under G.S. 105-130.11.

(c) Returns. - A payer must file a return with the Secretary and pay the withheld taxes to the Secretary in accordance with the requirements in G.S. 105-163.6.

(d) Annual Statement and Report. - A payer required to deduct and withhold from a contractor's compensation under this section must give the contractor a written statement that sets out the following information and any other information required by the Secretary:

(1) The payer's name, address, and taxpayer identification number.

(2) The contractor's name, address, and taxpayer identification number.

(3) The total amount of compensation paid during the calendar year.

(4) The total amount deducted and withheld under this section during the calendar year.

This statement is due by January 31 following the end of the calendar year, unless the personal services for which the payer is paying are completed before the end of the calendar year and the contractor requests the statement when the services are completed. In this circumstance, the statement is due within 45 days after the payer's last payment of compensation to the contractor.

Each payer shall file with the Secretary an annual report that compiles the information contained in each of the payer's statements to contractors and any other information required by the Secretary in the manner required by the Secretary. This report is due on the date prescribed by the Secretary and is in lieu of the information report required by G.S. 105-154.

(e) Records. - This subsection applies to a payer who pays compensation for personal services performed in connection with a performance, an entertainment, an athletic event, a speech, or the creation of a film, radio, or television program. If a payer does not withhold from payments to a nonresident entity because the entity is exempt from tax under G.S. 105-130.11, the payer must obtain from the entity documentation proving its exemption from tax. If a payer does not withhold from payments to a nonresident corporation or a nonresident limited liability company because the entity has obtained a certificate of authority from the Secretary of State, the payer must obtain from the entity its corporate identification number issued by the Secretary of State. If a payer does not withhold from payments to an individual because the individual is a resident, the payer must obtain the individual's address and social security number. If a payer does not withhold from a partnership because the partnership has a permanent place of business in this State, the payer must obtain the partnership's address and taxpayer identification number. The payer must retain this information with its records.

(f) Payer May Repay Amounts Withheld Improperly. - A payer may refund to a person any amount the payer withheld improperly from the person under this section, if the refund is made before the end of the calendar year and before the payer furnishes the person the annual statement required by subsection (d) of this section. An amount is withheld improperly if it is withheld from a payment to a person who is not a nonresident contractor or an ITIN contractor, if it is withheld from a payment that is not compensation, or if it is in excess of the amount required to be withheld under this section. A payer who makes a refund under this section must take the following actions:

(1) Not report the amount refunded on the annual statement required by subsection (d) of this section.

(2) Either not pay to the Secretary the amount refunded or, if the amount refunded has already been paid to the Secretary, reduce by the amount refunded the next payments to the Secretary of taxes withheld from the person. (1959, c. 1259, s. 1; 1973, c. 476, s. 193; 1989, c. 728, s. 1.42; 1989 (Reg. Sess., 1990), c. 945, s. 8; 1997-109, s. 2; 1998-98, ss. 11-13; 1998-162, s. 3; 2009-476, s. 2; 2013-414, s. 39(a).)

§ 105-163.4. Withholding does not create nexus.

A nonresident withholding agent's act in compliance with this Article does not in itself constitute evidence that the nonresident is doing business in this State. (1959, c. 1259, s. 1; 1989 (Reg. Sess., 1990), c. 945, s. 9; 1997-109, s. 2.)

§ 105-163.5. Employee exemptions allowable; certificates.

(a)   An employee receiving wages is entitled to the exemptions for which the employee qualifies under Article 4 of this Chapter.

(b)   Every employee shall, at the time of commencing employment, furnish his or her employer with a signed withholding exemption certificate informing the employer of the exemptions the employee claims, which in no event shall exceed the amount of exemptions to which the employee is entitled under the Code. If the employee fails to file the exemption certificate the employer, in computing amounts to be withheld from the employee's wages, shall allow the employee the exemption accorded a single person with no dependents.

(c)   Withholding exemption certificates shall take effect as of the beginning of the first payroll period that ends on or after the date on which the certificate is furnished, or if payment of wages is made without regard to a payroll period, then the certificate shall take effect as of the beginning of the miscellaneous payroll period for which the first payment of wages is made on or after the date on which the certificate is furnished.

(d)   If, on any day during the calendar year, the amount of withholding exemptions to which the employee is entitled is less than the amount of withholding exemptions claimed by the employee on the withholding exemption certificate then in effect with respect to the employee, the employee shall, within 10 days thereafter, furnish the employer with a new withholding exemption certificate stating the amount of withholding exemptions which the employee then claims, which shall in no event exceed the amount to which the employee is entitled on that day. If, on any day during the calendar year, the amount of withholding exemptions to which the employee is entitled is greater than the amount of withholding exemptions claimed, the employee may furnish the employer with a new withholding exemption certificate stating the amount of withholding exemptions which the employee then claims, which shall in no event exceed the amount to which the employee is entitled on that day.

(e)   Withholding exemption certificates must be in the form and contain the information required by the Secretary. As far as practicable, the Secretary shall cause the form of the certificates to be substantially similar to federal exemption certificates.

(f)   In addition to any criminal penalty provided by law, if an individual furnishes his or her employer an exemption certificate that contains information which has no reasonable basis and that results in a lesser amount of tax being withheld under this Article than would have been withheld if the individual had furnished reasonable information, the individual is subject to a penalty of fifty percent (50%) of the amount not properly withheld. (1959, c. 1259, s. 1; 1973, c. 476, s. 193; 1981 (Reg. Sess., 1982), c. 1277; 1989, c. 728, s. 1.43; 1997-109, s. 2.)

§ 105-163.6. When employer must file returns and pay withheld taxes.

(a) General. - A return is due quarterly or monthly as specified in this section. A return shall be filed with the Secretary in the manner required by the Secretary, shall report any payments of withheld taxes made during the period covered by the return, and shall contain any other information required by the Secretary.

Withheld taxes are payable quarterly, monthly, or semiweekly, as specified in this section. If the Secretary finds that collection of the amount of taxes this Article requires an employer to withhold is in jeopardy, the Secretary may require the employer to file a return or pay withheld taxes at a time other than that specified in this section.

(b) Quarterly. - An employer who withholds an average of less than two hundred fifty dollars ($250.00) of State income taxes from wages each month must file a return and pay the withheld taxes on a quarterly basis. A quarterly return covers a calendar quarter and is due by the last day of the month following the end of the quarter.

(c) Monthly. - An employer who withholds an average of at least two hundred fifty dollars ($250.00) but less than two thousand dollars ($2,000) from wages each month must file a return and pay the withheld taxes on a monthly basis. A return for the months of January through November is due by the 15th day of the month following the end of the month covered by the return. A return for the month of December is due the following January 31.

(d) Semiweekly. - An employer who withholds an average of at least two thousand dollars ($2,000) of State income taxes from wages each month shall file a return by the date set under the Code for filing a return for federal employment taxes attributable to the same wages and shall pay the withheld State taxes by the date set under the Code for depositing or paying federal employment taxes attributable to the same wages. The date set by the Code for depositing or paying federal employment taxes shall be determined without regard to § 6302(g) of the Code.

An extension of time granted to file a return for federal employment taxes attributable to wages is an automatic extension of time for filing a return for State income taxes withheld from the same wages, and an extension of time granted to pay federal employment taxes attributable to wages is an automatic extension of time for paying State income taxes withheld from the same wages. An employer who pays withheld State income taxes under this subsection is not subject to interest on or penalties for a shortfall in the amount due if the employer would not be subject to a failure-to-deposit penalty had the shortfall occurred in a deposit of federal employment taxes attributable to the same wages and the employer pays the shortfall by the date the employer would have to deposit a shortfall in the federal employment taxes.

(e) Category. - The Secretary shall monitor the amount of taxes withheld by an employer or estimate the amount of taxes to be withheld by a new employer and shall direct each employer to pay withheld taxes in accordance with the appropriate schedule. An employer shall file a return and pay withheld taxes in accordance with the Secretary's direction until notified in writing to file and pay under a different schedule. (1959, c. 1259, s. 1; 1973, c. 476, s. 193; c. 1287, s. 7; 1975, 2nd Sess., c. 979, s. 1; 1977, c. 488; 1987, c. 622, s. 9; c. 813, s. 24; 1989 (Reg. Sess., 1990), c. 945, s. 10; 1993, c. 450, s. 6; 1993 (Reg. Sess., 1994), c. 661, s. 1; 1997-109, s. 2; 2001-427, s. 5(a), (b); 2013-414, s. 39(b).)

§ 105-163.6A. Federal corrections.

If the amount of taxes an employer is required to withhold and pay under the Code is corrected or otherwise determined by the federal government, the employer must, within six months after being notified of the correction or final determination by the federal government, file a return with the Secretary reflecting the corrected or determined amount. The Secretary must propose an assessment for any additional tax due from the employer as provided in Article 9 of this Chapter. If there has been an overpayment of the tax, the Secretary must either refund the overpayment to the employer in accordance with G.S. 105-163.9 or credit the amount of the overpayment to the individual in accordance with G.S. 105-163.10. An employer who fails to comply with this section is subject to the penalties in G.S. 105-236 and forfeits the right to any refund due by reason of the determination. Failure of an employer to comply with this section does not, however, affect an individual's right to a credit under G.S. 105-163.10. (1993 (Reg. Sess., 1994), c. 582, s. 4; 2007-491, s. 17.)

§ 105-163.7. Statement to employees; information to Secretary.

(a) Every employer required to deduct and withhold from an employee's wages under G.S. 105-163.2 shall furnish to the employee in respect to the remuneration paid by the employer to such employee during the calendar year, on or before January 31 of the succeeding year, or, if the employment is terminated before the close of the calendar year, within 30 days after the date on which the last payment of remuneration is made, duplicate copies of a written statement showing the following:

(1)   The employer's name, address, and taxpayer identification number.

(2)   The employee's name and social security number.

(3)   The total amount of wages.

(4)   The total amount deducted and withheld under G.S. 105-163.2.

(b) The Secretary may require an employer to include information not listed in subsection (a) on the employer's written statement to an employee and to file the statement at a time not required by subsection (a). Every employer shall file an annual report with the Secretary that contains the information given on each of the employer's written statements to an employee and other information required by the Secretary. The annual report is due on the same date the employer's federal information return of federal income taxes withheld from wages is due under the Code. The report required by this subsection is in lieu of the report required by G.S. 105-154.

(c) Repealed by Session Laws 2002-72, s. 16, effective August 12, 2002. (1959, c. 1259, s. 1; 1973, c. 476, s. 193; 1989 (Reg. Sess., 1990), c. 945, s. 11; 1993 (Reg. Sess., 1994), c. 679, s. 8.3; 1997-109, s. 2; 2002-72, s. 16.)

§ 105-163.8. Liability of withholding agents.

(a) A withholding agent who withholds the proper amount of income taxes under this Article and pays the withheld amount to the Secretary is not liable to any person for the amount paid. A withholding agent who fails to withhold the proper amount of income taxes or pay the amount withheld to the Secretary is liable for the amount of tax not withheld or not paid. A withholding agent who fails to withhold the amount of income taxes required by this Article or who fails to pay withheld taxes by the due date for paying the taxes is subject to the penalties provided in Article 9 of this Chapter.

(b) Repealed by Session Laws 1998-212, s. 29A.14(g). (1959, c. 1259, s. 1; 1973, c. 476, s. 193; 1989 (Reg. Sess., 1990), c. 945, s. 12; 1997-109, s. 2; 1998-212, s. 29A.14(g).)

§ 105-163.9. Refund of overpayment to withholding agent.

A withholding agent who pays the Secretary more under this Article than the Article requires the agent to pay may obtain a refund of the overpayment by filing a request for a refund with the Secretary. No refund is allowed, however, if the withholding agent withheld the amount of the overpayment from the wages or compensation of the agent's employees or contractors. A withholding agent must file a request for a refund within the time period set in G.S. 105-241.6. Interest accrues on a refund as provided in G.S. 105-241.21. (1959, c. 1259, s. 1; 1973, c. 476, s. 193; 1975, c. 74, s. 1; 1981 (Reg. Sess., 1982), c. 1223, s. 3; 1989 (Reg. Sess., 1990), c. 945, s. 13; 1997-109, s. 2; 2007-491, s. 18; 2008-187, s. 15.)

§ 105-163.10. Withheld amounts credited to taxpayer for calendar year.

The amount deducted and withheld under this Article during any calendar year from the wages or compensation of an individual shall be allowed as a credit to that individual against the tax imposed by Article 4 of this Chapter for taxable years beginning in that calendar year. The amount deducted and withheld under this Article during any calendar year from the compensation of a nonresident entity shall be allowed as a credit to that entity against the tax imposed by Article 4 of this Chapter for taxable years beginning in that calendar year. If the nonresident entity is a pass-through entity, the entity shall pass through and allocate to each owner the owner's share of the credit.

If more than one taxable year begins in the calendar year during which the withholding occurred, the amount shall be allowed as a credit against the tax for the last taxable year so beginning. To obtain the credit allowed in this section, the individual or nonresident entity must file with the Secretary one copy of the withholding statement required by G.S. 105-163.3 or G.S. 105-163.7 and any other information the Secretary requires. (1959, c. 1259, s. 1; 1967, c. 1110, s. 4; 1973, c. 476, s. 193; 1989, c. 728, s. 1.44; 1991 (Reg. Sess., 1992), c. 930, s. 9; 1997-109, s. 2.)

§§ 105-163.11 through 105-163.14: Repealed by Session Laws 1985, c. 443, s. 1.

§ 105-163.15. Failure by individual to pay estimated income tax; interest.

(a) In the case of any underpayment of the estimated tax by an individual, the Secretary shall assess interest in an amount determined by applying the applicable annual rate established under G.S. 105-241.21 to the amount of the underpayment for the period of the underpayment.

(b) For purposes of subsection (a), the amount of the underpayment shall be the excess of the required installment, over the amount, if any, of the installment paid on or before the due date for the installment. The period of the underpayment shall run from the due date for the installment to whichever of the following dates is the earlier: (i) the fifteenth day of the fourth month following the close of the taxable year, or (ii) with respect to any portion of the underpayment, the date on which such portion is paid. A payment of estimated tax shall be credited against unpaid required installments in the order in which such installments are required to be paid.

(c) For purposes of this section there shall be four required installments for each taxable year with the time for payment of the installments as follows:

(1) First installment - April 15 of taxable year;

(2) Second installment - June 15 of taxable year;

(3) Third installment - September 15 of taxable year; and

(4) Fourth installment - January 15 of following taxable year.

(d) Except as provided in subsection (e), the amount of any required installment shall be twenty-five percent (25%) of the required annual payment. The term "required annual payment" means the lesser of:

(1) Ninety percent (90%) of the tax shown on the return for the taxable year, or, if no return is filed, ninety percent (90%) of the tax for that year; or

(2) One hundred percent (100%) of the tax shown on the return of the individual for the preceding taxable year, if the preceding taxable year was a taxable year of 12 months and the individual filed a return for that year.

(e) In the case of any required installment, if the individual establishes that the annualized income installment is less than the amount determined under subsection (d), the amount of the required installment shall be the annualized income installment, and any reduction in a required installment resulting from the application of this subsection shall be recaptured by increasing the amount of the next required installment determined under subsection (d) by the amount of the reduction and by increasing subsequent required installments to the extent that the reduction has not previously been recaptured.

In the case of any required installment, the annualized income installment is the excess, if any, of (i) an amount equal to the applicable percentage of the tax for the taxable year computed by placing on an annualized basis the taxable income for months in the taxable year ending before the due date for the installment, over (ii) the aggregate amount of any prior required installments for the taxable year. The taxable income shall be placed on an annualized basis under rules prescribed by the Secretary. The applicable percentages for the required installments are as follows:

(1) First installment - twenty-two and one-half percent (22.5%);

(2) Second installment - forty-five percent (45%);

(3) Third installment - sixty-seven and one-half percent (67.5%); and

(4) Fourth installment - ninety percent (90%).

(f) No interest shall be imposed under subsection (a) if the tax shown on the return for the taxable year reduced by the tax withheld under this Article is less than the amount set in section 6654(e) of the Code or if the individual did not have any liability for tax under Part 2 of Article 4 for the preceding taxable year.

(g) For purposes of this section, the term "tax" means the tax imposed by Part 2 of Article 4 minus the credits against the tax allowed by this Chapter other than the credit allowed by this Article. The amount of the credit allowed under this Article for withheld income tax for the taxable year is considered a payment of estimated tax, and an equal part of that amount is considered to have been paid on each due date of the taxable year, unless the taxpayer establishes the dates on which all amounts were actually withheld, in which case the amounts so withheld are considered payments of estimated tax on the dates on which the amounts were actually withheld.

(h) If, on or before January 31 of the following taxable year, the taxpayer files a return for the taxable year and pays in full the amount computed on the return as payable, no interest shall be imposed under subsection (a) with respect to any underpayment of the fourth required installment for the taxable year.

(i) Notwithstanding subsections (c), (d), (e), and (h) of this section, an individual who is a farmer or fisherman for a taxable year is subject to the provisions of this subsection.

(1) One installment. - The individual is required to make only one installment payment of tax for that taxable year. This installment is due on or before January 15 of the following taxable year. The amount of the installment payment must be the lesser of:

a. Sixty-six and two-thirds percent (66 2/3%) of the tax shown on the return for the taxable year, or, if no return is filed, sixty-six and two-thirds percent (66 2/3%) of the tax for that year; or

b. One hundred percent (100%) of the tax shown on the return of the individual for the preceding taxable year, if the preceding taxable year was a taxable year of 12 months and the individual filed a return for that year.

(2) Exception. - If, on or before March 1 of the following taxable year, the taxpayer files a return for the taxable year and pays in full the amount computed on the return as payable, no interest is imposed under subsection (a) of this section with respect to any underpayment of the required installment for the taxable year.

(3) Eligibility. - An individual is a farmer or fisherman for any taxable year if the individual's gross income from farming or fishing, including oyster farming,

for the taxable year is at least sixty-six and two-thirds percent (66 2/3%) of the total gross income from all sources for the taxable year, or the individual's gross income from farming or fishing, including oyster farming, shown on the return of the individual for the preceding taxable year is at least sixty-six and two-thirds percent (66 2/3%) of the total gross income from all sources shown on the return.

(j) In applying this section to a taxable year beginning on any date other than January 1, there shall be substituted, for the months specified in this section, the months that correspond thereto. This section shall be applied to taxable years of less than 12 months in accordance with rules prescribed by the Secretary.

(k) This section shall not apply to any estate or trust. (1959, c. 1259, s. 1; 1963, c. 785, ss. 3, 4; 1973, c. 476, s. 193; c. 1287, s. 7; 1977, c. 657, s. 5; c. 1114, s. 8; 1985, c. 443, s. 2; 1989, c. 692, s. 7.1; 1991 (Reg. Sess., 1992), c. 950, s. 1; 1997-109, s. 2; 1998-98, s. 71; 1998-212, s. 29A.14(h); 2000-126, s. 4; 2005-276, s. 6.37(l); 2007-491, s. 44(1)a.)

§ 105-163.16. Overpayment refunded.

If the amount of wages or compensation withheld at the source under this Article exceeds the tax imposed by Article 4 of this Chapter against which the withheld tax is credited under G.S. 105-163.10, the excess is considered an overpayment by the employee or contractor. If the amount of estimated tax paid under G.S. 105-163.15 exceeds the taxes imposed by Article 4 of this Chapter against which the estimated tax is credited under the provisions of this Article, the excess is considered an overpayment by the taxpayer. An overpayment shall be refunded as provided in Article 9 of this Chapter. (1959, c. 1259, s. 1; 1967, c. 702, s. 2; 1973, c. 476, s. 193; c. 903, s. 3; 1975, c. 74, s. 2; 1979, c. 801, s. 71; 1981 (Reg. Sess., 1982), c. 1223, s. 1; 1983, c. 663, s. 2; c. 865, s. 1; 1985, c. 443, s. 3; 1987 (Reg. Sess., 1988), c. 1063, s. 2; 1989, c. 728, s. 1.45; 1989 (Reg. Sess., 1990), c. 814, s. 23; 1991, c. 45, s. 22; 1993, c. 315, s. 2; 1997-109, s. 2.)

§§ 105-163.17 through 105-163.18: Repealed by Session Laws 1997, c. 109, s. 2.

§§ 105-163.19 through 105-163.21. Repealed by Session Laws 1967, c. 1110, s. 4.

§ 105-163.22. Reciprocity.

The Secretary may, with the approval of the Attorney General, enter into agreements with the taxing authorities of states having income tax withholding statutes with such agreements to govern the amounts to be withheld from the wages and salaries of residents of such other state or states under the provisions of this Article when such other state or states grant similar treatment to the residents of this State. Such agreements may provide for recognition of the anticipated tax credits allowed under the provisions of G.S. 105-151 in determining the amounts to be withheld. (1959, c. 1259, s. 1; 1973, c. 476, s. 193; 1997-109, s. 2.)

§ 105-163.23. Withholding from federal employees.

The Secretary is designated as the proper official to make request for and enter into agreements with the Secretary of the Treasury of the United States to provide for the compliance with this Article by the head of each department or agency of the United States in withholding of State income taxes from wages of federal employees and paying the same to this State. The Secretary is authorized, empowered, and directed to request and enter into these agreements. (1959, c. 1259, s. 1; 1973, c. 476, s. 193; 1997-109, s. 2.)

§ 105-163.24. Construction of Article.

This Article shall be liberally construed in pari materia with Article 4 of this Chapter to the end that taxes levied by Article 4 shall be collected with respect to wages and compensation by withholding agents' withholding of the appropriate amounts and by individuals' payments in installments of income tax with respect to income not subject to withholding. (1959, c. 1259, s. 1; 1997-109, s. 2.)

Article 4B.

Filing of Declarations of Estimated Income Tax and Installment Payments of Estimated Income Tax by Corporations.

§§ 105-163.25 through 105-163.37: Recodified as §§ 105-163.38 through 105-163.44.

Article 4C.

Filing of Declarations of Estimated Income Tax and Installment Payments of Estimated Income Tax by Corporations.

§ 105-163.38. Definitions.

The following definitions apply in this Article, unless the context requires otherwise:

(1)　Code. - Defined in G.S. 105-228.90.

(1a)　Corporation. - Defined in section 7701 of the Code.

(2)　Estimated tax. - The amount of income tax the corporation estimates as the amount imposed by Article 4 for the taxable year.

(3)　Fiscal year. - An accounting period of 12 months ending on the last day of any month other than December.

(4)　Secretary. - The Secretary of Revenue.

(5)　Taxable year. - The calendar year or fiscal year used as a basis to determine net income under Article 4. If no fiscal year has been established, "fiscal year" means the calendar year. In the case of a return made for a fractional part of the year under Article 4, or under rules prescribed by the Secretary, "taxable year" means the period for which the return is made. (1959, c. 1259, s. 1A; 1973, c. 476, s. 193; 1983, c. 713, s. 86; 1989 (Reg. Sess., 1990), c. 984, s. 15; 1991 (Reg. Sess., 1992), c. 922, s. 8; 1993, c. 12, s. 10.)

§ 105-163.39. Declarations of estimated income tax required.

(a) Declaration Required. - Every corporation subject to taxation under Article 4 shall submit a declaration of estimated tax to the Secretary. This declaration is due at the time established in G.S. 105-163.40, and payment of the estimated tax is due at the time and in the manner prescribed in that section.

(b) Content. - In the declaration of estimated tax, the corporation shall state its estimated total net income from all sources for the taxable year, the proportion of its total net income allocable to this State, its estimated tax, and any other information required by the Secretary.

(c) Amendments to Declaration. - Under rules prescribed by the Secretary, a corporation may amend a declaration of estimated tax. (1959, c. 1259, s. 1A; 1973, c. 476, s. 193; 1983, c. 713, s. 86.)

§ 105-163.40. Time for submitting declaration; time and method for paying estimated tax; form of payment.

(a) Due Dates of Declarations. - Declarations of estimated tax are due at the same time as the corporation's first installment payment. Installment payments are due as follows:

(1) If, before the 1st day of the 4th month of the taxable year, the corporation's estimated tax equals or exceeds five hundred dollars ($500.00), the corporation shall pay the estimated tax in four equal installments on or before the 15th day of the 4th, 6th, 9th and 12th months of the taxable year.

(2) If, after the last day of the 3rd month and before the 1st day of the 6th month of the taxable year, the corporation's estimated tax equals or exceeds five hundred dollars ($500.00), the corporation shall pay the estimated tax in three equal installments on or before the 15th day of the 6th, 9th and 12th months of the taxable year.

(3) If, after the last day of the 5th month and before the 1st day of the 9th month of the taxable year, the corporation's estimated tax equals or exceeds five hundred dollars ($500.00), the corporation shall pay the estimated tax in two equal installments on or before the 15th day of the 9th and 12th months.

(4) If, after the last day of the 8th month and before the 1st day of the 12th month of the taxable year, the corporation's estimated tax equals or exceeds five hundred dollars ($500.00), the corporation shall pay the estimated tax on or before the 15th day of the 12th month of the taxable year.

(b) Payment of Estimated Tax When Declaration Amended. - When a corporation submits an amended declaration after making one or more installment payments on its estimated tax, the amount of each remaining installment shall be the amount that would have been payable if the estimate in the amended declaration was the original estimate, increased or decreased as appropriate by the amount computed by dividing:

(1) The absolute value of the difference between:

a. The amount paid and

b. The amount that would have been paid if the estimate in the amended declaration was the original estimate by

(2) The number of remaining installments.

(c) Short Taxable Year. - Payment of estimated tax for taxable years of less than 12 months shall be made in accordance with rules promulgated by the Secretary.

(d) Form of Payment. - A corporation that is required under the Code to pay its federal-estimated corporate income tax by electronic funds transfer must pay its State-estimated tax by electronic funds transfer. (1959, c. 1259, s. 1A; 1973, c. 476, s. 193; 1983, c. 713, s. 86; 1989 (Reg. Sess., 1990), c. 984, s. 16; 1999-389, s. 7.)

§ 105-163.41. Underpayment.

(a) Except as provided in subsection (d), if the amount of estimated tax paid by a corporation during the taxable year is less than the amount of tax imposed upon the corporation under Article 4 of this Chapter for the taxable year, the corporation must be assessed interest in an amount determined by multiplying the amount of the underpayment as determined under subsection (b), for the period of the underpayment as determined under subsection (c), by the percentage established as the rate of interest on assessments under G.S. 105-241.21 that is in effect for the period of the underpayment. For the purpose of this section, the amount of tax imposed under Article 4 of this Chapter is the net amount after subtracting the credits against the tax allowed by this Chapter other than the credit allowed by this Article.

(b) The amount of the underpayment shall be the difference between:

(1) The amount of the installment the corporation would have been required to pay if the corporation's estimated tax equalled ninety percent (90%) of the tax imposed under Article 4 for the taxable year, assuming the same schedule of installments, or ninety percent (90%) of the tax imposed for the taxable year if the corporation made no installment payments; and

(2) The amount, if any, of the corresponding installment timely paid by the corporation.

(c) The period of the underpayment runs from the date the installment was required to be paid to the earlier of:

(1) The 15th day of the fourth month following the close of the taxable year, or

(2) With respect to any portion of the underpayment, the date on which the portion is paid. An installment payment of estimated tax is considered a payment of any previous underpayment only to the extent the payment exceeds the amount of the installment determined under subdivision (1) of subsection (b) for that installment date.

(d) Except as provided in subdivision (5) of this subsection, the interest for underpayment imposed by this section shall not be imposed if the total amount of all payments of estimated tax made on or before the last date prescribed for the payment of the installments equals or exceeds the amount that would have been required to be paid on or before that date if the estimated tax was equal to the least of:

(1) The tax shown on the return of the corporation for the preceding taxable year, if the corporation filed a return for the preceding taxable year and the preceding year was a taxable year of 12 months;

(2) An amount equal to the tax computed at the rates applicable to the taxable year but otherwise on the basis of the facts shown on the return of the corporation for, and the law applicable to, the preceding taxable year; or

(3) An amount equal to ninety percent (90%) of the tax for the taxable year computed by placing on an annualized basis the taxable income:

a. For the first three months of the taxable year, in the case of the installment required to be paid in the 4th month;

b. For the first three months or for the first five months of the taxable year, in the case of the installment required to be paid in the 6th month;

c. For the first six months or for the first eight months of the taxable year, in the case of the installment required to be paid in the 9th month; and

d. For the first nine months or for the first 11 months of the taxable year, in the case of the installment required to be paid in the 12th month of the taxable year.

(4) For purposes of this subdivision, the taxable income shall be placed on an annualized basis by multiplying by 12 the taxable income referred to in the preceding sentence, and dividing the resulting amount by the number of months in the taxable year (3, 5, 6, 8, 9, or 11 as the case may be) referred to in that sentence.

(5) In the case of a large corporation, as defined in section 6655 of the Code, subdivisions (1) and (2) of this subsection shall not apply. (1959, c. 1259, s. 1A; 1973, c. 476, s. 193; 1977, c. 1114, s. 9; 1983, c. 713, s. 86; 1987 (Reg. Sess., 1988), c. 994, ss. 2, 3; 2001-414, s. 13; 2005-276, s. 6.37(m); 2007-491, s. 44(1)a; 2013-414, s. 3.)

§ 105-163.42. Repealed by Session Laws 1985 (Regular Session, 1986), c. 820.

§ 105-163.43. Overpayment refunded.

If the amount of estimated tax paid under this Article exceeds the taxes against which the estimated tax is credited pursuant to this Article, the excess is considered an overpayment by the taxpayer and shall be refunded as provided in Article 9 of this Chapter. (1959, c. 1259, s. 1A; 1967, c. 1110, s. 5; 1973, c. 476, s. 193; 1983, c. 713, s. 86; 1993, c. 315, s. 1.)

§ 105-163.44: Repealed by Session Laws 2000-140, s. 66.

Article 5.

Sales and Use Tax.

§ 105-164: Repealed by Session Laws 1957, c. 1340, s. 5.

Part 1. Title, Purpose and Definitions.

§ 105-164.1. Short title.

This Article shall be known as the "North Carolina Sales and Use Tax Act." (1957, c. 1340, s. 5; 1998-98, s. 47.)

§ 105-164.2. Purpose.

The taxes herein imposed shall be in addition to all other license, privilege or excise taxes and the taxes levied by this Article are to provide revenue for the support of the public school system of this State and for other necessary uses and purposes of the government and State of North Carolina. (1957, c. 1340, s. 5.)

§ 105-164.3. Definitions.

The following definitions apply in this Article:

(1) Advertising and promotional direct mail. - Printed material that meets the definition of "direct mail" and the primary purpose of which is to attract public attention to a product, person, business, or organization, or to attempt to sell,

popularize, or secure financial support for a product, person, business, or organization. As used in this subdivision, "product" means tangible personal property, digital property, or a service.

(1a)　Analytical services. - Testing laboratories that are included in national industry 541380 of NAICS or medical laboratories that are included in national industry 621511 of NAICS.

(1b)　Ancillary service. - A service associated with or incidental to the provision of a telecommunications service. The term includes detailed communications billing, directory assistance, vertical service, and voice mail service. A vertical service is a service, such as call forwarding, caller ID, three-way calling, and conference bridging, that allows a customer to identify a caller or manage multiple calls and call connections.

(1c)　through (1e) Reserved for future codification purposes.

(1f)　Audio work. - A series of musical, spoken, or other sounds, including a ringtone.

(1g)　Audiovisual work. - A series of related images and any sounds accompanying the images that impart an impression of motion when shown in succession.

(1h)　Reserved for future codification purposes.

(1i)　Bundled transaction. - A retail sale of two or more distinct and identifiable products, at least one of which is taxable and one of which is exempt, for one nonitemized price. Products are not sold for one nonitemized price if an invoice or another sales document made available to the purchaser separately identifies the price of each product. A bundled transaction does not include the retail sale of any of the following:

a.　A product and any packaging item that accompanies the product and is exempt under G.S. 105-164.13(23).

b.　A sale of two or more products whose combined price varies, or is negotiable, depending on the products the purchaser selects.

c.　A sale of a product accompanied by a transfer of another product with no additional consideration.

d. A product and the delivery or installation of the product.

e. A product and any service necessary to complete the sale.

(1j) Reserved for future codification purposes.

(1k) Business. - An activity a person engages in or causes another to engage in with the object of gain, profit, benefit, or advantage, either direct or indirect. The term does not include an occasional and isolated sale or transaction by a person who does not claim to be engaged in business.

(1l) Reserved for future codification purposes.

(1m) Cable service. - The one-way transmission to subscribers of video programming or other programming service and any subscriber interaction required to select or use the service.

(2) Candy. - A preparation of sugar, honey, or other natural or artificial sweeteners in combination with chocolate, fruits, nuts, or other ingredients or flavorings in the form of bars, drops, or pieces that do not require refrigeration. The term does not include any preparation that contains flour.

(3) Clothing. - All human wearing apparel suitable for general use including coats, jackets, hats, hosiery, scarves, and shoes.

(4) Clothing accessories or equipment. - Incidental items worn on the person or in conjunction with clothing including jewelry, cosmetics, eyewear, wallets, and watches.

(4a) Combined general rate. - The State's general rate of tax set in G.S. 105-164.4(a) plus the sum of the rates of the local sales and use taxes authorized by Subchapter VIII of this Chapter for every county in this State.

(4b) Computer. - An electronic device that accepts information in digital or similar form and manipulates it for a result based on a sequence of instructions.

(4c) Computer software. - A set of coded instructions designed to cause a computer or automatic data processing equipment to perform a task.

(4d) Computer supply. - An item that is considered a "school computer supply" under the Streamlined Agreement.

(5) Consumer. - A person who stores, uses, or otherwise consumes in this State tangible personal property, digital property, or a service purchased or received from a retailer either within or without this State.

(5a) Reserved for future codification purposes.

(5b) Custom computer software. - Computer software that is not prewritten computer software. The term includes a user manual or other documentation that accompanies the sale of the software.

(5c) Datacenter. - A facility that provides infrastructure for hosting or data processing services and that has power and cooling systems that are created and maintained to be concurrently maintainable and to include redundant capacity components and multiple distribution paths serving the computer equipment at the facility. Although the facility must have multiple distribution paths serving the computer equipment, a single distribution path may serve the computer equipment at any one time. The following definitions apply in this subdivision:

a. Concurrently maintainable. - Capable of having any capacity component or distribution element serviced or repaired on a planned basis without interrupting or impeding the performance of the computer equipment.

b. Multiple distribution paths. - A series of distribution paths configured to ensure that failure on one distribution path does not interrupt or impede other distribution paths.

c. Redundant capacity components. - Components beyond those required to support the computer equipment.

(5d) Repealed by Session Laws 2009-451, s. 27A.3(d), effective January 1, 2010, and applicable to sales made on or after that date.

(6) Delivery charges. - Charges imposed by the retailer for preparation and delivery of personal property or services to a location designated by the consumer.

(6a) Development tier. - The classification assigned to an area pursuant to G.S. 143B-437.08.

(7) Dietary supplement. - A product that is intended to supplement the diet of humans and is required to be labeled as a dietary supplement under federal law, identifiable by the "Supplement Facts" box found on the label.

(7a) Digital code. - A code that gives a purchaser of the code a right to receive an item by electronic delivery or electronic access. A digital code may be obtained by an electronic means or by a tangible means. A digital code does not include a gift certificate or a gift card.

(7c) Direct mail. - Printed material delivered or distributed by the United States Postal Service or other delivery service to a mass audience or to addresses on a mailing list provided by the purchaser or at the direction of the purchaser when the cost of the items is not billed directly to the recipients. The term includes tangible personal property supplied directly or indirectly by the purchaser to the direct mail seller for inclusion in the package containing the printed material. The term does not include multiple items of printed material delivered to a single address.

(8) Direct-to-home satellite service. - Programming transmitted or broadcast by satellite directly to the subscribers' premises without the use of ground equipment or distribution equipment, except equipment at the subscribers' premises or the uplink process to the satellite.

(8a) Drug. - A compound, substance, or preparation or a component of one of these that meets any of the following descriptions and is not food, a dietary supplement, or an alcoholic beverage:

a. Is recognized in the United States Pharmacopoeia, Homeopathic Pharmacopoeia of the United States, or National Formulary.

b. Is intended for use in the diagnosis, cure, mitigation, treatment, or prevention of disease.

c. Is intended to affect the structure or function of the body.

(8b) Durable medical equipment. - Equipment that meets all of the conditions of this subdivision. The term includes repair and replacement parts for the equipment. The term does not include mobility enhancing equipment.

a. Can withstand repeated use.

b. Primarily and customarily used to serve a medical purpose.

c. Generally not useful to a person in the absence of an illness or injury.

d. Not worn in or on the body.

(8c) Durable medical supplies. - Supplies related to use with durable medical equipment that are eligible to be covered under the Medicare or Medicaid program.

(8d) Electronic. - Relating to technology having electrical, digital, magnetic, wireless, optical, electromagnetic, or similar capabilities.

(8e) Eligible Internet datacenter. - A datacenter that satisfies each of the following conditions:

a. The facility is used primarily or is to be used primarily by a business engaged in software publishing included in industry 511210 of NAICS or an Internet activity included in industry 519130 of NAICS.

b. The facility is comprised of a structure or series of structures located or to be located on a single parcel of land or on contiguous parcels of land that are commonly owned or owned by affiliation with the operator of that facility.

c. The facility is located or to be located in a county that was designated, at the time of application for the written determination required under sub-subdivision d. of this subdivision, either an enterprise tier one, two, or three area or a development tier one or two area pursuant to G.S. 105-129.3 or G.S. 143B-437.08, regardless of any subsequent change in county enterprise or development tier status.

d. The Secretary of Commerce has made a written determination that at least two hundred fifty million dollars ($250,000,000) in private funds has been or will be invested in real property or eligible business property, or a combination of both, at the facility within five years after the commencement of construction of the facility.

(8f) Eligible railroad intermodal facility. - Defined in G.S. 105-129.95.

(8g) Energy Star qualified product. - A product that meets the energy efficient guidelines set by the United States Environmental Protection Agency and the United States Department of Energy and is authorized to carry the Energy Star label.

(9) Engaged in business. - Any of the following:

a. Maintaining, occupying, or using permanently or temporarily, directly or indirectly, or through a subsidiary or agent, by whatever name called, any office, place of distribution, sales or sample room, warehouse or storage place, or other place of business for selling or delivering tangible personal property, digital property, or a service for storage, use, or consumption in this State, or permanently or temporarily, directly or through a subsidiary, having any representative, agent, sales representative, or solicitor operating in this State in the selling or delivering. The fact that any corporate retailer, agent, or subsidiary engaged in business in this State may not be legally domesticated or qualified to do business in this State is immaterial.

b. Maintaining in this State, either permanently or temporarily, directly or through a subsidiary, tangible personal property or digital property for the purpose of lease or rental.

c. Making a remote sale, if one of the conditions listed in G.S. 105-164.8(b) is met.

d. Shipping wine directly to a purchaser in this State as authorized by G.S. 18B-1001.1.

(10) Food. - Substances that are sold for ingestion or chewing by humans and are consumed for their taste or nutritional value. The substances may be in liquid, concentrated, solid, frozen, dried, or dehydrated form. The term does not include an alcoholic beverage, as defined in G.S. 105-113.68, or a tobacco product, as defined in G.S. 105-113.4.

(11) Food sold through a vending machine. - Food dispensed from a machine or another mechanical device that accepts payment.

(12) Gross sales. - The sum total of the sales price of all retail sales of tangible personal property, digital property, and services.

(13) Hub. - Either of the following:

a. An interstate air courier's hub is the interstate air courier's principal airport within the State for sorting and distributing letters and packages and from which the interstate air courier has, or expects to have upon completion of construction, no less than 150 departures a month under normal operating conditions.

b. An interstate passenger air carrier's hub is the airport in this State that meets both of the following conditions:

1. The air carrier has allocated to the airport under G.S. 105-338 more than sixty percent (60%) of its aircraft value apportioned to this State.

2. The majority of the air carrier's passengers boarding at the airport are connecting from other airports rather than originating at that airport.

(14) In this (the) State. - Within the exterior limits of the State of North Carolina, including all territory within these limits owned by or ceded to the United States of America.

(14a) Information service. - A service that generates, acquires, stores, processes, or retrieves data and information and delivers it electronically to or allows electronic access by a consumer whose primary purpose for using the service is to obtain the processed data or information.

(14c) Interstate air business. - An interstate air courier, an interstate freight air carrier, or an interstate passenger air carrier.

(15) Interstate air courier. - A person whose primary business is the furnishing of air delivery of individually addressed letters and packages for compensation, in interstate commerce, except by the United States Postal Service.

(15b) Interstate freight air carrier. - A person whose primary business is scheduled freight air transportation, as defined in the North American Industry Classification System adopted by the United States Office of Management and Budget, in interstate commerce.

(16) Interstate passenger air carrier. - A person whose primary business is scheduled passenger air transportation, as defined in the North American Industry Classification System adopted by the United States Office of Management and Budget, in interstate commerce.

(17) Lease or rental. - A transfer of possession or control of tangible personal property for a fixed or indeterminate term for consideration. The term does not include any of the following:

a. A transfer of possession or control of property under a security agreement or deferred payment plan that requires the transfer of title upon completion of the required payments.

b. A transfer of possession or control of property under an agreement that requires the transfer of title upon completion of required payments and payment of an option price that does not exceed the greater of one hundred dollars ($100.00) or one percent (1%) of the total required payments.

c. The providing of tangible personal property along with an operator for a fixed or indeterminate period of time if the operator is necessary for the equipment to perform as designed. For the purpose of this sub-subdivision, an operator must do more than maintain, inspect, or set up the tangible personal property.

(17a) Repealed by Session Laws 2009-451, s. 27A.3(d), effective January 1, 2010, and applicable to sales made on or after that date.

(18) Repealed by Session Laws 2009-451, s. 27A.3(g), effective August 7, 2009.

(19) Major recycling facility. - Defined in G.S. 105-129.25.

(20) Manufactured home. - A structure that is designed to be used as a dwelling and is manufactured in accordance with the specifications for manufactured homes issued by the United States Department of Housing and Urban Development.

a., b. Repealed by Session Laws 2003-400, s. 13, effective January 1, 2004, and applicable to sales of modular homes on and after that date.

(21) Mobile telecommunications service. - A radio communication service carried on between mobile stations or receivers and land stations and by mobile stations communicating among themselves and includes all of the following:

a. Both one-way and two-way radio communication services.

b. A mobile service that provides a regularly interacting group of base, mobile, portable, and associated control and relay stations for private one-way or two-way land mobile radio communications by eligible users over designated areas of operation.

c. Any service for which a federal license is required in a personal communications service.

(21a) Mobility enhancing equipment. - Equipment that meets all of the conditions of this subdivision. The term includes repair and replacement parts for the equipment. The term does not include durable medical equipment.

a. Primarily and customarily used to provide or increase the ability of an individual to move from one place to another.

b. Appropriate for use either in a home or motor vehicle.

c. Not generally used by a person with normal mobility.

d. Not normally provided on a motor vehicle by a motor vehicle manufacturer.

(21b) Modular home. - A factory-built structure that is designed to be used as a dwelling, is manufactured in accordance with the specifications for modular homes under the North Carolina State Residential Building Code, and bears a seal or label issued by the Department of Insurance pursuant to G.S. 143-139.1.

(21c) Modular homebuilder. - A person who furnishes for consideration a modular home to a purchaser that will occupy the modular home. The purchaser can be a person that will lease or rent the unit as real property.

(22) Moped. - A vehicle that has two or three wheels, no external shifting device, and a motor that does not exceed 50 cubic centimeters piston displacement and cannot propel the vehicle at a speed greater than 30 miles per hour on a level surface.

(23) Motor vehicle. - A vehicle that is designed primarily for use upon the highways and is either self-propelled or propelled by a self-propelled vehicle, but does not include:

a. A moped.

b. Special mobile equipment.

c. A tow dolly that is exempt from motor vehicle title and registration requirements under G.S. 20-51(10) or (11).

d. A farm tractor or other implement of husbandry.

e. A manufactured home, a mobile office, or a mobile classroom.

f. Road construction or road maintenance machinery or equipment.

(23a) NAICS. - Defined in G.S. 105-228.90.

(24) Net taxable sales. - The gross retail sales of the business of a retailer taxed under this Article after deducting exempt sales and nontaxable sales.

(25) Nonresident retail or wholesale merchant. - A person who does not have a place of business in this State, is registered for sales and use tax purposes in a taxing jurisdiction outside the State, and is engaged in the business of acquiring, by purchase, consignment, or otherwise, tangible personal property or digital property and selling the property outside the State or in the business of providing a service.

(25a) Other direct mail. - Any direct mail that is not advertising and promotional mail regardless of whether advertising and promotional direct mail is included in the same mailing.

(25b) Over-the-counter drug. - A drug that contains a label that identifies the product as a drug as required by 21 C.F.R. § 201.66. The label includes either of the following:

a. A "Drug Facts" panel.

b. A statement of its active ingredients with a list of those ingredients contained in the compound, substance, or preparation.

(26) Person. - Defined in G.S. 105-228.90.

(26a) Place of primary use. - The street address representative of where the use of a customer's telecommunications service primarily occurs. The street address must be the customer's residential street address or primary business street address. For mobile telecommunications service, the street address must be within the licensed service area of the service provider. If the customer who contracted with the telecommunications provider for the telecommunications service is not the end user of the service, the end user is considered the customer for the purpose of determining the place of primary use.

(26b) Prepaid calling service. - A right that meets all of the following requirements:

a. Authorizes the exclusive purchase of telecommunications service.

b. Must be paid for in advance.

c. Enables the origination of calls by means of an access number, authorization code, or another similar means, regardless of whether the access number or authorization code is manually or electronically dialed.

d. Is sold in predetermined units or dollars whose number or dollar value declines with use and is known on a continuous basis.

(27) Prepaid telephone calling service. - Prepaid calling service or prepaid wireless calling service.

(27a) Prepaid wireless calling service. - A right that meets all of the following requirements:

a. Authorizes the purchase of mobile telecommunications service, either exclusively or in conjunction with other services.

b. Must be paid for in advance.

c. Is sold in predetermined units or dollars whose number or dollar value declines with use and is known on a continuous basis.

(28) Prepared food. - Food that meets at least one of the conditions of this subdivision. Prepared food does not include food the retailer sliced, repackaged, or pasteurized but did not heat, mix, or sell with eating utensils.

a. It is sold in a heated state or it is heated by the retailer.

b. It consists of two or more foods mixed or combined by the retailer for sale as a single item. This sub-subdivision does not include foods containing raw eggs, fish, meat, or poultry that require cooking by the consumer as recommended by the Food and Drug Administration to prevent food borne illnesses.

c. It is sold with eating utensils provided by the retailer, such as plates, knives, forks, spoons, glasses, cups, napkins, and straws.

(29) Prescription. - An order, formula, or recipe issued orally, in writing, electronically, or by another means of transmission by a physician, dentist, veterinarian, or another person licensed to prescribe drugs.

(29a) Prewritten computer software. - Computer software, including prewritten upgrades, that is not designed and developed by the author or another creator to the specifications of a specific purchaser. The term includes software designed and developed by the author or another creator to the specifications of a specific purchaser when it is sold to a person other than the specific purchaser.

(30) Production company. - A person engaged in the business of making original motion picture, television, or radio images for theatrical, commercial, advertising, or educational purposes.

(30a) Professional motorsports racing team. - A racing team that satisfies all of the following conditions:

a. The team is operated for profit.

b. The team does not claim a deduction under section 183 of the Code.

c. The team competes in at least sixty-six percent (66%) of the races sponsored in a race series in a single season by a motorsports sanctioning body.

(30b) Prosthetic device. - A replacement, corrective, or supporting device worn on or in the body that meets one of the conditions of this subdivision. The term includes repair and replacement parts for the device.

a. Artificially replaces a missing portion of the body.

b. Prevents or corrects a physical deformity or malfunction.

c. Supports a weak or deformed portion of the body.

(31) Protective equipment. - Items for human wear and designed as protection of the wearer against injury or disease or as protection against damage or injury of other persons or property but not suitable for general use including breathing masks, face shields, hard hats, and tool belts.

(32) Purchase. - Acquired for consideration, regardless of any of the following:

a. Whether the acquisition was effected by a transfer of title or possession, or both, or a license to use or consume.

b. Whether the transfer was absolute or conditional regardless of the means by which it was effected.

c. Whether the consideration is a price or rental in money or by way of exchange or barter.

(33) Purchase price. - The term has the same meaning as the term "sales price" when applied to an item subject to use tax.

(33b) Related member. - Defined in G.S. 105-130.7A.

(33c) Remote sale. - A sale of tangible personal property or digital property ordered by mail, by telephone, via the Internet, or by another similar method, to a purchaser who is in this State at the time the order is remitted, from a retailer who receives the order in another state and delivers the property or causes it to be delivered to a person in this State. It is presumed that a resident of this State who remits an order was in this State at the time the order was remitted.

(34) Retail sale or sale at retail. - The sale, lease, or rental for any purpose other than for resale, sublease, or subrent.

(35) Retailer. - A person engaged in the business of any of the following:

a. Making sales at retail, offering to make sales at retail, or soliciting sales at retail of tangible personal property, digital property, or services for storage, use, or consumption in this State. When the Secretary finds it necessary for the efficient administration of this Article to regard any sales representatives, solicitors, representatives, consignees, peddlers, or truckers as agents of the dealers, distributors, consignors, supervisors, employers, or persons under whom they operate or from whom they obtain the items sold by them regardless of whether they are making sales on their own behalf or on behalf of these dealers, distributors, consignors, supervisors, employers, or persons, the Secretary may so regard them and may regard the dealers, distributors, consignors, supervisors, employers, or persons as "retailers" for the purpose of this Article.

b. Delivering, erecting, installing, or applying tangible personal property for use in this State, regardless of whether the property is permanently affixed to real property or other tangible personal property.

c. Making a remote sale, if one of the conditions listed in G.S. 105-164.8(b) is met.

(35c) Ringtone. - A digitized sound file that is downloaded onto a device and that may be used to alert the user of the device with respect to a communication.

(36) Sale or selling. - The transfer for consideration of title, license to use or consume, or possession of tangible personal property or digital property or the performance for consideration of a service. The transfer or performance may be conditional or in any manner or by any means. The term includes the following:

a. Fabrication of tangible personal property for consumers by persons engaged in business who furnish either directly or indirectly the materials used in the fabrication work.

b. Furnishing or preparing tangible personal property consumed on the premises of the person furnishing or preparing the property or consumed at the place at which the property is furnished or prepared.

c. A transaction in which the possession of the property is transferred but the seller retains title or security for the payment of the consideration.

d. A lease or rental.

e. Transfer of a digital code.

(37) Sales price. - The total amount or consideration for which tangible personal property, digital property, or services are sold, leased, or rented. The consideration may be in the form of cash, credit, property, or services. The sales price must be valued in money, regardless of whether it is received in money.

a. The term includes all of the following:

1. The retailer's cost of the property sold.

2. The cost of materials used, labor or service costs, interest, losses, all costs of transportation to the retailer, all taxes imposed on the retailer, and any other expense of the retailer.

3. Charges by the retailer for any services necessary to complete the sale.

4. Delivery charges.

5. Installation charges.

6. Repealed by Session Laws 2007-244, s. 1, effective October 1, 2007.

7. Credit for trade-in.

8. Discounts that are reimbursable by a third party and can be determined at the time of sale through any of the following:

I. Presentation by the consumer of a coupon or other documentation.

II. Identification of the consumer as a member of a group eligible for a discount.

III. The invoice the retailer gives the consumer.

b. The term does not include any of the following:

1. Discounts that are not reimbursable by a third party, are allowed by the retailer, and are taken by a consumer on a sale.

2. Interest, financing, and carrying charges from credit extended on the sale, if the amount is separately stated on the invoice, bill of sale, or a similar document given to the consumer.

3. Any taxes imposed directly on the consumer that are separately stated on the invoice, bill of sale, or similar document given to the consumer.

(37a) Satellite digital audio radio service. - A radio communication service in which audio programming is digitally transmitted by satellite to an earth-based receiver, whether directly or via a repeater station.

(37b) School instructional material. - Written material commonly used by a student in a course of study as a reference and to learn the subject being taught. The following is an all-inclusive list:

a. Reference books.

b. Reference maps and globes.

c. Textbooks.

d. Workbooks.

(37d) School supply. - An item that is commonly used by a student in the course of study and is considered a "school supply" or "school art supply" under the Streamlined Agreement.

(38) Secretary. - The Secretary of the North Carolina Department of Revenue.

(38b) Service contract. - A warranty agreement, a maintenance agreement, a repair contract, or a similar agreement or contract by which the seller agrees to maintain or repair tangible personal property.

(39) Repealed by Session Laws 2002-16, s. 3, effective August 1, 2002, and applicable to taxable services reflected on bills dated after August 1, 2002.

(40) Soft drink. - A nonalcoholic beverage that contains natural or artificial sweeteners. The term does not include beverages that contain one or more of the following:

a. Milk or milk products.

b. Soy, rice, or similar milk substitutes.

c. More than fifty percent (50%) vegetable or fruit juice.

(41) Special mobile equipment. - Any of the following:

a. A vehicle that has a permanently attached crane, mill, well-boring apparatus, ditch-digging apparatus, air compressor, electric welder, feed mixer, grinder, or other similar apparatus is driven on the highway only to get to and from a nonhighway job and is not designed or used primarily for the transportation of persons or property.

b. A vehicle that has permanently attached special equipment and is used only for parade purposes.

c. A vehicle that is privately owned, has permanently attached fire-fighting equipment, and is used only for fire-fighting purposes.

d. A vehicle that has permanently attached playground equipment and is used only for playground purposes.

(42) Sport or recreational equipment. - Items designed for human use and worn in conjunction with an athletic or recreational activity that are not suitable for general use including ballet shoes, cleated athletic shoes, shin guards, and ski boots.

(43) State agency. - A unit of the executive, legislative, or judicial branch of State government, such as a department, a commission, a board, a council, or The University of North Carolina. The term does not include a local board of education.

(44) Storage. - The keeping or retention in this State for any purpose, except sale in the regular course of business, of tangible personal property or digital property purchased from a retailer. The term does not include a purchaser's storage of tangible personal property or digital property in any of the following circumstances:

a. When the purchaser is able to document that at the time the purchaser acquires the property the property is designated for the purchaser's use outside the State and the purchaser subsequently takes it outside the State and uses it solely outside the State.

b. When the purchaser acquires the property to process, fabricate, manufacture, or otherwise incorporate it into or attach it to other property for the purchaser's use outside the State and, after incorporating or attaching the purchased property, the purchaser subsequently takes the other property outside the State and uses it solely outside the State.

(45) Repealed by Session Laws 2009-451, s. 27A.3(g), effective August 7, 2009.

(45a) Streamlined Agreement. - The Streamlined Sales and Use Tax Agreement as amended as of May 24, 2012.

(46) Tangible personal property. - Personal property that may be seen, weighed, measured, felt, or touched or is in any other manner perceptible to the senses. The term includes electricity, water, gas, steam, and prewritten computer software.

(47) Taxpayer. - Any person liable for taxes under this Article.

(48) Telecommunications service. - The electronic transmission, conveyance, or routing of voice, data, audio, video, or any other information or signals to a point, or between or among points. The term includes any transmission, conveyance, or routing in which a computer processing application is used to act on the form, code, or protocol of the content for purposes of the transmission, conveyance, or routing, regardless of whether it is referred to as voice-over Internet protocol or the Federal Communications Commission classifies it as enhanced or value added. The term does not include the following:

a. An information service.

b. The sale, installation, maintenance, or repair of tangible personal property.

c. Directory advertising and other advertising.

d. Billing and collection services provided to a third party.

e. Internet access service.

f. Radio and television audio and video programming service, regardless of the medium of delivery, and the transmission, conveyance, or routing of the service by the programming service provider. The term includes cable service and audio and video programming service provided by a mobile telecommunications service provider.

g. Ancillary service.

h. Digital property that is delivered or accessed electronically, including an audio work, an audiovisual work, or any other item subject to tax under G.S. 105-164.4(a)(6b).

(49) Use. - The exercise of any right, power, or dominion whatsoever over tangible personal property, digital property, or a service by the purchaser of the property or service. The term includes withdrawal from storage, distribution, installation, affixation to real or personal property, and exhaustion or consumption of the property or service by the owner or purchaser. The term does not include the following:

a. A sale of property or a service in the regular course of business.

b. A purchaser's use of tangible personal property or digital property in any of the circumstances that would exclude the storage of the property from the definition of "storage" in subdivision (44) of this section.

(50) Use tax. - The tax imposed by Part 2 of this Article.

(50c) Video programming. - Programming provided by, or generally considered comparable to programming provided by, a television broadcast station, regardless of the method of delivery.

(51) Wholesale merchant. - A person engaged in the business of any of the following:

a. Making wholesale sales.

b. Buying or manufacturing tangible personal property, digital property, or a service and selling it to a registered resident or nonresident retail or wholesale merchant for resale.

c. Manufacturing, producing, processing, or blending any articles of commerce and maintaining a store, warehouse, or any other place that is separate and apart from the place of manufacture or production for the sale or distribution of the articles, other than bakery products, to another for the purpose of resale.

(52) Wholesale sale. - A sale of tangible personal property, digital property, or a service for the purpose of resale. The term includes a sale of digital property for reproduction into digital or tangible personal property offered for sale. The term does not include a sale to a user or consumer not for resale or, in the case of digital property, not for reproduction and sale of the reproduced property. (1957, c. 1340, s. 5; 1959, c. 1259, s. 5; 1961, c. 1213, s. 1; 1967, c. 1110, s. 6; 1973, c. 476, s. 193; c. 1287, s. 8; 1975, c. 104; c. 275, s. 6; 1979, c. 48, s. 2; c. 71; c. 801, s. 72; 1983, c. 713, ss. 87, 88; 1983 (Reg. Sess., 1984), c. 1097, ss. 4, 5; 1985, c. 23; 1987, c. 27; c. 557, s. 3.1; c. 854, ss. 2, 3; 1987 (Reg. Sess., 1988), c. 1044, s. 3; c. 1096, ss. 1-3; 1989, c. 692, s. 3.2; 1989 (Reg. Sess., 1990), c. 813, s. 13; 1991, c. 45, s. 15; c. 79, ss. 1, 3; c. 689, s. 190.1(a); 1991 (Reg. Sess., 1992), c. 949, s. 3; 1993, c. 354, s. 16; c. 484, s. 1; c. 507, s. 1; 1995 (Reg. Sess., 1996), c. 649, s. 2; 1996, 2nd Ex. Sess., c. 14, ss. 13, 14; 1997-6, s. 7; 1997-370, s. 1; 1997-426, s. 4; 1998-22, s. 4; 1998-55, ss. 7, 13; 1998-98, ss. 13.1(a), 106; 1999-337, s. 28(a), (b); 1999-360, s. 6(a)-(c); 1999-438, s. 4; 2000-153, s. 4; 2000-173, s. 9; 2001-347, ss. 2.1-2.7; 2001-414, s. 14; 2001-424, s. 34.17(b); 2001-430, ss. 1, 2; 2001-476, s. 18(a); 2001-489, s. 3(a); 2002-16, ss. 1, 2, 3; 2002-170, s. 6; 2003-284, s. 45.2; 2003-400, ss. 13, 14; 2003-402, s. 12; 2004-124, s. 32B.3; 2004-170, ss. 18, 19; 2005-276, ss. 33.2, 33.3; 2006-33, s. 1; 2006-66, ss. 24.10(a), 24.17(a); 2006-151, s. 2; 2006-162, s. 5(a); 2006-168, ss. 4.1, 4.3; 2006-252, ss. 2.25(a), (a1), (c), 2.26; 2007-244, s. 1; 2007-323, ss. 31.14(a), 31.20(a), 31.23(b); 2008-107, s. 28.12(a); 2009-445, s. 11; 2009-451, s. 27A.3(d), (g); 2010-91, ss. 1, 2; 2010-166, s. 3.3; 2011-330, ss. 15(a), (b), 31(c); 2012-79, s. 2.7; 2013-316, s. 6(a); 2013-414, ss. 8, 23(a).)

Part 2. Taxes Levied.

§ 105-164.4. Tax imposed on retailers.

(a) A privilege tax is imposed on a retailer at the following percentage rates of the retailer's net taxable sales or gross receipts, as appropriate. The general rate of tax is four and three-quarters percent (4.75%).

(1) The general rate of tax applies to the sales price of each item or article of tangible personal property that is sold at retail and is not subject to tax under another subdivision in this section.

(1a) The general rate applies to the sales price of each manufactured home sold at retail, including all accessories attached to the manufactured home when it is delivered to the purchaser.

(1b) The rate of three percent (3%) applies to the sales price of each aircraft or boat sold at retail, including all accessories attached to the item when it is delivered to the purchaser. The maximum tax is one thousand five hundred dollars ($1,500) per article.

(1c), (1d) and (1e) Repealed by Session Laws 2005-276, s. 33.4(b), effective January 1, 2006.

(1f) (See note for delayed repeal of subdivision) The rate of two and eighty-three-hundredths percent (2.83%) applies to the sales price of electricity that is measured by a separate meter or another separate device and sold to a commercial laundry or to a pressing and dry-cleaning establishment for use in machinery used in the direct performance of the laundering or the pressing and cleaning service.

a. Repealed by Session Laws 2007-397, s. 10(b), effective October 1, 2007, and applicable to sales occurring on or after that date.

b. Repealed by Session Laws 2006-66, s. 24.19(a), effective July 1, 2007, and applicable to sales made on or after that date.

c. Repealed by Session Laws 2007-397, s. 10(b), effective October 1, 2007, and applicable to sales occurring on or after that date.

(1g) Repealed by Session Laws 2004-110, s. 6.1, effective October 1, 2004, and applicable to sales of electricity made on or after that date.

(1h) Expired pursuant to Session Laws 2004-110, s. 6.4, effective for sales made on or after October 1, 2007.

(1i) Repealed by Session Laws 2007-397, s. 10(a), effective October 1, 2007, and applicable to sales occurring on or after that date.

(1j) Repealed by Session Laws 2007-397, s. 10(f), effective July 1, 2010, and applicable to sales occurring on or after that date.

(2) The applicable percentage rate applies to the gross receipts derived from the lease or rental of tangible personal property by a person who is engaged in the business of leasing or renting tangible personal property, or is a retailer and leases or rents property of the type sold by the retailer. The applicable percentage rate is the rate and the maximum tax, if any, that applies to a sale of the property that is leased or rented. A person who leases or rents property shall also collect the tax imposed by this section on the separate retail sale of the property.

(3) A tax at the general rate applies to the gross receipts derived from the rental of an accommodation. The tax does not apply to (i) a private residence or cottage that is rented for fewer than 15 days in a calendar year; (ii) an accommodation rented to the same person for a period of 90 or more continuous days; or (iii) an accommodation arranged or provided to a person by a school, camp, or similar entity where a tuition or fee is charged to the person for enrollment in the school, camp, or similar entity.

Gross receipts derived from the rental of an accommodation include the sales price of the rental of the accommodation. The sales price of the rental of an accommodation is determined as if the rental were a rental of tangible personal property. The sales price of the rental of an accommodation marketed by a facilitator includes charges designated as facilitation fees and any other charges necessary to complete the rental.

A person who provides an accommodation that is offered for rent is considered a retailer under this Article. A facilitator must report to the retailer with whom it has a contract the sales price a consumer pays to the facilitator for an accommodation rental marketed by the facilitator. A retailer must notify a facilitator when an accommodation rental marketed by the facilitator is completed and the facilitator must send the retailer the portion of the sales price the facilitator owes the retailer and the tax due on the sales price no later than 10 days after the end of each calendar month. A facilitator that does not send the retailer the tax due on the sales price is liable for the amount of tax the facilitator fails to send. A facilitator is not liable for tax sent to a retailer but not remitted by the retailer to the Secretary. Tax payments received by a retailer from a facilitator are held in trust by the retailer for remittance to the Secretary. A retailer that receives a tax payment from a facilitator must remit the amount received to the Secretary. A retailer is not liable for tax due but not received from a facilitator. The requirements imposed by this subdivision on a retailer and a facilitator are considered terms of the contract between the retailer and the facilitator.

A person who, by written contract, agrees to be the rental agent for the provider of an accommodation is considered a retailer under this Article and is liable for the tax imposed by this subdivision. The liability of a rental agent for the tax imposed by this subdivision relieves the provider of the accommodation from liability. A rental agent includes a real estate broker, as defined in G.S. 93A-2.

The following definitions apply in this subdivision:

a. Accommodation. - A hotel room, a motel room, a residence, a cottage, or a similar lodging facility for occupancy by an individual.

b. Facilitator. - A person who is not a rental agent and who contracts with a provider of an accommodation to market the accommodation and to accept payment from the consumer for the accommodation.

(4) Every person engaged in the business of operating a dry cleaning, pressing, or hat-blocking establishment, a laundry, or any similar business, engaged in the business of renting clean linen or towels or wearing apparel, or any similar business, or engaged in the business of soliciting cleaning, pressing, hat blocking, laundering or linen rental business for any of these businesses, is considered a retailer under this Article. A tax at the general rate of tax is levied on the gross receipts derived by these retailers from services rendered in engaging in any of the occupations or businesses named in this subdivision. The tax imposed by this subdivision does not apply to receipts derived from coin, token, or card-operated washing machines, extractors, and dryers. The tax imposed by this subdivision does not apply to gross receipts derived from services performed for resale by a retailer that pays the tax on the total gross receipts derived from the services.

(4a) (See note for delayed repeal of subdivision) The rate of three percent (3%) applies to the gross receipts derived from sales of electricity, other than sales of electricity subject to tax under another subdivision in this section. A person who sells electricity is considered a retailer under this Article.

(4b) A person who sells tangible personal property at a specialty market, other than the person's own household personal property, is considered a retailer under this Article. A tax at the general rate of tax is levied on the sales price of each article sold by the retailer at the specialty market. The term "specialty market" has the same meaning as defined in G.S. 66-250.

(4c)   The combined general rate applies to the gross receipts derived from providing telecommunications service and ancillary service. A person who provides telecommunications service or ancillary service is considered a retailer under this Article. These services are taxed in accordance with G.S. 105-164.4C.

(4d)   The sale or recharge of prepaid telephone calling service is taxable at the general rate of tax. The tax applies regardless of whether tangible personal property, such as a card or a telephone, is transferred. The tax applies to a service that is sold in conjunction with prepaid wireless calling service. Prepaid telephone calling service is taxable at the point of sale instead of at the point of use and is sourced in accordance with G.S. 105-164.4B. Prepaid telephone calling service taxed under this subdivision is not subject to tax as a telecommunications service.

(5)   Repealed by Session Laws 1998-212, s. 29A.1(a), effective May 1, 1999.

(6)   The combined general rate applies to the gross receipts derived from providing video programming to a subscriber in this State. A cable service provider, a direct-to-home satellite service provider, and any other person engaged in the business of providing video programming is considered a retailer under this Article.

(6a)   The general rate applies to the gross receipts derived from providing satellite digital audio radio service. For services received by a mobile or portable station, the service is sourced to the subscriber's business or home address. A person engaged in the business of providing satellite digital audio radio service is a retailer under this Article.

(6b)   The general rate applies to the sales price of digital property that is sold at retail and that is listed in this subdivision, is delivered or accessed electronically, is not considered tangible personal property, and would be taxable under this Article if sold in a tangible medium. The tax applies regardless of whether the purchaser of the item has a right to use it permanently or to use it without making continued payments. The tax does not apply to a service that is taxed under another subdivision of this subsection or to an information service. The following property is subject to tax under this subdivision:

a. An audio work.

b. An audiovisual work.

c. A book, a magazine, a newspaper, a newsletter, a report, or another publication.

d. A photograph or a greeting card.

(7) The combined general rate applies to the sales price of spirituous liquor other than mixed beverages. As used in this subdivision, the terms "spirituous liquor" and "mixed beverage" have the meanings provided in G.S. 18B-101.

(8) The general rate applies to the sales price of each modular home sold at retail, including all accessories attached to the modular home when it is delivered to the purchaser. The sale of a modular home to a modular homebuilder is considered a retail sale. A person who sells a modular home at retail is allowed a credit against the tax imposed by this subdivision for sales or use tax paid to another state on tangible personal property incorporated in the modular home. The retail sale of a modular home occurs when a modular home manufacturer sells a modular home to a modular homebuilder or directly to the end user of the modular home.

(9) (Effective July 1, 2014) The combined general rate applies to the gross receipts derived from sales of electricity and piped natural gas.

(10) The general rate of tax applies to admission charges to an entertainment activity listed in this subdivision. Offering any of these listed activities is a service. An admission charge includes a charge for a single ticket, a multioccasion ticket, a seasonal pass, an annual pass, and a cover charge.

An admission charge does not include a charge for amenities. If charges for amenities are not separately stated on the face of an admission ticket, then the charge for admission is considered to be equal to the admission charge for a ticket to the same event that does not include amenities and is for a seat located directly in front of or closest to a seat that includes amenities.

When an admission ticket is resold and the price of the admission ticket is printed on the face of the ticket, the tax does not apply to the face price. When an admission ticket is resold and the price of the admission ticket is not printed on the face of the ticket, the tax applies to the difference between the amount the reseller paid for the ticket and the amount the reseller charges for the ticket.

Admission charges to the following entertainment activities are subject to tax:

a. A live performance or other live event of any kind.

b. A motion picture or film.

c. A museum, a cultural site, a garden, an exhibit, a show, or a similar attraction or a guided tour at any of these attractions.

(11) The general rate of tax applies to the sales price of a service contract.

(b) The tax levied in this section shall be collected from the retailer and paid by him at the time and in the manner as hereinafter provided. Provided, however, that any person engaging or continuing in business as a retailer shall pay the tax required on the net taxable sales of such business at the rates specified when proper books are kept showing separately the gross proceeds of taxable and nontaxable sales of tangible personal property in such form as may be accurately and conveniently checked by the Secretary or his duly authorized agent. If such records are not kept separately the tax shall be paid as a retailer on the gross sales of business and the exemptions and exclusions provided by this Article shall not be allowed. The tax levied in this section is in addition to all other taxes whether levied in the form of excise, license or privilege or other taxes.

(c) Certificate of Registration. - Before a person may engage in business as a retailer or a wholesale merchant, the person must obtain a certificate of registration from the Department in accordance with G.S. 105-164.29. (1957, c. 1340, s. 5; 1959, c. 1259, s. 5; 1961, c. 826, s. 2; 1963, c. 1169, ss. 3, 11; 1967, c. 1110, s. 6; c. 1116; 1969, c. 1075, s. 5; 1971, c. 887, s. 1; 1973, c. 476, s. 193; c. 1287, s. 8; 1975, c. 752; 1977, c. 903; 1977, 2nd Sess., c. 1218; 1979, c. 17, s. 1; c. 22; c. 48, s. 1; c. 527, s. 1; c. 801, s. 73; 1981, c. 984, ss. 1, 2; 1981 (Reg. Sess., 1982), cc. 1207, 1273; 1983, c. 510; c. 713, ss. 89, 93; c. 805, ss. 1, 2; 1983 (Reg. Sess., 1984), c. 1065, ss. 1, 2, 4; c. 1097, ss. 6, 13; 1985, c. 704; 1985 (Reg. Sess., 1986), c. 925; c. 1005; 1987, c. 557, ss. 4, 5; c. 800, ss.

2, 3; c. 854, s. 1; 1987 (Reg. Sess., 1988), c. 1044, s. 4; 1989, c. 692, ss. 3.1, 3.3, 8.4(8); c. 770, s. 74.4; 1989 (Reg. Sess., 1990), c. 813, ss. 14, 15; 1991, c. 598, s. 5; c. 689, s. 311; c. 690, s. 1; 1993, c. 372, s. 1; c. 484, s. 2; 1995, c. 17, s. 6; c. 477, s. 1; 1996, 2nd Ex. Sess., c. 13, ss. 1.1, 9.1, 9.2; 1997-475, s. 1.1; 1998-22, s. 5; 1998-55, ss. 8, 14; 1998-98, ss. 13.2, 48(a), (b); 1998-121, ss. 3, 5; 1998-197, s. 1; 1998-212, s. 29A.1(a); 1999-337, ss. 29, 30; 1999-360, s. 3(a), (b); 1999-438, s. 1; 2000-140, s. 67(a); 2001-424, ss. 34.13(a), 34.17(a), 34.23(b), 34.25(a); 2001-430, ss. 3, 4, 5; 2001-476, ss. 17(b)-(d), (f); 2001-487, ss. 67(b), 122(a)-(c); 2002-16, s. 4; 2003-284, s. 38.1; 2003-400, s. 15; 2004-110, ss. 6.1, 6.2, 6.3; 2005-144, s. 9.1; 2005-276, ss. 33.1, 33.4(a), (b); 2006-33, ss. 2, 11; 2006-66, ss. 24.1(a), (b), (c), 24.19(a), (b); 2006-151, s. 3; 2007-145, s. 9(a); 2007-323, ss. 31.2(a), (b), 31.16.3(h); 31.16.4(g); 2007-397, s. 10(a)-(f); 2009-451, s. 27A.2(b), (e); 2010-31, s. 31.6(a); 2010-123, s. 10.2; 2011-330, s. 16; 2013-316, ss. 3.1(a), 4.1(c), (e), 5(b), 6(b); 2013-414, ss. 9, 40.)

§ 105-164.4A: Repealed by Session Laws 2005-276, s. 33.5, effective January 1, 2006.

§ 105-164.4B. Sourcing principles.

(a)   General Principles. - The following principles apply in determining where to source the sale of a product. These principles apply regardless of the nature of the product, except as otherwise noted in this section:

(1)   When a purchaser receives a product at a business location of the seller, the sale is sourced to that business location.

(2)   When a purchaser or purchaser's donee receives a product at a location specified by the purchaser and the location is not a business location of the seller, the sale is sourced to the location where the purchaser or the purchaser's donee receives the product.

(3)   When subdivisions (1) and (2) of this subsection do not apply, the sale is sourced to the location indicated by an address for the purchaser that is available from the business records of the seller that are maintained in the ordinary course of the seller's business when use of this address does not constitute bad faith.

(4) When subdivisions (1), (2), and (3) of this subsection do not apply, the sale is sourced to the location indicated by an address for the purchaser obtained during the consummation of the sale, including the address of a purchaser's payment instrument, if no other address is available, when use of this address does not constitute bad faith.

(5) When subdivisions (1), (2), (3), and (4) of this subsection do not apply, including the circumstance in which the seller is without sufficient information to apply the rules, the location will be determined based on the following:

a. Address from which tangible personal property was shipped,

b. Address from which the digital good or the computer software delivered electronically was first available for transmission by the seller, or

c. Address from which the service was provided.

(b) Periodic Rental Payments. - When a lease or rental agreement requires recurring periodic payments, the payments are sourced as follows:

(1) For leased or rented property, the first payment is sourced in accordance with the principles set out in subsection (a) of this section and each subsequent payment is sourced to the primary location of the leased or rented property for the period covered by the payment. This subdivision applies to all property except a motor vehicle, an aircraft, transportation equipment, and a utility company railway car.

(2) For leased or rented property that is a motor vehicle or an aircraft but is not transportation equipment, all payments are sourced to the primary location of the leased or rented property for the period covered by the payment.

(3) For leased or rented property that is transportation equipment, all payments are sourced in accordance with the principles set out in subsection (a) of this section.

(4) For a railway car that is leased or rented by a utility company and would be transportation equipment if it were used in interstate commerce, all payments are sourced in accordance with the principles set out in subsection (a) of this section.

(c) Transportation Equipment Defined. - As used in the section, the term "transportation equipment" means any of the following used to carry persons or property in interstate commerce: a locomotive, a railway car, a commercial motor vehicle as defined in G.S. 20-4.01, or an aircraft. The term includes a container designed for use on the equipment and a component part of the equipment.

(d) Exceptions. - This section does not apply to the following:

(1) Telecommunications services. - Telecommunications services are sourced in accordance with G.S. 105-164.4C.

(2) Direct mail. - Direct mail is sourced in accordance with G.S. 105-164.4E.

(3) Florist wire sale. - A florist wire sale is sourced to the business location of the florist that takes an order for the sale. A "florist wire sale" is a sale in which a retail florist takes a customer's order and transmits the order to another retail florist to be filled and delivered.

(e) Accommodations. - The rental of an accommodation, as defined in G.S. 105-164.4(a)(3), is sourced to the location of the accommodation.

(f) Digital Property. - A purchaser receives digital property when the purchaser takes possession of the property or makes first use of the property, whichever comes first. (2001-347, s. 2.9; 2002-16, s. 5; 2003-284, s. 45.3; 2004-170, s. 20; 2006-33, s. 3; 2006-66, s. 24.13(a); 2008-187, s. 42; 2009-445, s. 12; 2010-31, s. 31.6(b); 2010-123, s. 10.2; 2011-330, s. 29; 2012-79, s. 2.8; 2013-414, s. 23(b).)

§ 105-164.4C. Telecommunications service and ancillary service.

(a) General. - The gross receipts derived from providing telecommunications service or ancillary service in this State are taxed at the rate set in G.S. 105-164.4(a)(4c). Telecommunications service is provided in this State if the service is sourced to this State under the sourcing principles set out in subsections (a1) and (a2) of this section. Ancillary service is provided in this State if the telecommunications service to which it is ancillary is provided in this State. The definitions and provisions of the federal Mobile

Telecommunications Sourcing Act apply to the sourcing and taxation of mobile telecommunications services.

(a1)   General Sourcing Principles. - The following general sourcing principles apply to telecommunications services. If a service falls within one of the exceptions set out in subsection (a2) of this section, the service is sourced in accordance with the exception instead of the general principle.

(1)   Flat rate. - A telecommunications service that is not sold on a call-by-call basis is sourced to this State if the place of primary use is in this State.

(2)   General call-by-call. - A telecommunications service that is sold on a call-by-call basis and is not a postpaid calling service is sourced to this State in the following circumstances:

a.   The call both originates and terminates in this State.

b.   The call either originates or terminates in this State and the telecommunications equipment from which the call originates or terminates and to which the call is charged is located in this State. This applies regardless of where the call is billed or paid.

(3)   Postpaid. - A postpaid calling service is sourced to the origination point of the telecommunications signal as first identified by either the seller's telecommunications system or, if the system used to transport the signal is not the seller's system, by information the seller receives from its service provider.

(a2)   Sourcing Exceptions. - The following telecommunications services and products are sourced in accordance with the principles set out in this subsection:

(1)   Mobile. - Mobile telecommunications service is sourced to the place of primary use, unless the service is prepaid wireless calling service or is air-to-ground radiotelephone service. Air-to-ground radiotelephone service is a postpaid calling service that is offered by an aircraft common carrier to passengers on its aircraft and enables a telephone call to be made from the aircraft. The sourcing principle in this subdivision applies to a service or product provided as an adjunct to mobile telecommunications service if the charge for the service or product is included within the term "charges for mobile telecommunications services" under the federal Mobile Telecommunications Sourcing Act.

(2) Prepaid. - Prepaid telephone calling service is sourced in accordance with G.S. 105-164.4B.

(3) Private. - Private telecommunications service is sourced in accordance with subsection (e) of this section.

(b) Repealed by Session Laws 2006-33, s. 4, effective January 1, 2007.

(c) (1) through (10) Repealed by Session Laws 2006-33, s. 4, effective January 1, 2007.

(11) Repealed by Session Laws 2005-276, s. 33.7, effective October 1, 2005.

(12) through (16) Repealed by Session Laws 2006-33, s. 4, effective January 1, 2007.

(d) Recodified as G.S. 105-164.4D by Session Laws 2006-151, s. 4, effective January 1, 2007.

(e) Private Line. - The gross receipts derived from private telecommunications service are sourced as follows:

(1) If all the customer's channel termination points are located in this State, the service is sourced to this State.

(2) If all the customer's channel termination points are not located in this State and the service is billed on the basis of channel termination points, the charge for each channel termination point located in this State is sourced to this State.

(3) If all the customer's channel termination points are not located in this State and the service is billed on the basis of channel mileage, the following applies:

a. A charge for a channel segment between two channel termination points located in this State is sourced to this State.

b. Fifty percent (50%) of a charge for a channel segment between a channel termination point located in this State and a channel termination point located in another state is sourced to this State.

(4) If all the customer's channel termination points are not located in this State and the service is not billed on the basis of channel termination points or channel mileage, a percentage of the charge for the service is sourced to this State. The percentage is determined by dividing the number of channel termination points in this State by the total number of channel termination points.

(f) Call Center Cap. - The gross receipts tax on telecommunications service that originates outside this State, terminates in this State, and is provided to a call center that has a direct pay permit issued by the Department under G.S. 105-164.27A may not exceed fifty thousand dollars ($50,000) a calendar year. This cap applies separately to each legal entity.

(g) Credit. - A taxpayer who pays a tax legally imposed by another state on a telecommunications service taxable under this section is allowed a credit against the tax imposed in this section.

(h) Definitions. - The following definitions apply in this section:

(1) Ancillary service. - Defined in G.S. 105-164.3.

(1a) Call-by-call basis. - A method of charging for a telecommunications service whereby the price of the service is measured by individual calls.

(2) Call center. - Defined in G.S. 105-164.27A.

(3) Mobile telecommunications service. - Defined in G.S. 105-164.3.

(4) Place of primary use. - Defined in G.S. 105-164.3.

(5) Postpaid calling service. - A telecommunications service that is charged on a call-by-call basis and is obtained by making payment at the time of the call either through the use of a credit or payment mechanism, such as a bank card, travel card, credit card, or debit card, or by charging the call to a telephone number that is not associated with the origination or termination of the telecommunications service. A postpaid calling service includes a service that meets all the requirements of a prepaid telephone calling service, except the exclusive use requirement.

(6) Prepaid telephone calling service. - Defined in G.S. 105-164.3.

(7) Private telecommunications service. - Telecommunications service that entitles a subscriber of the service to exclusive or priority use of a communications channel or group of channels.

(8) Telecommunications service. - Defined in G.S. 105-164.3. (2001-430, s. 6; 2001-487, ss. 67(a), (c), 69(b); 2002-16, s 10; 2002-16, ss. 6, 7, 8, 9, 11, 14; 2003-416, s. 16(a); 2005-276, ss. 33.6, 33.7; 2006-33, s. 4; 2006-151, s. 4; 2011-330, s. 17; 2013-414, s. 41.)

§ 105-164.4D. Bundled transactions.

(a) Tax Application. - Tax applies to the sales price of a bundled transaction unless one of the following applies:

(1) Fifty percent (50%) test. - All of the products in the bundle are tangible personal property, the bundle includes one or more of the exempt products listed in this subdivision, and the price of the taxable products in the bundle does not exceed fifty percent (50%) of the price of the bundle:

a. Food exempt under G.S. 105-164.13B.

b. A drug exempt under G.S. 105-164.13(13).

c. Medical devices, equipment, or supplies exempt under G.S. 105-164.13(12).

(2) Allocation. - The bundle includes a service, and the retailer determines an allocated price for each product in the bundle based on a reasonable allocation of revenue that is supported by the retailer's business records kept in the ordinary course of business. In this circumstance, tax applies to the allocated price of each taxable product in the bundle.

(3) Ten percent (10%) test. - The price of the taxable products in the bundle does not exceed ten percent (10%) of the price of the bundle, and no other subdivision in this subsection applies.

(b) Determining Threshold. - A retailer of a bundled transaction subject to this section may use either the retailer's cost price or the retailer's sales price to determine if the transaction meets the fifty percent (50%) test or the ten percent

(10%) test set out in subdivisions (a)(1) and (a)(3) of this section. A retailer may not use a combination of cost price and sales price to make this determination. If a bundled transaction subject to subdivision (a)(3) of this section includes a service contract, the retailer must use the full term of the contract in determining whether the transaction meets the threshold set in the subdivision. (2006-151, ss. 4, 5; 2007-244, s. 2.)

§ 105-164.4E. Direct Mail.

(a) Advertising and Promotional Direct Mail. - The following sourcing principles apply to advertising and promotional direct mail.

(1) To the location where the direct mail is delivered if it is purchased pursuant to a direct pay permit issued under G.S. 105-164.27A(a1), or if it is purchased with an exemption certificate claiming direct mail and bearing the direct mail permit number issued under G.S. 105-164.27A(a1).

(2) To the location where the direct mail is delivered if the purchaser provides the seller with information to show the jurisdictions to which the direct mail is to be delivered.

(3) To the location from which the direct mail was shipped if subdivision (1) or (2) of this subsection does not apply.

(b) Other Direct Mail. - The following sourcing principles apply to other direct mail:

(1) To the location indicated by an address for the purchaser that is available from the business records of the seller that are maintained in the ordinary course of the seller's business when use of this address does not constitute bad faith.

(2) To the jurisdictions where the direct mail is delivered if it is purchased pursuant to a direct pay permit issued under G.S. 105-164.27A(a1), or if it is purchased with an exemption certificate claiming direct mail and bearing the direct mail permit number issued under G.S. 105-164.27A(a1).

(c) Relief From Liability. - In the absence of bad faith, a seller is relieved of:

(1) All obligations to collect, pay, or remit any tax on any direct mail transaction where the purchaser issues a direct pay permit issued under G.S.

105-164.27A(a1), or if it is purchased with an exemption certificate claiming direct mail and bearing the direct mail permit number issued under G.S. 105-164.27A(a1).

(2) Further obligation to collect any additional tax on the sale of advertising and promotional direct mail where the seller sourced the sale according to delivery information provided by the purchaser. (2013-414, s. 23(c).)

§ 105-164.5: Repealed by Session Laws 1998-121, s. 2, as amended by Session Laws 1998-217, s. 59.

§ 105-164.5A: Repealed by Session Laws 1961, c. 1213, s. 3.

§ 105-164.6. Complementary use tax.

(a) Tax. - An excise tax at the applicable rate set in G.S. 105-164.4 is imposed on the products listed below. The applicable rate is the rate and maximum tax, if any, that would apply to the sale of the product. A product is subject to tax under this section only if it is subject to tax under G.S. 105-164.4.

(1) Tangible personal property or digital property purchased inside or outside this State for storage, use, or consumption in this State. This subdivision includes property that becomes part of a building or another structure.

(2) Tangible personal property or digital property leased or rented inside or outside this State for storage, use, or consumption in this State.

(3) Services sourced to this State.

(b) Liability. - The tax imposed by this section is payable by the person who purchases, leases, or rents tangible personal property or digital property or who purchases a service. If the property purchased becomes a part of a building or other structure in the State and the purchaser is a contractor or subcontractor, the contractor, the subcontractor, and the owner of the building are jointly and severally liable for the tax. The liability of a contractor, a subcontractor, or an owner who did not purchase the property is satisfied by receipt of an affidavit from the purchaser certifying that the tax has been paid.

(c) Credit. - A credit is allowed against the tax imposed by this section for the following:

(1) The amount of sales or use tax paid on the item to this State, provided the tax is stated and charged separately on the invoice or other document of the retailer given to the purchaser at the time of the sale, except as otherwise provided in G.S. 105-164.7, or provided the retailer remitted the tax subsequent to the sale and the purchaser obtains such documentation. Payment of sales or use tax to this State on an item by a retailer extinguishes the liability of a purchaser for the tax imposed under this section.

(2) The amount of sales or use tax due and paid on the item to another state. If the amount of tax paid to the other state is less than the amount of tax imposed by this section, the difference is payable to this State. The credit allowed by this subdivision does not apply to tax paid to a state that does not grant a similar credit for sales or use taxes paid in North Carolina.

(d), (e) Repealed by Session Laws 2005-276, s. 33.8, effective October 1, 2005.

(f) Registration. - Before a person may engage in business in this State selling or delivering tangible personal property, digital property, or a service for storage, use, or consumption in this State, the person must obtain a certificate of registration from the Department. To obtain a certificate of registration, a person must register with the Department.

The holder of the certificate of registration must pay the tax levied under this Article. A certificate of registration is valid unless it is revoked for failure to comply with the provisions of this Article or becomes void. A certificate issued to a retailer becomes void if, for a period of 18 months, the retailer files no returns or files returns showing no sales.

(g) Repealed by Session Laws 1995, c. 7, s. 1. (1957, c. 1340, s. 5; 1959, c. 1259, s. 5; 1961, c. 826, s. 2; 1967, c. 1110, s. 6; 1973, c. 476, s. 193; 1979, c. 17, s. 2; c. 48, ss. 3, 4; c. 179, s. 3; c. 527, s. 2; 1979, 2nd Sess., c. 1100, s. 1; c. 1175; 1981, cc. 18, 65; 1983, c. 713, s. 90; 1983 (Reg. Sess., 1984), c. 1065, s. 3; 1989, c. 692, s. 3.4; 1991, c. 689, s. 312; c. 690, s. 3; 1995, c. 7, s. 1; c. 17, s. 7; 1998-121, s. 4; 1999-438, s. 1.1; 2001-414, s. 15; 2003-416, ss. 17, 24(a); 2005-276, s. 33.8; 2006-162, s. 6; 2009-451, s. 27A.3(h); 2011-330, s. 25(a); 2013-414, s. 10.)

§ 105-164.6A. Voluntary collection of use tax by sellers.

(a) Voluntary Collection Agreements. - The Secretary may enter into agreements with sellers pursuant to which the seller agrees to collect and remit on behalf of its customers State and local use taxes due on items of tangible personal property, digital property, or services the seller sells. For the purpose of this section, a seller is a person who is engaged in the business of selling tangible personal property, digital property, or services for use in this State and who does not have sufficient nexus with this State to be required to collect use tax on the sales.

(b) Mandatory Provisions. - The agreements must contain the following provisions:

(1) The seller is not liable for use tax not paid to it by a customer.

(2) A customer's payment of a use tax to the seller relieves the customer of liability for the use tax.

(3) The seller must remit all use taxes it collects from customers on or before the due date specified in the agreement, which may not be later than 31 days after the end of a quarter or other collection period. The collection period cannot be more often than annually if the seller's State and local tax collections are less than one thousand dollars ($1,000) in a calendar year.

(4) A seller who fails to remit use taxes collected on behalf of its customers by the due date specified in the agreement is subject to the interest and penalties provided in Article 9 of this Chapter with respect to the taxes to the same extent as if the seller were a retailer and were required to collect use taxes under this Article.

(c) Optional Provisions. - The agreements may contain the following provisions:

(1) The seller will collect the use tax only on items that are subject to the general rate of tax.

(2) The seller will collect local use taxes only to the extent they are at the same rate in every unit of local government in the State.

(3) The seller will remit the tax and file reports in the form prescribed by the Secretary.

(4) Other provisions establishing the types of transactions on which the seller will collect tax and prescribing administrative procedures and requirements. (1996, 2nd Ex. Sess., c. 14, s. 11; 2000-120, s. 4; 2003-284, s. 45.4; 2009-451, s. 27A.3(i).)

Vision Books Order Form

Fax Orders:	1-980-299-5965
Phone Orders:	1-704-898-0770
E-mail Orders:	www.visionbooks.org
Mail Orders:	Vision Books, LLC P.O. Box 42406 Charlotte, NC 28215

Shipp To:
Name_____
Address_____
City_____State_____Zip_____
Phone_____Fax_____
Email_____@_____

Bill To: We can bill a third party on your behalf.
Name_____
Address_____
City_____State_____Zip_____
Phone____(_____)_____Fax_____
Email_____@_____

Pamphlet Number ($15.00 Each)	Qty	Total Cost
_____	_____	_____
_____	_____	_____
_____	_____	_____
_____	_____	_____
_____	_____	_____
_____	_____	_____
_____	_____	_____
<u>Full Volume Set 1-92</u>	<u>92 Pamphlets</u>	<u>1,380.00</u>

Free Shipping Shipping & Handling on Full Volume Orders
Add $1.00 Shipping & Handling per pamphlet $_____

Total Cost $_____

Thank you for your support. Management!

DID YOU ENJOY THIS BOOK?

Vision Books, LLC would like to hear from you! If you or someone you know has been fasely imprisoned, we would like to hear your story. If the 'North Carolina Criminal Law and Procedure' has had an effect in your life or if you have suggestions, we would like to hear from you. Send your letters to:

Vision Books, LLC
Attn: Staff Writers
P.O. Box 42406
Charlotte, NC 28215
Email: staff@visionbooks.org

Order Additional Copies:

Fax Orders:	1-980-299-5965
Phone Orders:	1-704-898-0770
E-mail Orders:	www.visionbooks.org
Mail Orders:	Vision Books, LLC P.O. Box 42406 Charlotte, NC 28215

www.ingramcontent.com/pod-product-compliance
Lightning Source LLC
Chambersburg PA
CBHW051629170526
45167CB00001B/118